MOUNTAINS OF SILVER

MOUNTAINS OF SILVER

LIFE IN COLORADO'S RED MOUNTAIN MINING DISTRICT

P. DAVID SMITH

WESTERN REFLECTIONS
PUBLISHING COMPANY

Library of Congress Cataloging-in-Publication Data

Smith, P. David.
     Mountains of silver : the story of Colorado's Red Mountain mining
district / P. David Smith.
     p.   cm.
     Includes bibliographical references and index.
     1. Red Mountain Mining District (Colo.) – History. 2. Silver mines
and mining – Colorado – Red Mountain Mining District – History.
I. Title.
F782.R36S65   1994
338.2'7421'097883–dc20   94-4318
                                                                 CIP

ISBN 1-890437-36-0

Cover design by Laurie Goralka Design

Western Reflections Publishing Company
219 Main Street
Montrose, Co 81401
USA

This book is dedicated to the brave and hardy men and women who lived, worked, and died at Red Mountain.

The rain, gust-driven, veils the distant pines
Upon the hill,
Yet cannot hide the skeletons of mines
And silent mill;
And through an empty street the cold wind whines
With hag voice shrill.
How many tragedies the eye may read
In this dead mart;
From cabins, windowless, faint voices plead
And specters start.
I pause and turn upon the hillside's crown,
And vision groups
Where gleam the rain-washed cabin roofs far down
The darkening slopes;
But now the night has closed upon the town
Of buried hopes.

Arthur Chapman
"In a Deserted Mining Camp"

Contents

Acknowledgments

There are many people who have helped in some way to make this book a reality. I would particularly like to thank Barbara Muntyan, Curator of the Ouray County Historical Society; Robert Larson, co-owner and geologist, Monadnock Mineral Services of Ouray; Professor Sam Romberger of Colorado School of Mines; Allen Nossaman, Curator of the San Juan County Historical Society; and Jack Swanson of Ouray, for reading my manuscript for historical or geological accuracy. Also, many thanks go to the staffs of the Colorado Historical Society, Denver Public Library, and The Center for Southwest Studies at Fort Lewis College Library for help with research and especially for help with photographs and maps. A special thank-you goes to Stan Oliner of the Colorado Historical Society for his help in obtaining many hard-to-find newspapers and books. Finally, but not by any means least, I thank my wife Jan for her help in typing the manuscript and for many hours of forbearance while I did research or wrote the book.

Foreword

Red Mountain! The name rings with the allure, the excitement, of the mining West. Red Mountain emerged as an important part of the San Juan mining region, one of the significant mining areas in American history. Its history is the epic of western mining and the pioneers who came to develop and settle this fascinating land.

Permanent mining and settlement came to the San Juans in the early 1870s. The rush to the "silver ribbed" Red Mountain district occurred in the early 1880s. New York's respected *Engineering and Mining Journal*, on October 21, 1882, noted "excitement over discoveries of rich mineral on Red Mountain increases." The reporter went on to say that although "unusually inclement weather" blanketed the vicinity, it "is literally covered with prospectors." Within a year Ouray's outspoken *Solid Muldoon* proclaimed about forty mines were working; Red Mountain had come of age. Reports like this convinced even "the most skeptical" of the "wonderful future in store" for this district.

P. David Smith captures the story of these years in *Mountains of Silver*. The struggle to maintain mining and settlement was paramount. The rivalry of little camps – Red Mountain, Ironton, and Guston, for example – bring an urban flavor to the story that is so familiar in western mining. So, too, is the larger conflict between the mining towns of Silverton and Ouray to dominate this district and tie it firmly into their economic spheres. Like their major counterparts Back East, neither of these communities was going to let the other gain an advantage, and both considered Red Mountain in its economic hinterland.

Improved transportation held the key to a profitable future, and in the nineteenth century that meant one thing – the railroad. Otto Mears built his Silverton Railroad into the Red Mountain district, and it was an engineering marvel, but he found profits less than were expected. The winter season also played havoc with his line and his train schedule, as it did everywhere else in the San Juans. The railroad worked no miracles in this district. It did, however, help make Red Mountain a tourist attraction, part of the famed "Circle Route" out of Denver.

There is failure here, and accomplishment, too. As historian Bruce Catton wrote, "America is equally a tale of might-have-beens and used-to-bes, of ghost towns and shuttered mills . . ." The golden beckoning of the West promised failure as well as success, something most chose to ignore. Ambition and determination at Red Mountain trailed into obscurity for the unsung, average folks who lived and worked there. Yet their saga needs to be told, so continue into the pages of *Mountains of Silver* and join the adventure in a time long gone, an adventure that tells much about the past, and the present, as well.

Duane A. Smith

INTRODUCTION

Today, when a visitor stands in the cold, crisp winter air at the summit of Red Mountain Pass, the impact of the scenery is immediately overwhelming. But after a few moments the visual senses peak, and then the silence seems all-encompassing. An occasional car may go whizzing by on U.S. Highway 550. Several times a day a snowplow driver may stop to take a short break, gather his wits, and rest his snow-burned eyes before returning down the mountain to Ouray or Silverton. If a major storm is approaching, the wind may whistle through the trees. But as the twentieth century draws to a close, little moves and few sounds can be heard on Red Mountain Pass. One could easily imagine that civilization had disappeared from this little corner of the earth. It is now especially hard to envision that, a century ago, several thousand people lived in half a dozen towns within a few miles of Red Mountain Divide.

It may be a little easier to catch a glimpse of past history during the short San Juan summer, which attracts tens of thousands of tourists to the spectacular scenery of the Red Mountains. During late June, July, and August, the whine of four-wheel vehicles can usually be heard. Families often picnic among the alpine wildflowers, or hikers pick their way among the fallen trees. A hint of what transpired is on occasion uncovered when a visitor finds a piece of a shoe, or perhaps a bottle or a nail. The dumps of the mines are commonly

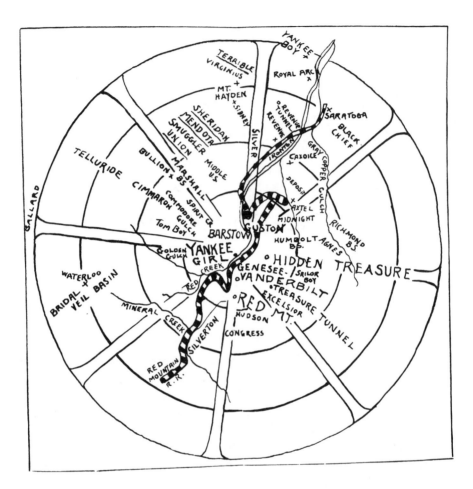

The prospectus for the Red Mountain Railroad, Mining & Smelting Company shows the intense promotion that went on at the Red Mountain district (note the prospectus's Philadelphia address at right). It included this map, which shows most of the valuable San Juan mines; however, the majority of them were not potential customers. (*Author's collection*)

searched, and sometimes small but beautiful mineral specimens are uncovered. Not much is left to chronicle what happened here in the Red Mountain Mining District. The same winds, deep snows, acids, fires, and snowslides that made life so dangerous and difficult for the 1880s prospector trying to gain a foothold at Red Mountain have also quickly destroyed what he left behind.

But dreamers once lived here – and they lived well. Most of the inhabitants of Red Mountain expected their district to grow into one of the richest mining camps on earth. As opposed to the typically squalid and polluted

mining camp, Red Mountain was touted as one of the healthiest spots in Colorado. It had lots of pure, clean air and water. Even under cramped and crowded conditions, where as many as twenty men might pay a dollar each for the privilege of spending the night on the dirt floor of a small cabin, there were reportedly only four people over a twenty-year span who died from sickness. Yet many a man did meet his Maker on Red Mountain as a result of mining accidents, snowslides, or gunfights.

The story of Red Mountain is perhaps an amalgam of many of the western boom-and-bust mining cycles. The setting for the drama that was to eventually unfold took place in some of the most spectacularly beautiful mountains in North America. In the first few years after Red Mountain's discovery, only a small number of prospectors made a few meager strikes. When the first rich silver strikes were made, development was rapid, and half a dozen towns were hastily built throughout the eight-square-mile district. Thousands of prospectors and other fortune hunters poured into what was called "the new Leadville." The land promoters and mining speculators usually stood to do as well as the original prospectors, who in turn were often able to sell their basically unproven claims for fantastic sums. Lawyers and stockbrokers made small fortunes. Merchants, saloonkeepers, and prostitutes made quick, easy money. The first freighters were extremely well paid for bringing supplies into Red Mountain with their long pack trains of burros or mules and, in turn, packing the rich ore out. Even the poorly paid miner had a real chance to make his fortune in the Red Mountains, because many a man would grubstake other prospectors while he toiled in the mines for ten or twelve hours a day, six days a week, to earn money to buy needed supplies.

Better transportation routes were desperately needed to bring out the rich ore from the mines. It didn't take long before wagon roads were being blasted out of solid "impassable" cliffs. The result was the now-famous Million Dollar Highway. Close behind was the Silverton Railroad – "The Rainbow Route" – one of the most isolated and spectacular train lines in the world. This short little twenty-mile railroad is gone today but is known to every narrow-gauge train buff in North America.

The local prospectors and miners faced some terrible hardships. Besides the normal hazards of the mines, they braved problems that were unique to Red Mountain. Most of the rich veins went straight down, necessitating the use of large, expensive pumps to keep the water out of the depths and creating dangerous vertical shafts that followed the ore into the bowels of the earth. One slip and a man could fall a thousand feet. These dangers were compounded at Red Mountain because the exposure of the local iron and sulfur ores to air created sulfuric acid in the water. The acid ate through pumps, rails, shovels, and other mine machinery—it would even eat the shirt right off a man's back! Nails dissolved in the rungs of ladders, planks fell from the ceilings, and cables turned to rust in a month's time.

Dangers didn't only lurk in the depths of the mines at Red Mountain. When on the surface, the men faced heavy snows and bitter cold. In the winter, the snow could pile up so deep that all outside work came to a complete standstill. Even after the railroad came up and over the top of Red Mountain Divide, the mines often had to supply armies of men just to keep the tracks clear. At such times the stages were rigged like sleighs, and sometimes anchors were dragged behind freight wagons (to act as brakes) going down the steep slopes. Scores of men were killed by avalanches or simply by freezing to death.

And the men (and in some cases, the women) laughed and danced and sang and died. A few churches were built, but there were twenty times as many saloons. Gamblers, prostitutes, and con men flocked to the Red Mountain district. Gunfights occurred, claims were jumped, lawsuits were filed, and heroic deeds were performed. In the process, a great deal of damage was done to the most beautiful country in the world; whole forests of trees were cut and roadbeds were blasted into almost vertical cliffs—but some of the most picturesque ruins in North America were the result.

Millions of dollars in capital were poured into the Red Mountain Mining District, mainly supplied by wealthy investors from Europe or the East Coast of the United States—all of whom were as anxious to strike it rich as were the local prospectors. Millions of dollars in silver ore were taken out of the Red Mountains. There were even some men lucky enough to make a profit! In the first decade after its discovery, the Red Mountain Mining District had an output of precious metals that was second in Colorado only to Leadville, whose own rush had begun in 1877. All told, it is estimated that upwards of thirty million dollars in silver, lead, zinc, copper, and gold were taken from

Both Ouray and Silverton were towns whose economies were based on supplying goods and services to the mines in the nearby mountains. These burros rest in Ouray before their trip to the mines. Their loads include a blacksmith's bellows, dynamite, and a stove along with the other supplies. (*W. H. Jackson photo; author's collection*)

the Red Mountain Mining District in a few short decades. At today's prices, the production would come close to a value of a quarter-billion dollars.

The nearby towns of Ouray and Silverton fought fiercely for the right to furnish the necessary supplies to the rich Red Mountain mines. Both the Silverton and Ouray papers constantly extolled the benefits of their localities and warned of the dangers to those brave souls who dared to visit the other settlement. Silverton had the early advantage, because the first discoveries were made on the south side of Red Mountain Divide, and a rough road already ran from that town to the edge of the district. But Ouray soon built a good wagon road into the very heart of the new discoveries. At about the same time, it became evident that the really rich ore was on the Ouray side of the divide. Whatever advantage Ouray took was soon countered by the arrival of the Denver and Rio Grande Railroad at Silverton and the eventual extension of the Silverton Railroad to the Red Mountain district.

After the Silver Panic of 1893, Red Mountain mining was never the same, and the district died slowly. The Silverton Railroad cut back on service, shortened the line, and even eliminated winter routes before finally being abandoned in 1922. After the silver heyday some gold was discovered, and the first successful economic recovery of zinc was made at the Red Mountain district. Red Mountain Town burned in 1892, was reconstructed, burned again in 1895, was partially rebuilt, and was finally destroyed in 1939 by a forest fire. Around the turn of the century, millions of dollars were invested in the Meldrum and Joker tunnels—last-ditch efforts to continue to tap ores that were declining in value.

The last inhabitants of the Red Mountain district were Harry and Milton Larson, who, beginning in the 1920s, lived and prospected near Ironton. Harry died in the 1940s, but Milton continued to live there until he died in the mid-1960s. The last great mine of the Red Mountain district—the Idarado—closed in 1978.

Now Red Mountain is silent. The outline of the railroad grade is faintly visible. A handful of mine buildings still stands. A few men continue to keep up the equipment and do environmental cleanup at the Idarado Mine. But every year less and less of man's accomplishments remain, and more and more of the land returns to its original state. Geologists speculate that rich chimneys of ore may still remain hidden in the mountains. Large reserves of low-grade ore are known to exist. It is only a matter of metal prices rising to the point where the ore can be mined economically again. Red Mountain will come to life once more.

ONE

∞∞∞◦◎◦◎◦∞∞∞

THE LAND

The San Juan Mountains of southwestern Colorado spread out over some twelve thousand square miles and cover approximately one-eighth of the present state of Colorado. They contain some of the highest, most rugged, and richly mineralized country in North America. Hundreds of peaks and ridges rise to over thirteen thousand feet above sea level; many rise to over fourteen thousand feet. The San Juans are so mineralized that more than forty percent of their territory was eventually incorporated into mining districts. However, the majority of the San Juan minerals are concentrated in a much smaller region of about 250 square miles, basically bounded by Silverton on the south, Lake City on the east, Ouray on the north, and Ophir on the west. The Red Mountains lie at the very core of this rich zone.

Although its geologic history is estimated to have begun 350 million years ago, the forces that created the San Juan Mountains themselves are relatively recent. Sixty-five million years ago, the lush tropical period of the dinosaurs was interrupted in the San Juans by a time of intense volcanic activity. Large amounts of molten lava pushed up on the older rocks, which then composed the surface of the earth, breaking and pushing them apart. The San Juan Mountains were the scene of an enormous geologic upheaval, so much so that they have been said to have more country standing on edge than any other place in the world.[1] The earth was cracked deeply in many places. Great amounts

7

of superheated groundwater and mineralized steam from deep within the earth were injected upward into these cracks and, as they cooled, they formed many of the valuable ore veins that run throughout the San Juans. Although the volcanic activity caused the San Juan terrain to grow to be much higher in elevation than it is today, the area did not have its current ruggedness. Instead, the San Juan country was an extensively raised dome that was almost twenty-five thousand feet higher than the surrounding plains. Gradually, over millions of years, the dome was mostly worn flat again by erosion.[2]

Approximately thirty-five million years ago, when the San Juans had again become an almost flat plain, another major series of volcanic eruptions occurred. At least eight thousand cubic miles of a dark gray rock, eventually named the San Juan Formation, was spewed out over the region. Then, for five million years, erosion again worked on the land. About thirty million years ago, more intense volcanic activity occurred. This time, the fine ash from the San Juan volcanoes spread out over thousands of square miles. The ash had a leveling effect, filling in the crevices and canyons caused by the previous erosion. Eventually, another four thousand cubic miles of light lava was blown into the air. These materials settled and weathered into the red- or pink-colored rocks that have come to be known in the San Juans as the Silverton and Potosi volcanics. Together, these volcanic eruptions composed what was one of the largest outpourings of volcanic rock that ever occurred in the Rocky Mountains. The Red Mountains are formed, in large part, by these materials.[3]

As the magma chamber was emptied by the massive eruptions, large empty spaces were left under the earth's surface. The volcanoes would some-times collapse into these underground voids, which formed more or less circu-lar craters or depressions on the surface, referred to as "calderas." Calderas were usually much larger than the actual volcanoes that caused them to form. One of the largest calderas is the elliptically shaped San Juan volcanic depression, which extends some fifty miles from Silverton to Lake City and has an average width of about fifteen miles. The surface of the land inside this caldera sank from one thousand to three thousand feet about twenty-seven to thirty million years ago. This sinking, and a great deal of the erosion that followed, is not apparent today because the basin was filled with volcanic material about a million years later when additional volcanic activity occurred. Eventually, several other smaller calderas were formed within the San Juan volcanic depres-sion. Geologically speaking, this activity occurred only yesterday, so the San Juan Mountains have not yet had time to be worn down. Give the area another ten or fifteen million years and the San Juans will probably be flat again, as they have been at least twice before in the history of our earth.

Twenty-six million years ago, the San Juans' volcanic activity was basically finished, although for many millions of years thereafter there were still ore-bearing solutions being injected into the fractures and faults that had been formed by the intense forces at work. Unlike the San Juan volcanic depression, the outlines of the smaller calderas within are still fairly easy to discern, since they were not later filled with ash. The outside rings of these calderas are generally well defined by a series of faults or sunken areas, and streams and valleys tended to occur in these lower spots. Red Mountain Creek, Mineral Creek, and the Animas River define the outer edge of the depression caused by the Silverton Caldera.

Near the end of this intense geological activity, an unusual phenomenon occurred at the Red Mountains. Mineralized water, gases, and vapors from the underground magma chambers were once again pushed up from deep in the earth. But instead of forming veins in the cracks and fractures, these mineral deposits occurred in nearly vertical cylinders that were round or elliptical and that geologists call "chimneys." Generally, the ore at Red Mountain was formed in these chimneys like a layer cake. The first layer, near the surface, was usually composed of lead and zinc ores – often galena, which is a silver and lead ore. The next layer down was predominantly copper and silver ore. At the bottom were usually low-grade copper ores that often contained very small amounts of gold and that, overall, were the least valuable of all the minerals in the chimneys.

The size of the ore chimneys varied radically. Typical low-grade chimneys were three hundred to two thousand feet deep and one hundred to twelve hundred feet wide. The notably rich pipes of ore (which were sometimes formed within the larger chimneys) were usually much smaller, typically fifteen to thirty feet wide and one hundred to three hundred feet deep. When the conditions were just right, these pipes were often capped or sealed with cementlike silica. If this occurred at or near the surface, the caps would usually be harder than the surrounding territory and stand out as hills slightly higher than the surrounding terrain. What came to be called "The Knob," located near Red Mountain Town, is the perfect example of a capped pipe – a very round, tall hill sitting by itself near the saddle of Red Mountain Pass.[4] At other times, the cap occurred some distance below the surface. In either case, the minerals below the seal in these pipes are much richer than those above the seal or in other pipes that have no seal, because surface waters are then prevented from seeping in and leaching out the minerals.

Besides the pipes and chimneys, yet another surprising geologic phenomenon happened at Red Mountain. As the last of the volcanism occurred, the rising gases and vapors were very acidic. These acids often attacked the softer breccia inside the pipes and leached it out in many places, causing large empty spots (or chambers) to occur in the chimneys. The walls of the pipes were sometimes altered into soft mineralized clays, creating rich mineral caves just waiting to be discovered by the lucky prospectors.

Most of the major ore bodies of the San Juans were deposited by the same type of hot waters that occurred at Red Mountain; however, as already mentioned, the minerals were usually deposited not in chimneys but in veins or fissures that filled much earlier-formed long cracks (in the earth). Some of these large veins of ore radiated out long distances from the Silverton Caldera and ran through the Red Mountain Mining District. For the most part, these particular veins contained relatively low-grade minerals; but, for short distances they could contain some very valuable ore. As a result, the overall geology of the Red Mountains became so complex that it still contains many secrets and surprises for the geologist.

We now know that most of the pipes, chimneys, and veins that were eventually formed at the Red Mountains lined up in a rich mineral belt that occurred on the northwest side of the Silverton Caldera. This belt runs from Anvil Mountain on the south toward Red Mountain No. 1 on the north in the direction of Mount Sneffels. It varies in width from three thousand to seven thousand feet and extends vertically at least five thousand feet. The entire belt is full of low-grade ore. In a smaller zone between Red Mountain Pass and the south end of Ironton Park (and extending to a width of about three thousand feet) were many extremely rich pockets of minerals. Some of these chimneys were so rich that at least one early writer thought that *all* of the lodes and veins of the surrounding San Juan Mountains converged at these points.[5] Although this theory turned out to be false, there was fabulously rich ore in the vicinity of the Red Mountains—enough that a man's wildest dreams could be fulfilled and fantastic fortunes made.

Most people envision the rugged present-day San Juan Mountains as having risen up out of the ground because of intense volcanic activity. In fact, most of the steep, rugged features of the San Juans came about because of glaciers that created many of the large canyons by slowly grinding their way through the upraised dome that had been created by the previous volcanic activity. The ash and lava spewed out by the volcanoes actually tended to level out the high and low spots, so that during periods of volcanic activity the San Juans grew higher but more rounded, much as an ant hill grows upward as grains of sand are thrown to the outside.

Instead of the volcanoes, it was the water, snow, and ice of several ice ages that formed much of the San Juans' rough features. The gray and red volcanic rocks were etched deep by massive glaciers that left long, deep, curving

FIGURE 11.—Diagrammatic cross section showing the physiographic evolution of the San Juan region since the beginning of Tertiary time." *a*, Pre-Cambrian schist and gneiss; *b*, Algonkian quartzites; *c*, Pre-Cambrian granitic intrusion; *d*, Paleozoic and Mesozoic rocks; *e*, Ridgway till and Telluride conglomerate; *f*, middle and late Tertiary volcanics; *g*, Tertiary intrusives.

This sketch shows just how much the San Juans have been reduced and shaped by erosion over millions of years. The original mountains were 25,000 feet high! Now the highest peaks are a little over 14,000 feet. *(Reprinted from Wallace Atwood, "Eocene Glacial Deposits in Southwest Colorado," USGS Professional Paper 95-B, June 12, 1915, page 23)*

valleys as they slowly moved away from the center of the San Juans. The sides of these valleys we now think of as mountains. The glaciers were followed by large creeks and rivers, which further eroded the land and caused gullies, jagged pinnacles, and deep crevices to appear. Near Red Mountain, one glacial system moved north toward Ouray and another moved south toward Silverton, thus leaving Red Mountain Divide—the steep-sided yet somewhat flat-topped ridge that runs from Red Mountain No. 3 westward toward Trico Peak. The San Juan glacial periods came and went for millions of years, but the last such period was only about ten thousand years ago—a few seconds in the past in geologic terms!

As a result of all the volcanic and glacial activity, the San Juan Mountains are rugged, broken, and extremely irregular. So much so, that today when rain or snow falls on the north side of Red Mountain Divide the water will flow in a mostly northerly direction down Red Mountain Creek to the Uncompahgre River, from there into the Gunnison River, and, finally, into the Colorado River at Grand Junction. From that point, the flow will change to the south and southwest through Utah and Arizona. A drop of rain or a flake of snow that falls even a few inches south of Red Mountain Divide will follow a very different path down Mineral Creek, south to the Animas River and, thence, into the San Juan River. At this point, the flow will shift to a westerly direction until the San Juan meets the Colorado River near Rainbow Bridge National Monument, a few dozen miles above the Utah-Arizona border, some three hundred miles from its starting point.

Although a glacier carved out the large valley running north away from Red Mountain Pass, another geological phenomenon occurred a few miles north of Red Mountain Divide that changed the expected topography. A huge landslide moved down what is now called Hendrick Gulch and blocked the valley. This in turn caused a silt-filled lake to back up toward the divide. The extremely flat, broad, swampy valley called Ironton Park was the result.

A major landslide came down Hendrick's Gulch thousands of years ago and filled Red Mountain Canyon. Ever since, Ironton Park has been swampy, and in the 1880s large amounts of grass grew there. Red Mountain No. 1 is left of center in the photograph; Red Mountain No. 2 and No. 3 are to the right. *(W. H. Jackson photo; author's collection)*

At one time, the valley was very grassy. Eastern travel writer Earnest Ingersoll reported that, in 1885, the valley was covered with "prairies of long grass that every autumn is mowed for hay."[6] With the onset of mining, mostly willows filled the park; but recently with mining operations at a standstill, the grass has begun to return to the valley.

Today, as the crow flies, the historic mining towns of Silverton and Ouray are situated about twenty miles apart; and at an almost equal distance from each town lies the formidable mountain barrier known as Red Mountain Pass. It is the center of the Red Mountain Mining District and it is here that our story is set. But we should keep in mind that "Red Mountain" is actually three separate mountains – numbered 1, 2, and 3 from north to south. Eventually, two towns coexisted on the slopes of Red Mountain No. 3, and both were called "Red Mountain." The divide, the creek, and the mining district all bore the name "Red Mountain." All of this makes it easy to see why "Red Mountain" has been a considerable source of confusion to historians, geologists, and the public at large.

The brilliant hues of red, yellow, and orange rocks that cover the Red

Mountain slopes obviously gave the region its name. The red color comes from the weathering of pyrite that covers its slopes. The mountains have so much pyrite that they actually seem to glow after rains, standing out like beacons from the mists and low-hanging clouds. In just the right kind of light, the mountains look as if someone poured bright red and yellow paint down their sides. Early-day writers called them "the Scarlet Peaks,"[7] the "Crimson Domes,"[8] or referred to them as being "gaudier than a cardinal's hat."[9] In 1874, geologist Ferdinand W. Hayden was the first to officially and scientifically investigate the Red Mountains. In his 1876 report he mentioned that the Red Mountains were "originally white; the presence of ferric oxygen compounds gradually changed this color to yellow, orange, red and brown . . . Decomposition of pyrite releases the sulphur and changes the iron . . . This, in varying percentages, produces the colors and shades above enumerated. This mineral (pyrite) was probably segregated during the period of the cooking of the rock. Its presence denotes nothing save the existence and ejection of a large amount of iron and sulphur at the time of eruption."[10]

The prospectors didn't care about the rhetoric. They only knew that the bright colors were clues to possible rich ore bodies. The pyrite was the result of an alteration of the volcanic rock by hot sulfuric and acidic waters. Even if the Red Mountains were only composed of this highly oxidized red-colored low-grade ore (technically most of the rocks are composed of an aggregate of clay materials, diaspore, alunite, and quartz), the early prospectors knew that the same volcanic activity and acidic waters that formed the Red Mountains might have formed rich silver veins nearby. The reports of Hayden and other early explorers were, therefore, to draw many a prospector to the vicinity of the Red Mountains.

Getting to the Red Mountain Mining District was not easy. It was located high up in the mountains, the lower elevations being about ninety-five hundred feet at the south and north bases of Red Mountain Pass and rising up to over thirteen thousand feet at the tops of the surrounding mountains. Most of the rich mines were discovered at between ten thousand and eleven thousand feet in elevation – just slightly below the tree line (the imaginary line above which trees will not grow) in what is called the subalpine life zone. It was a harsh and cold climate that awaited the prospectors, very similar to living in northern Canada. Heavy stands of Engelmann spruce and subalpine fir predominate on the divide, although aspen may be found in the lower areas (the Canadian life zone). Sometimes the trees could fall and twist together in such as way as to make an impassable barrier. Only a few scrawny and twisted limber and bristlecone pines could be found on exposed windblown ridges and in the rocky soils that cover the higher parts of the Red Mountain Mining District. A local prospector was almost sure of having too much or too little timber available nearby for his needs.

On the more enchanting side of life, an enormous variety of mountain wildflowers did well in the subalpine life zone. The heavy winter snows melted slowly, thereby supplying plenty of moisture to the flowers of early summer while they waited for the late-summer thunderstorms to arrive. Spring came late to the Red Mountains – sometimes not until May or June. Once it did come, everything on the mountain was a deep, soggy mud. There were many swampy areas that remained throughout the summer and fall. In the winter, which sometimes returned to Red Mountain by late September or early October, the ground would freeze and the snow and ice would tend to level out the terrain, often actually making travel easier.[11]

The harshness of the climate at Red Mountain always has been dramatically influenced by both altitude and exposure to the sun. Every thousand feet that a prospector increased his elevation was the equivalent of traveling 350 miles to the north at sea level. Due to a lack of sunlight, a north-facing slope usually had the very same climate as a south-facing slope that was several thousand feet higher in elevation. Red Mountain prospectors faced weather that was generally dry and sunny, but there were wide fluctuations in temperature from day to night. When the sun was out, the temperature usually felt warmer than it actually was because of the rarefied air and the effect of solar heating. Men could often work comfortably during the day in below-freezing weather without wearing a coat. The temperatures in the valleys, which lay at either side of Red Mountain Divide, were often much lower than at the top of the divide (frigid air settles); therefore, extremely cold temperatures were generally not a major problem on the Red Mountains, although the thermometer could drop far below zero for short periods of time.

In the winter, the sky was usually cloudless between snowstorms, which could be expected to arrive every four or five days. The weather often would be mild and balmy one day and cold and snowy the next. The wind was normally light (blowing only at the beginning of snowstorms), which helped keep the chill factor close to the actual temperature and kept drifting snow down to a minimum. Although the temperature would only occasionally fall to below zero, the snow, wind, and cold could, on occasion, combine to bring deadly windchill factors of thirty or forty degrees below zero.

The San Juans are one of the wettest areas of Colorado, which as a whole is in a rather dry zone. In the summer, the Red Mountain weather was normally crystal clear and sunny in the mornings, but clouds usually formed by lunchtime, and light rain showers could be expected in the afternoons.

Yet most of the year's average of forty inches of precipitation came in the winter in the form of light snow. Twelve to thirty-six inches of snow could fall on Red Mountain Divide in a single day, but that snow might contain less than half an inch of water. Because of the heavy snows, steep terrain, and warm days, avalanches often roared down the mountains in the winter—especially in the months of January, February, and March.

The rain and the deep snows left the divide covered with small streams in all but the coldest parts of the winter. In fact, many of the small streamlets simply started from water that oozed up out of the ground. Some of the clearest, purest water known to man was on Red Mountain Divide, yet a dozen yards away a stream might have become so polluted from the natural minerals in the ground that the water would be undrinkable. The surface, where not rocky, was generally boggy because water collected in every little depression on the divide at any time the ground was not frozen. In the summer and fall, quite a few small lakes provided a natural habitat for the ducks, geese, and other waterfowl that were passing through.

Although at times the Red Mountains were a harsh environment, most wildlife thrived there, and the local animal populations included deer, marmots (whistle pigs), ptarmigan, bear, elk, rabbits, squirrels, and occasionally mountain sheep and coyotes. The lush, tall grasses in the marshes and nearby heavy timber were perfect for their habitation. Many of the trees had been knocked to the ground by the heavy snows or by avalanches, thereby allowing sunlight to reach the many small parks and providing protection for the smaller animals. In the summer, the rich soil provided the perfect base for wild raspberries, strawberries, chokecherries, and many other edible plants. However, as soon as the divide became heavily populated, the animals began to migrate out of the vicinity and the vegetation began to disappear.

William L. Marshall, who passed through the Red Mountains with the Wheeler survey party in 1875, left a vivid early description of Red Mountain Divide—"the mountains . . . are of rounded slopes, which, though still retaining the characteristic steepness common to the mountains of this entire region, are, as a rule, covered with Alpine grasses, and the soil, though often boggy from the melting snow, offers a foothold for animals in their attempts at climbing or crossing them. The most marked feature of this portion of the divide are the two [sic] brilliant scarlet red peaks between the headwaters of Cement Creek and the Red Fork of the Uncompahgre. They are not of a very great height, but the decomposition of the pyrites in the trachytes composing them leaves the entire surface of those beautiful cones a brilliant red which contrasts strongly with the green bold pates or the somber brown of the trachytic masses of the neighboring peaks."[12]

The Red Mountains constituted a severe yet bountiful land that waited for the first explorers and prospectors. The environment would demand everything from the men who searched the slopes for riches, but the district promised everything that a prospector could dream of in return. Nature had set the stage. Fantastic scenery awaited the traveler. Fabulous riches awaited discovery by the prospector. It was time for man to come upon the scene.

TWO

———≈◦◦◦◦◦◦◉◦◦◦◦◦◦≈———

THE EXPLORERS

Although even today a harsh and rugged land, the central portion of the San Juan Mountains was an especially uninviting place some ten thousand years ago when glaciers filled the mountain valleys. By that time, prehistoric peoples had begun to roam throughout what was to become southwestern Colorado. Over the next nine thousand years, the Clovis, Folsom, Fremont, and Anasazi cultures all flourished within forty or fifty miles of Red Mountain, but there is little indication that they ventured very far into or stayed for very long in the cold and uninviting San Juans. The nomadic Utes inhabited the southwestern portion of Colorado from about A.D. 1300 until they were expelled by the United States government in 1881. The Utes also avoided travel into the central San Juans except on occasional hunting and foraging trips in the summer. Even then, they were usually just passing through the area on their way somewhere else. A few Ute hunting trails, arrowheads, and flint knives have been found in the vicinity of Red Mountain, but not nearly to the extent that they are found at the fringes of the San Juans or in most other parts of Colorado.

The San Juan country was so challenging and uninviting that the early official Spanish and American explorers who probed this newly discovered land either avoided the rugged San Juan Mountains altogether or suffered grave and often tragic consequences. Don Juan Mirade Rivera's Spanish expedition

17

passed some fifty miles to the south and west of the Red Mountains when looking for gold in 1765. Eleven years later, friars Escalante and Dominguez skirted the San Juans fifteen miles to the north and west while looking for a trade route to California. However, the Escalante–Dominguez diaries and maps show that at the time of their expedition, most of the prominent mountains and rivers of the San Juans had established Spanish names–a sure sign that unauthorized prospectors had been frequenting the area. Some of the Spanish names even indicated *la plata*–Spanish for silver! Vague and inexact tales of lost San Juan gold and silver mines were to precede many of the early American explorers–again at least an indication that earlier but unrecorded prospectors had been in the San Juans and may have discovered precious metals.

By the early part of the nineteenth century, American fur traders began to venture into what was to become western Colorado. In the 1830s, Antoine Robidoux established a "fort" about sixty miles north of Red Mountain near present-day Delta. He had several dozen men working traps in the surrounding mountains and, although no actual confirmation of such has been found, one or more of the trappers is very likely to have ventured into the Red Mountains in search of beaver pelts.

In 1848, the United States government sent John C. Fremont to explore a region that included the San Juans, and in 1853 Captain John W. Gunnison was dispatched to investigate the uncharted lands that bordered the San Juans to the north. Both men were given the specific assignment of looking for feasible transcontinental railroad routes. Both expeditions met with disaster. Gunnison not only found his route to be too rugged for a railroad, but he was later killed by Paiutes in Utah. Fremont had hardly left the San Luis Valley on his way into the San Juan Mountains before his pack mules froze and were eaten by his starving men. Eleven of his contingency of thirty-three men perished in the deep winter snows of the San Juan Mountains. It now seems like a miracle that the whole group wasn't destroyed. Somehow one of Fremont's party did manage to find placer gold about a dozen miles east of Silverton, near the headwaters of the San Juan River. He initially kept his strike a secret and returned the next year to officially locate his claim. Even though the overwrought man searched frantically, he was unable to find his original discovery. No recorded account exists of mining activity in the San Juans at this time, but existing arrastras (devices to crush ore) and signs of previous placer mining activity were reported by the first American prospectors.

In 1859, during the Pikes Peak gold rush, more than fifty thousand prospectors flooded into present-day Colorado (then part of Kansas Territory). Some lucky individuals had immediate success, but there was too little placer gold on the eastern slopes of the Rocky Mountains to satisfy the hordes of men who had traveled hundreds of miles to strike it rich. Almost half of the prospectors quickly returned home. A scattering of hopeful locations were staked by those who remained. A few claims were even successfully worked for placer gold. But most of the diggings soon played out, and the stalwarts of the "fifty-niners" began to spread into other parts of the Rocky Mountains to search for their riches.

By the spring of 1860, the first American prospectors had taken their search for gold and silver to the vicinity of the Red Mountains. Many were following rumors that gold could be found in what later came to be known as Baker's Park, the high mountain valley that encompasses present-day Silverton. In July 1860, Charles Baker led a group of seven men into the park that would bear his name. The men had only limited success in prospecting for gold, but Baker returned again in 1861, and this time several hundred men accompanied him. Quite a large amount of silver was discovered, but it could not easily be extracted by panning. In fact, most of the prospectors had no desire to mine for silver. They were looking for rich and easy-to-pan placer gold similar to what had been found in California.

Some of Baker's prospectors traveled north out of Baker's Park and looked for gold in or near the Red Mountains. It was reported that they explored to the east, north, and west of Baker's Park, "passing over the high mountains to the headwaters of the Gunnison, Uncompahgre and San Miguel rivers, prospecting all their head tributaries and gulches . . . ."[1] But the men who had been attracted by Baker's discovery soon went away frustrated. One disappointed man wrote the Denver-based *Rocky Mountain News* that many experienced miners "say the country does not look right for gold country . . . Baker is either deceived himself, or the most outrageous deceiver that ever lived."[2]

During the winter of 1861, another group of frustrated gold seekers called "the Wright party" left Fort Garland and crossed the Continental Divide over Cochetopa Pass. They panned for gold near present-day Ridgway Lake and traveled into the large bowl that became the future site of Ouray, but like their counterparts in Baker's Park, they found only small amounts of gold and nearly starved to death. Unlike Baker's party, this group didn't even have the consolation of finding silver. The Wright party left as soon as the snow had melted enough to make travel possible.

Terrible hardships were faced by these early pioneers. The San Juans were too remote, the weather was too harsh, and the men were frequently harassed by Utes (on whose land they were trespassing). The United States had become embroiled in the Civil War, and many a would-be prospector left the Rocky Mountains to join the fighting. The war also caused an acute shortage of soldiers

This very early sketch of Silverton and Baker's Park has stylized the mountains so that they look more rugged than they actually were but otherwise presents a fairly accurate picture of the early days of the settlement. The San Juan country was already being publicized heavily throughout the United States by the time this illustration was published. *(Reprinted from* Frank Leslie's Illustrated Newspaper, *May 8, 1875; author's collection)*

who were needed by those miners who did decide to stay in the San Juan Mountains to protect them from the justly upset Ute Indians. All significant prospecting activity, therefore, came to an end in the San Juans for nearly a decade.

It wasn't until 1870 that gold seekers returned in any number to Baker's Park, and it was an additional five years before they made their way back to the present-day Ouray–Ridgway valley. Silver, although not as valuable as gold, was becoming a mineral of consequence. This time, most prospectors were actually excited to make new discoveries of silver; and some, like Miles T. Johnson, who prospected at the Little Giant Mine in Baker's Park, even found considerable amounts of gold.

Approximately fifty men prospected in or near Baker's Park in the summer of 1871, although most left for more comfortable quarters as soon as winter descended upon the high mountain valley. In August 1872, mining had progressed to the point that a small ore mill was shipped to the Little

The early San Juan prospectors faced the constant threat of a Ute attack. The problem was not that the Utes were particularly ferocious (in fact, they were quite peaceful) but that the whites couldn't seem to keep their promises to stay off Ute land, again and again taking land that they had promised the Utes was theirs "forever." (*Drawing by W. A. Rogers for* Harper's Weekly, *October 25, 1879; author's collection*)

Giant Mine one small piece at a time by pack mule or burro. It didn't matter that, under a United States treaty in 1868, the San Juans had been solemnly pledged to be the sovereign territory of the Ute Indians. Hundreds of prospectors headed toward Baker's Park in the spring of 1872.

The rush to the San Juans gained so much momentum that it was obvious that something had to be done about the Utes' possession of the land. No town could be platted, no title to a mine could become legal, until the Utes' land could be taken from them. Although the federal government sent soldiers into the San Juans in an attempt to keep the overly eager prospectors out of Ute territory, it was only a temporary measure. Ultimately the politicians were not about to anger hundreds of its citizens because of a few Ute Indians; and the prospectors were adamant that Washington should take whatever action necessary to get possession of the San Juans.[4]

On the other hand, although the Utes were upset that the "great white father" of the United States couldn't seem to keep his word, the local Native Americans were content as long as the whites did their mining in the isolated and out-of-the-way mountains. Chief Ouray summed up the Utes' feelings during the Brunot Treaty negotiations of 1873 when he stated: "We are perfectly willing to sell our mountain lands, and hope the miners will find heaps of gold and silver. We have no wish to molest or make them any trouble. We do not want they should go down into our valleys, however, and kill or scare away our game."[5] The Utes only hunted on occasion in the San Juans, and just a few prospectors spent more than the summer season in the mountainous portion of their land. However, the Americans had several times promised the Utes that they would be able to keep the San Juans forever. Many Utes questioned whether the Americans would ever be satisfied.

The answer to what seemed to be a stalemate came when the Ute chief, Ouray, was promised an extremely tempting bribe—if he would get the Utes to sign a treaty to give up the San Juans, the United States government would find his long-lost son. After lengthy negotiations, a relatively small sixty- by seventy-five-mile section of the mountains was settled on as something the Utes were willing to relinquish. The Utes reserved the right to continue hunting

This photograph was taken in 1874 in Washington, D.C., during the signing of the Brunot Treaty, which deeded the San Juans to the United States. Otto Mears is at the far right in the second row; Ouray and his wife, Chipeta, are in the center of the first row. (*Colorado Historical Society*)

in the San Juans – a condition that made the miners quite nervous, but one with which they were willing to live. After the signing of the treaty and ratification by the United States Senate in 1874, a tour was arranged by the United States government to show the Utes the new boundaries of their land and to show off some of the more successful mines in the territory that had been ceded. The latter part of the offer was something that did not interest the Utes.

By 1874, the local prospectors realized that their mining claims could soon be legalized. The potential value of the San Juan mines was recognized as far away as the eastern United States because the region was being described in glowing terms by writers in various mining journals. It was not gold that was causing the excitement. Most thoughts of placer mining for gold had long been abandoned. It was the rich silver quartz veins that now attracted attention.

Notwithstanding the large amount of publicity and excitement over the mineral potential of the San Juans, the remoteness and ruggedness of the local mountains caused mining and prospecting to continue at a slow pace. F. H. Endlich of the Hayden Survey wrote: "At the time of my visit at the San Juan mines in August and September, 1874, but comparatively little work had been done. The greater portion of the miner's time and energy was devoted to prospecting, and but a few had developed their lodes to any extent. One difficulty under which they labored was want of available capital, and of places where the ore might be converted into cash."[6]

The locale that eventually became the community of Silverton had been settled as early as 1873. The signing of the Brunot Treaty, however, prompted the town's official foundation in 1874. The name of the new town itself reflected the predominance of silver in the district. There was now at least some limited capital for local development and, perhaps of even greater importance, the locals had a determined attitude that they would overcome all obstacles, no matter how difficult they might be. Silverton and nearby Howardsville quickly began to take on the appearance of true frontier towns now that the Ute "threat" was over. About fifty prospectors even spent the winter of 1874–1875 "holed up" in Baker's Park.

In the early 1870s, the United States government decided that great surveys must be made of the vast uncharted portions of the western United States and its territories. In 1873, the Wheeler survey group was authorized by the United States War Department to investigate the unexplored land to the west of Denver. In particular, they were to look for possible railroad or wagon routes through the mountains and were to prepare detailed maps of the territory. In 1874 and again in 1875 the Wheeler group made its way into the San Juans. Those same years, the Hayden survey expedition was also sent into the San Juan Mountains by the Department of the Interior. Their basic purpose was to check the local geology, flora, fauna, drainage, and topography. Eventually, in 1877, Hayden published a detailed atlas of his group's findings and of his surveys, which, by then, covered the entire western portion of the new state of Colorado. His efforts are especially remembered in the Red Mountains, where the long, tall ridge to the west of Ironton Peak came to carry the name of this great explorer.

Franklin Rhoda was one of the first members of the Hayden Survey to explore the Red Mountains. He traveled from Silverton directly over Red Mountain Divide in the summer of 1874 and later reported that "having camped overnight at the junction of Bear [South Fork] and Mineral Creeks, the next morning [September 3] we moved up the latter, and made stations 27 and 28 on a high ridge between Mineral and Cement Creeks . . . Camping near the head of the creek, the following day we crossed the Pass at its head and passed over to the head of the Uncompahgre River."[7] Rhoda had crossed Red Mountain Divide but, before doing so, had noted that Mineral Creek was so full of iron, sulfur, and other minerals as to be totally unfit for drinking. It was an obvious sign of heavy mineralization, but no major note was made of the discovery.

Rhoda continued: "The elevation of this pass is 11,100 feet above the sea. It is entirely covered with timber. The slope to the south is quite gradual but to the north, down the Uncompahgre, the fall is 800 feet in two miles. Then for several miles the stream flows comparatively smoothly, till it finally enters a deep box-canyon, where the fall is very great. Traveling for some distance is both difficult and dangerous. At the bottom of the first steep slope a great area of fallen timber commences. The logs so cover the ground that traveling is very nearly impossible."[8] Rhoda reported that there were two existing trails that led over Red Mountain Pass to the head of the Uncompahgre River, but since the box canyon on the north (near the present-day Riverside Slide tunnel) barred all possible access, there was no need for further description.

In August 1875, William Marshall of the Wheeler Survey was surveying the same area and noted that "the Red Mountains attract the eye instantly from any point of view by their brilliancy and are a well-known landmark."[9] He reported that a new mining town was already in existence in "Red Mountain Valley" (today called Ironton Park). He believed the name of the new settlement to be "Park City." Although very short-lived, it was probably the first settlement in what is now Ouray County. Marshall confirmed the Hayden party's opinion that the Uncompahgre Canyon was "utterly impassable" and declared that the new mining town of Park City was only accessible from Silverton, "except by a rough and steep trail from the headwaters of the Uncompahgre" (the present-day Engineer Mountain–Poughkeepsie route).

The southern section of Uncompahgre Canyon was composed of walls so sheer and high that it prompted early U.S. surveyors to label the canyon totally "impassable." Less than ten years later Otto Mears had conquered the canyon, but to do so he had had to literally hang the road from the walls in places. *(W. H. Jackson photo; Colorado Historical Society)*

Marshall pointed out, with considerable foresight, that transportation within the entire San Juan region would be very difficult, but that "it is conceded that the mines of San Juan, La Plata and Hinsdale counties [at this time what were later to be Ouray and San Miguel counties were also included] are valuable, rich, and extensive, this problem of routes of communication must touch these towns . . . and make for them and for the transportation companies the prospective traffic of this rich mining and producing region an alluring prize."[10]

Although traveling in "unexplored territory," the Wheeler and Hayden expeditions lived in comparative comfort at their base camp in Baker's Park. In 1874, Hayden wrote: "A camp was set up in the upper end of Baker's Park, in which was left all extra material in charge of two or three men, and then, traveling with but few animals and very light packs, rapid side trips were made into all the strongholds and fastness of the grandest mountains in all of Colorado."[11] By 1875, William Marshall reported Howardsville, Eureka, Animas Forks, and Silverton to be good-size towns. He predicted the whole of Baker's Park to be filled with houses and mills within five to ten years. It seemed a likely prediction, since the population of Silverton and Howardsville had already risen to several hundred by the summer of 1875.

This photograph was taken at the Hayden Survey's base camp near Silverton in the summer of 1874. From here, smaller groups ranged into the nearby mountains – one group explored the Red Mountains. The Survey returned to finish the job the next year. *(W. H. Jackson photo; Colorado Historical Society)*

On the other side of Red Mountain Divide, the settlement of Ouray was founded on August 28, 1875. During the winter of 1875–1876, a few prospectors stayed in the bowl that now encompasses the city of Ouray, and the settlement grew as quickly as Silverton when rich mines were discovered nearby. In 1876, Ouray was officially platted and boasted a population of more than four hundred. By 1880, Silverton and Ouray had grown to the point that they were the two largest towns in the San Juans, although Silverton was approximately twice the size of Ouray.

The steep ravines and the tall mountains that lay between Ouray and Silverton stymied the building of a road directly between these two towns. The route that had to be taken was circuitous and passable only on horseback. Even in good summer weather it could take a day or more to travel from one town to the other. The early-day route was not the same as at present; rather, from Silverton one would travel up the Animas River to the small settlement at Mineral Point and then down the Uncompahgre River (along the route of the present-day Engineer Road) to its confluence with Red Mountain Creek and on north to Ouray. Although circuitous, it was still the quickest route because the southern portion of the Uncompahgre Canyon

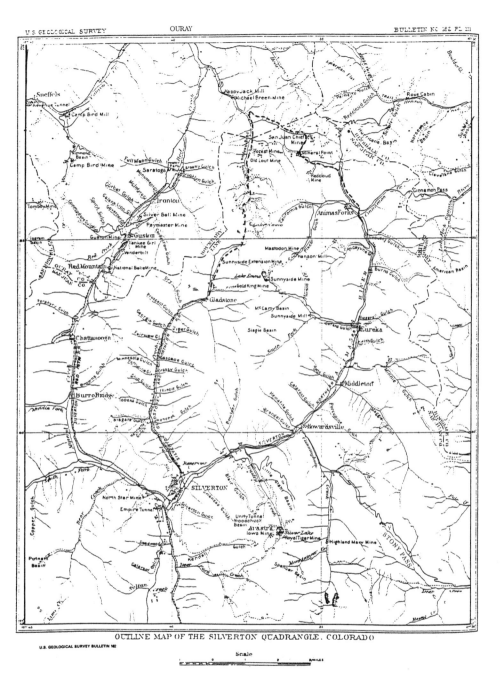

OUTLINE MAP OF THE SILVERTON QUADRANGLE, COLORADO

U.S. GEOLOGICAL SURVEY BULLETIN 182

Scale

Early explorers went into the Howardsville area over Stony Pass (*lower right*) or Cinnamon Pass (*upper right*). Early travel between Ouray and Silverton was by Howardsville and Animas Forks or, for the really hardy traveler, through Gladstone and Poughkeepsie Gulch. The Red Mountain route was considered impassable in the 1870s. (*Reprinted from* U.S. Geological Survey Bulletin 182; *author's collection*) continued to prove as impossible to traverse as Hayden and Marshall had originally described.[12]

A shorter trail (but one that was barely passable) was to travel from Ouray up the Uncompahgre River through Poughkeepsie Gulch to near the top of Red Mountain No. 1 and then down Cement Creek to Silverton. This was the rough, steep path described by Wheeler. Although this route was shorter in distance, it was so difficult and tortuous near the end of Poughkeepsie Gulch that it was still quicker to travel between the towns by way of Mineral Point.

Despite the rugged terrain and lack of decent wagon roads, as soon as the news of the discovery of silver and gold began to leak out, a torrent of men began to flood into the central San Juans. These early prospectors knew the mountains and their secrets well; they traveled lightly and lived off the land. They need to be distinguished from many later prospectors who were basically city men hoping to quickly strike it rich. The "greenhorn prospector" depended, in great part, upon guidebooks and the advice of the old-timers. One local guidebook suggested that every new San Juan prospector should be equipped with kitchen utensils, three double blankets, a poncho, one pound of flour, half a pound of beef for each day in the mountains, mules, drills, sledgehammer, pick, shovel, and powder and fuse. As if this weren't enough, an additional three hundred to five hundred dollars in cash was suggested! The guide went on to detail local temperatures, composition of ore, railway routes to the mines, cost of living in various towns, distances between towns, mining laws, and the necessary forms for filing claims.[13]

Whether a prospector was a grizzled old-timer or a tenderfoot, he needs to be distinguished from the miner. Prospectors were the men who scoured the mountains looking for a bonanza discovery. They drifted in and out of a mining district depending on the current rumors. When they found promising ore, they staked their claim by marking the corners, recorded it with the authorities, and did the necessary assessment work. This gave the prospector legal ownership of the minerals located on his discovery, but very seldom would he be able to afford (or have the desire) to carry out any kind of extensive development. It was usually much too expensive for the poor prospector to come up with the vast sums of money needed to extensively and properly develop a mine and thereby receive a patent (or total legal ownership) from the federal government.

Besides, the prospector was usually quite anxious to quickly sell his new mine and move on to look for new discoveries. It gave him an instant profit and left no further financial risk. It was then up to those investors who had the necessary money to bring in the heavy equipment and hire the miners to do the backbreaking work needed to take the great majority of the precious minerals from the claim. As opposed to the prospector, the miner usually stayed to work at a single mine until it closed. He was usually paid regular daily wages or perhaps a fixed amount of wages for a fixed amount of work. A miner's life was not easy, but his income was relatively secure and he could "settle down" in one place.

By the end of 1876, most of the major mineral-producing districts in the San Juans had been discovered, and a large influx of capital was making serious mining activity possible along the Animas River near Silverton, in Imogene and Yankee Boy basins near Ouray, and in the vicinity of Mineral Point. In 1876, Frank Fosset, a travel writer, wrote that although the San Juans "remained a *terra incognita* through all the years that the other Colorado mining districts were discovered and developed, the region bids fair to surpass all others in the enormous size and length of its silver-bearing veins."[14]

Although other districts flourished throughout the San Juans, no important discoveries were immediately made in the Red Mountains. The first prospectors were working under some major disadvantages. As previously mentioned, the crust of the earth in the vicinity of Red Mountain had been subjected to a variety of geologic alterations that often overlapped, making any type of geologic predictions difficult. The valuable minerals at Red Mountain were in the small pipes hidden within the larger chimneys that themselves did not carry particularly valuable ore; the richest minerals were usually found some distance below the surface. Because of the heavy snows, there was only a short time during the year when the ground could be examined for ore, and even then there were very few exposed veins or outcroppings on the surface for the prospectors to discover.

San Juan prospectors normally looked for veins, not chimneys or pipes. It was such a common occurrence for rich veins to outcrop on the surface in the San Juans that one local mining guide boasted in 1877 that "the surface croppings are so distinct that, without previous experience, the would-be prospector will invariably discern the 'signs' and with pick and hammer secure a piece of 'blossom' rock which assures him that he has 'struck it rich.'"[15] It was also an axiom in the San Juans that ore increased in value the higher in elevation it was formed, but this rule turned out to be only partially true in the Red Mountain district. Some of the pipes within the chimneys were extremely rich, but most of the ore at the top of the chimneys, although high in elevation, was low-grade. It was only after digging down into the chimney that the prospector would usually find the high-grade ore. Because of all the prospecting problems, only a few persistent men continued to work the Red

Because most Red Mountain ores were in chimney deposits, the typical mining method was to dig vertical shafts rather than horizontal tunnels. In the discovery depicted here, the prospectors have yet to determine whether their "find" has any value. (*Reprinted from* Harper's Weekly, *November 10, 1883; author's collection*)

Mountain slopes in the late 1870s. They were convinced that the signs indicated they should be able to make a rich strike. A few staked claims, but the Red Mountain ore always seemed to be of a low grade.

At the same time, the attention of many Colorado prospectors and capitalists was drawn away from the San Juans. The new excitement was the discovery of rich strikes of silver in Leadville. For years, Leadville silver had been overlooked in the mad search for gold. Finally, in 1877, the value of the dark "worthless" sand, which the local prospectors had cursed in their pans, was recognized. It turned out that Leadville was sitting on a mountain of silver, and the district exploded with activity like no previous rush known in Colorado. By 1878, tens of thousands of prospectors and merchants swarmed into Leadville, and a good many of them came from the San Juans. Throughout Colorado, thoughts of gold were nearly forgotten. During the late 1870s and 1880s, it was silver that was the object of a prospector's search – not just in the San Juans, but in the entire new state of Colorado. By the end of the decade, Colorado had surpassed all other states or territories in terms of silver production.

The Red Mountain prospectors continued to search, and they were not experiencing total failure. Several promising silver mines were located during the late 1870s. However, the ore, although valuable, was not of an extremely rich grade and, since silver was worth only a sixteenth of an equal weight of gold, it took much larger quantities of silver-bearing ore to turn a profit, or, alternatively, the costs of silver production needed to be kept low. Easy and inexpensive transportation of silver ore was, therefore, of great concern. Places like Leadville, at the end of the Arkansas River Valley, were quickly supplied with a railroad. Transportation was not easy in the late 1870s in the San Juans. Neither Ouray nor Silverton had a railroad, and Red Mountain's ore had to be hauled some two hundred miles by mules or burros to the smelters.

Most of the mining activity that did take place at the Red Mountain Mining District was at the extreme northern end of the Mineral Creek valley in the vicinity of what was later known as Chattanooga. Two of the principal mines were the Silver Crown and the Silver Ledge. The Silver Crown group was located in 1878, and its string of claims took up all of Mill Creek Gulch, which lay directly to the west of the eventual location of the town of Chattanooga. The Silver Ledge was located near the source of Mineral Creek and just a short distance to the south of Red Mountain Pass. By the end of the 1870s, both mines showed large bodies of a low-grade silver ore.

Although greater total amounts of silver were deposited in the Silver Ledge and Silver Crown pipes, they were not nearly as concentrated as in the chimneys that were later discovered. With either high silver prices or extremely cheap transportation, their low-grade ores were economical to produce. But, even though the mines were relatively close to Silverton, there was only a pack trail to connect them. Transportation was not cheap, and silver prices were not especially high. The Silver Crown and Silver Ledge mines were, therefore, only marginal producers at the time.

Prospectors continued to scour the Red Mountain district at the end of the 1870s, even though nothing but low-grade ore had been exposed. A momentary rush of excitement occurred when Leadville mining millionaire Horace Tabor purchased mines at the head of Poughkeepsie Gulch, on the border of the western slopes of Red Mountain No. 1. A small village called Poughkeepsie was built high above and on the south end of the gulch from which it took its name. George Croffutt, another early-day travel writer, described it as "the biggest little mining camp in the San Juan country." Tabor toured the central San Juans in 1879, proclaiming that his claims were "worth nearly or about the same now, I suppose, as my interests in Leadville."[16] The *Ouray Times* tried to use the event to stir up business by reporting that "the excitement is intense; our streets are becoming deserted and he who cannot get a pack animal shoulders his blanket and grub and takes his way towards Red Mountain Park."[17] However, most results were disappointing. Ore was found, but it was low-grade, and without high silver prices or inexpensive transportation to get it to the mills, the ore wasn't worth shipping.

There was, however, good reason to be optimistic. By 1880, all of the San Juan locals realized that cheaper transportation was coming soon. Although by different routes, the Denver and Rio Grande Railroad was headed toward both Silverton and Ouray. Most felt that a wagon road, or even a railroad, could be built from at least one of those towns up the divide to Red Mountain. The low-grade ores that lay on the dumps might soon be worth shipping to market.

By 1880, both Ouray and Silverton ranked in the top ten Colorado cities, and both were pushing hard to get a railroad because of the many mining districts that surrounded them. In 1880, either town would have been in a position to build a road and supply provisions to the men working at Red Mountain, but there didn't seem to be a need because of the consistent low-grade quality of the ore that had been discovered.

In 1881, due to extensive prospecting activity in the area, the Red Mountain Mining District was officially formed. A significant number of patented claims would now be governed by their owners' own rules and regulations. It was also recognition that the district contained a large amount of mineralization. Although its exact geographic boundaries were never defined, the district has always included much more territory than just the Red Mountains proper—usually including McMillan Peak (12,804 feet), Trico Peak (13,321 feet), Telluride Peak (13,508 feet), and the long ridges down each side of Ironton Peak (Hayden Mountain on the west and Brown Mountain on the east). Later, the district was often extended south to the base of Red Mountain Divide at Chattanooga. However, it was just as often defined as ending at the Ouray–San Juan county line. A few mining men extended the Red Mountain district to cover the eastern Red Mountain slopes that drain into Cement Creek. But to most geologists, the Red Mountain district was defined as extending from Ironton Park on the north to Chattanooga on the south, and east and west to the ridge lines of the neighboring mountains—an area about eight miles long and not quite that wide.

Because of the severity of the winters, the inaccessibility of the location, and the lack of adequate roads or trails, the prospectors continued to flow slowly into the Red Mountain country. In San Juan County, J. G. Haines, Adams, and Craves located the Congress Mine in July 1881. History would only later prove it to be one of the great mines of the district. That summer, the men at the Congress sank a shaft some thirty-five feet deep, and the entire seven-by-nine-foot hole was found to be solid in minerals. Unfortunately, the owners of the Congress were unfamiliar with the character of the low-grade copper and silver ore and didn't realize that it also contained a fair amount of gold. As was common at the time, they assayed the ore for silver alone and, believing

By the late 1880s, Silverton had grown to be one of the largest cities in Colorado. This scene looks north on Green Street. The large building on the left is the Grand Imperial Hotel. Its upper floors served as the San Juan County courthouse for many years. (*Author's collection*)

it to be only low-grade, they discontinued work for the rest of the year. Although gold wasn't present in sizeable quantities, if it had been detected, the ore would have been found to be worth shipping. The Senate, Salem, St. Paul, and Carbon Lake claims were also located in the summer of 1881, and they eventually came to be worked with the Congress as a recognized mining group located on the southern slopes of Red Mountain No. 3. But they, too, caused no great excitement. As far as their owners were aware, their group was basically composed of low-grade ores.

On the other side of Red Mountain Divide, in Ouray County, the Guston Mine was located on August 21, 1881, by August Dietlaf, Andrew Meldrum, John Robinson, and Albert Lang. The Guston didn't seem to be a bonanza strike either. It was operated mainly because it had high levels of lead, which was badly needed as a flux (a substance that helped extract silver) at the Pueblo Smelter and Refining Company in Ouray. At this early point in its development, the silver content of the Guston ore wasn't by itself of sufficient value to warrant shipping to market.

In the spring of 1882, those prospectors who had forsaken their low-grade mines during the long, harsh winter returned once more with the eternal hope that this time they would strike it rich. There was even good reason to be optimistic. In August 1881, the Denver and Rio Grande Railroad had reached Durango and construction had immediately continued due north toward Silverton. The arrival of the railroad at Silverton in the summer of 1882 meant that some of the lower-grade ore, which had been piling up on the Red Mountain dumps, could be shipped inexpensively to the smelters and mills. Perhaps the freight charges would be low enough for the mines to make a profit, even with the moderate silver prices of the time.

The first real excitement of the summer of 1882 came when tests done in June showed that the Congress ore was, in fact, valuable enough to ship. Two men were hired to continually work its main shaft, which they quickly deepened to fifty feet through a solid, although low-grade, ore. On the other side of the divide, D. C. Hartwell, agent for the Ouray smelter, was still anxious to continue obtaining lead ores, and induced the Guston's owners to return and even increase the output of the Guston Mine.[18]

With the prospect of relatively cheap transportation imminent, some of the Red Mountain ore seemed to have economic value. By July 1882, the Congress Mine had been sold for twenty-one thousand dollars and then was sold again to Silverton parties. Drifts were run out from the main Congress shaft, and the new owners learned that what had previously been thought to be low-grade ore was, in fact, a richer copper ore that contained from one-half to two ounces of gold and up to fifty ounces of silver per ton. The Congress's main shaft was immediately deepened to eighty feet, but at that point the workers hit foul air, making it necessary for them to stop work until additional machinery could be brought to the site and a tunnel driven into the side of the shaft to improve the ventilation. The Congress ore realized a little more than sixty dollars per ton in Silverton, which made it profitable to work, but with the high transportation costs from Red Mountain, the Congress still fell far short of being considered a bonanza.

The same phenomenon was taking place at some other Red Mountain mines. Since the Hudson's discovery in 1881, only minimal assessment work had been done on its shaft, but twelve feet down the owners hit a low-grade ore that spread across the entire width and breadth of the shaft. The Genessee Mine was also located in the summer of 1882 by Jasper Brown and Adelbert Parsell. Although they were doing only modest work on their prospect, they also had hit a large amount of good low-grade ore.

One of the biggest events in the history of San Juan mining was the arrival of the Denver and Rio Grande Railroad in Silverton on July 8, 1882. The railroad's shipping rate from Silverton to the smelters in Pueblo was only twelve dollars per ton. Most of the Red Mountain ore appeared to be low-grade, and the apparent location of the majority of the ore was on the Silverton side of Red Mountain Pass. Silverton seemed to be the town that would supply the Red Mountain Mining District. However, unforeseen events were about to occur that would change forever the attitude of mining men toward what looked like an extensive but unimpressive supply of low-grade ore at Red Mountain.

THREE

———⸺⋙∘∘∘∘◉∘◉∘∘∘⋘⸺———

THE MINES

August 14, 1882 was a hot day even high in the mountains at the Guston Mine. John Robinson needed meat and, typical of the prospectors in the Red Mountain district, he picked up his rifle and headed uphill to the south to kill what he needed. In the rarefied air of ten thousand feet above sea level, he soon was breathing hard and sat down for a moment's rest.[1] Robinson was an experienced prospector, one who was always looking for signs of "color," and a fragment from a nearby boulder soon attracted his attention. The moment he picked up the rock he knew there was something special in his hand. It was much too heavy for its size – a sure sign of precious metals within. And, sure enough, when broken open it revealed itself to be a rich piece of solid galena (a lead mineral commonly rich in silver). Robinson knew instantly that he might well be rich, but little did he dream of the events he was about to set in motion.[2]

All thoughts of deer hunting were quickly forgotten. Robinson began a search for the exposed ledge of ore from which the rock had come. It was soon discovered nearby and officially claimed and staked for himself and Andrew Meldrum, A. E. "Gus" Lang, and August Dietlaf, his three partners at the Guston Mine. However, exciting as the original discovery had been, it wasn't until Robinson and his partners went to work and dug a shallow twelve-foot shaft that they discovered "the mother lode." It was the first of

"STRUCK IT RICH."

Judging by the small pile of dirt in this scene, it is evident that there hadn't been much digging before the prospectors felt they had struck it rich. At Red Mountain, this scene was often repeated in actuality. (*Reprinted from* Harper's Weekly, *June 9, 1883; author's collection*)

the rich Red Mountain chimneys to be exposed. The four men had located the Yankee Girl Mine, which was to become one of the richest and most famous silver mines in the history of mining in the United States.

It was obvious that a large body of valuable ore had been discovered – one that had no visible limits on any of the four sides of the shaft. Since it was impossible to determine the exact course of the "vein," the locators, as a safety precaution, staked adjoining claims on each of the four sides of the Yankee Girl. As events turned out, the really rich ore wasn't in a vein at all, but rather in vertical chimneys. Nevertheless, two of the additional claims, the Orphan Boy and Robinson, proved to have their own rich ore chimneys that were almost as valuable as those of the Yankee Girl Mine.

The original Yankee Girl locators were soon able to send a long burro train to Ouray loaded with forty-five hundred pounds of ore. Their first mill run contained an average of eighty-eight ounces of silver per ton and was fifty-six percent lead. It was a rich discovery – good enough that only a month later, when the discovery shaft was merely twenty feet deep, the mine was sold for $125,000. The new owners put twenty miners to work night and day. Ore was shipped regularly by mule train to Silverton. The new owners were not to be disappointed, because every foot of digging showed the same or an even richer body of ore.

Meanwhile, the four original owners of the Yankee Girl began to work the Orphan Boy and Robinson claims, using the money they had received from the sale of the Yankee Girl. Their new mine was soon producing almost as much rich ore as their original strike. Silverton's newspaper, *The La Plata Miner,* didn't need any more evidence. It optimistically proclaimed that the Yankee Girl, including surrounding claims, was simply the biggest strike ever made in Colorado: "The pay streak of the Yankee Girl is three times larger than we have ever seen in any other mine in the country."[3]

It was the discovery at the Yankee Girl Mine that opened the floodgates to the Red Mountain Mining District. A torrent of prospectors, speculators, carpenters, and merchants soon were headed toward the Scarlet Peaks. Almost every week the Denver papers carried articles on Red Mountain with captions such as "Encouraging News from the Mines at Red Mountain – Brilliant Prospects Ahead." The resultant mining boom ignited in numbers that hadn't been matched since Leadville five years earlier. Earnest Ingersoll, a famous Eastern travel writer who happened to be traveling through the district at the time, noted that "claim stakes dotted the mountain as thick as poles in a hop-field, and astonishing success attended nearly every digging . . . ."[4]

The purchasers of the Yankee Girl were O. P. Posey (an easterner who had recently moved to Silverton), George Crawford of Pittsburgh, L. J. Atwood of Waterbury, Connecticut, and James Irvine of Lima, Ohio. Posey and Crawford were investors who would play important roles throughout the history of the Red Mountain district. Their purchase was a good sign that outside capital was beginning to trickle toward the Red Mountain mines. The Yankee Girl Mining Company was incorporated in 1883 for $2.5 million, and the company (which by then also owned the Orphan Boy claim) rewarded its stockholders for their faith. Successive mill runs showed values of 110, 167, and then 174 ounces of silver per ton. The ore was getting richer as the shaft went down! Two new shafts were driven 250 feet apart to test just how much of the rich ore was present. The result was an estimate (at the time only somewhat overly optimistic) that eight men working at the Yankee Girl Mine could produce ore that, at today's prices, would be worth over one hundred thousand dollars per week.

The feverish excitement at the Yankee Girl served to bring attention to the other mines that had already been doing reasonably well on the San Juan County side of Red Mountain Divide. In September 1882, the owners of the Hudson were confident enough of their future that they built living quarters

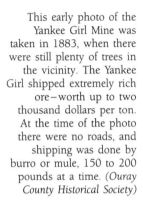

This early photo of the Yankee Girl Mine was taken in 1883, when there were still plenty of trees in the vicinity. The Yankee Girl shipped extremely rich ore—worth up to two thousand dollars per ton. At the time of the photo there were no roads, and shipping was done by burro or mule, 150 to 200 pounds at a time. *(Ouray County Historical Society)*

near the mine so that their miners could work all winter. In that same month, the Congress Mine shipped ore that now assayed at eighty to one hundred dollars per ton and that on occasion contained ore that ran sixty percent copper, three and one-half ounces of gold, and eighty ounces of silver. Every time the ore of the Congress Mine was assayed, it contained ever larger and richer amounts of copper ore. An eighteen-foot-wide deposit of its rich ore had been exposed, and a shaft, drifts, and crosscuts were being driven. The Congress became the first of the Red Mountain mines to start making regular daily shipments of ore, each and every day sending to Silverton about five tons of ore that by late summer contained a steady value of about one hundred dollars per ton. The very first signs of a permanent settlement were beginning to appear around its workings.

Back in the midsummer of 1882, Red Mountain's worth had hardly even been recognized. By October, only sixty days after the big discoveries, it was obvious that the region would become one of the major mining districts in the San Juans—perhaps in the entire United States. By November, the *La Plata Miner* pronounced the Red Mountain Mining District "officially open" and predicted a half-million dollars in ore would be produced during the winter of 1882–1883.[5] In December, the same paper acknowledged that "people are in a habit of making a most liberal allowance for exaggerated newspaper reports as well as any verbal reports which come to them in reference to the mineral wealth of a country. The Red Mountain district has not been exaggerated, nor has it been puffed to the extent which its merits warrant."[6]

By the end of 1882, the whole stage for the district's development had been set. Every day exciting new discoveries were made. On the northern slopes of Red Mountain a forty-foot tunnel had been driven at the Guston, and it showed a streak of solid rich ore five feet wide. The lead and copper ores at the Yankee Girl continued to run high in silver. The Orphan Boy, Robinson, and Yankee Girl were operated as a group. Over a thousand tons of rich silver ore had been shipped to Silverton from just this one group, even though it had to be packed out 150 to 250 pounds at a time on the backs of mules and burros. At the top of Red Mountain Divide, the National Belle had been discovered by Richard Journey. Although the claim was not yet spectacular, he had uncovered a four-foot-wide body of good galena ore, which was often mixed with various carbonates.

South of the divide, the Congress temporarily stopped shipping ore because of the problems connected with freighting in the winter. It did, however, continue to do development work, operations needed to make it easier to mine the ore but that didn't produce ore. In this case the development work was a tunnel that, it was hoped, would solve many problems. This "adit" would drain water from the original vertical shaft, provide better ventilation throughout the mine, and make it easier to get the ore out. The Senate, St. Paul, Carbon Lake, and Salem claims were all now worked in connection with the Congress. In October, the Hudson Mine came into prominence only two thousand feet north of the Congress but on the other side of the divide. Its owners had developed a forty-six-foot shaft that produced ore that averaged thirty-two percent copper, twenty-nine ounces of silver, and half an ounce of gold per ton. The Hudson was one of the first of the Red Mountain mines to make the decision to stockpile ore during the harsh winter and ship only in the summer. The move was a wise one, because it saved up to seven dollars per ton in shipping costs. Many of the other mines soon did the same. The Yankee Girl was still shipping about ten tons of rich ore a day; however, it was reported that "no other mine will attempt to ship until spring."[7]

In December 1882, the Salem became the first of the Red Mountain mines to actually shut down because of water flooding its shaft. Nonetheless, by the second week of January 1883, a force pump had been brought in by sled through the deep snow, and the mine was put into operation again.

Soon the Congress Mine was also reported as having trouble with water seepage. The owners ordered a pump that was four times larger than their first one, which had itself only been put into operation a few months before.

These men display most of the equipment needed to begin the process of mining—drills, picks, fuses, and so on—but this type of small operation could only last a short time before ore cars, boilers, and other heavy machinery were needed. As a result, many small miners were forced to look for investors. *(Ouray County Historical Society)*

The problem that was to plague most Red Mountain mines was becoming apparent. Their shafts followed the rich ore chimneys straight down into the earth—there was no way for the water to naturally flow from the workings. This necessitated the use of huge boilers that produced steam to activate the large pumps used to get the water out of the shafts. The boilers used massive amounts of wood and coal, which had to be brought in over large distances. All of this was expensive, and the operation got even more costly as the shaft got deeper. Nevertheless, the owners of the Congress were optimistic, and the mine was soon back in operation. It continued to produce two and a half tons of valuable galena ore each day.

In February, the Congress, the Salem, and Carbon Lake became the first Red Mountain mines to apply for their patents, which officially transferred ownership of the mine from the United States to the new owners. The next month, the Silver Crown Mine was proclaimed to be developing "an immense body of mineral," and the owners of the nearby Silver Ledge Mine announced

In the first hectic days at Red Mountain, claims were often staked when the snow was still so deep that the prospectors had to "snow-shoe" in and couldn't even examine the ground for minerals. But many prospectors did just that – counting on there being silver wherever they put the stakes. *(Reprinted from* Harper's Weekly, *June 9, 1883; author's collection)*

that they had discovered one of the largest bodies of ore yet. Meanwhile, because of the problems they had with winter production, even the Yankee Girl was forced to reduce its work force to two men. Even so, the mine had already produced and shipped galena ore containing 32,000 ounces of silver and 408,000 pounds of lead.

The activity in those mines that did continue during the winter of 1882–1883 was remarkable because, in light of the harsh and bitter conditions, most Red Mountain mines couldn't produce or ship any ore at all. It was simply too hard to work in the deep snow, too hard to transport the ore out or to ship in supplies. Only the local newspapers didn't seem to be affected by the deep snow. Their articles became more and more glorious as they reported the mineral wonders of the Red Mountain region. Especially vocal were the *Red Mountain Review* at Red Mountain City and *The Red Mountain Pilot* at Red Mountain Town. The papers on the Ouray side of the divide announced that "the Hudson is visited daily by many people who come away astonished at its richness and the amount of ore in sight."[8] The Silverton press boasted that "the Congress . . . is one of the wonders of Red Mountain and with the coming season will develop into one of the richest mines of Colorado . . . Recent developments have proven that the ore increases in richness and quantity as the shafts are extended, a fact that, as a natural consequence, greatly enhanced the value of the Congress, and one, too, that will continue to increase its intrinsic worth."[9] It was reported that the Congress ore needed no sorting and was shipped just as fast as it came out of the shaft. However, despite the glowing reports of the Red Mountain newspapers, the actual statistics reveal that at the time the stories were printed, the Congress had only shipped ore worth $15,674.40, and the Hudson Mine hadn't done any better.

The expectations for the entire new mining district ran extraordinarily high at both newspapers on Red Mountain Divide. *The Red Mountain Review* boasted that "in the first six months of her existence Red Mountain has shown greater progress than did Leadville in its first two years."[10] It reported that the Yankee Girl kept a pack train of seventy-five mules busy the entire winter packing ore to the railroad in Silverton, where it was taken all the way to St. Louis for treatment. The mine was reported to have already paid for itself. "The roof is mineral, the walls or sides are mineral, and everything is mineral except the open space through which we entered," boasted one reporter.[11] One very special piece of Yankee Girl ore was supposed to have assayed at twenty-five hundred ounces of silver per ton!

Although it was difficult to work in the winter, development resumed quickly at all of the mines as the first signs of spring appeared in 1883. By late April, the Congress's drainage tunnel had intersected its shaft, but the tunnel was now eight feet higher than the bottom of the eighty-foot-deep shaft, since work had also continued there. It was reported that the adit went through solid ore the last eight feet before it hit the shaft, which indicated that the ore body could be twenty to thirty feet wide. Its ore contained about twenty to thirty ounces of silver, three-eighths to one and one-half ounces of gold, and was at least twenty-five percent copper—an average value of one hundred dollars per ton.

In the spring of 1883, the National Belle Mine, located within the city limits of Red Mountain Town, quickly became one of the top-producing mines of the Red Mountain district. Its work force concentrated on a large ore body that was fourteen feet in width. "This valuable property is being developed by skillful management and is beyond a doubt one of the great bonanzas of the district."[12] Once again, at the time of the newspaper report, only about one hundred tons of ore had actually been shipped from the National Belle, but its ore was valuable. One mill run showed that a ton of its ore contained an average of one hundred ounces of silver, five dollars in gold, fifty percent lead, and a fair percentage of copper.

The Red Mountain Review was quick to boast that the Hudson also contained an immense body of mineral at its lower level "that shows a richer and better ore, which the work done demonstrates beyond a doubt that the supply is almost unlimited . . ." But the same issue gave credit where credit was due: "the Silver Ledge [in San Juan County] is still on the front as a mine of undoubted value. Through the center of an immense vein of galena there runs an almost pure streak of grey copper averaging 6 inches in width."[13]

Seldom did the early prospectors who made the initial rich strikes actually get much money by shipping ore from the mine. By the summer of 1883, many capitalists had moved into the Red Mountain district. Their aim was to purchase the richer mines from the initial discoverers. The precious metals were not nuggets lying on the ground to be picked up: They were locked up in hard quartz veins or deep within the chimneys of the Red Mountains. Working the hard quartz fissure lodes or the deep volcanic pipes required not only a lot of labor but also the purchase of expensive machinery such as pumps, winches, and drills. Only rich investors or stock companies could provide this kind of money.

A large percentage of Red Mountain's needed capital came from the East Coast and from as far away as Europe. The Yankee Girl, the National Belle, and the Guston mines eventually raised huge sums of money from these sources. The National Belle raised so much outside capital that it definitely became overcapitalized by borrowing much more money than was logical to repay, thereby dooming its stockholders to certain loss.[14] The economic need for capital at Red Mountain and the ensuing speculation meant that many of the small prospectors were quickly bought out by big businessmen. The new owners hired large numbers of daily-wage earners to work the mines. Unfortunately, most of these miners made relatively low pay for the extremely dangerous conditions under which they worked.

Although the really big mines didn't seem to have much trouble getting capital for development, many of the owners of small operations had to rely on their own sweat and blood to expand their operations. "There is no let up on the amount of development work being done in the district. While there is as yet comparatively little capital invested in our mines, yet the men who own them are pushing work to their fullest extent, firmly believing that it is only a matter of time when Red Mountain properties will be eagerly sought after by capital, and they are determined to have something to show when

The mining is starting to get serious at this mine, which has almost finished its new shaft house. The horse at the right, in harness, could rotate the drum and wind the cable up out of the shaft. Notice the several children who have appeared on their donkeys to look over the situation. *(Denver Public Library, Western History Department)*

the time comes. This is a most healthy sign and shows there is a permanency and bottom to our district which it will do to bank on."[15]

The fervid speculation meant that the prices being paid for the Red Mountain mines kept going up and up. On May 26, the Guston was sold to eastern capitalists for $100,000 cash. Then the Hudson sold for $140,000. The June 11 issue of the *Red Mountain Pilot* announced that the owners of the National Belle had turned down an offer of $160,000. The new owners continued to hire additional miners and bring in bigger machinery. Quite a few of the mines began to ship the lower-grade ore that had been piling up on their dumps. This ore could not be sold at a profit; the new owners evidently felt that even if the ore was ultimately sold for less than the cost of production, its revenue could still help offset current expenses. If the mine was up for sale or was selling stock, the low-grade ore could also help boost the mine's total record of ore produced.

Plenty of valuable new ore was being found daily in the Red Mountain mines—a fact that helped feed the local frenzy. By June 1883, the men at the Guston were working a six-foot vein of solid galena that contained up to two hundred ounces of silver per ton. The National Belle had driven a 115-foot tunnel that was used to access a large ore body that was a full twelve feet high and six feet across. Some of the hand-picked ore from the Yankee Girl

Mine continued to contain an unbelievable two thousand to twenty-two hundred ounces of silver per ton! The June 23 *Red Mountain Pilot*, located in the settlement of Red Mountain City, optimistically reported that just those mines in the immediate vicinity of its newspaper office would produce two million dollars in ore by the end of the year.

The truly incredible news occurred in July 1883. Under banner headlines of "Wonderful, Miraculous, Astonishing" and "Greatest Discovery in the World," the *Red Mountain Pilot* announced the rich strike. It happened while workmen were crosscutting the one-hundred-foot tunnel of the National Belle to determine the width of the ore vein. At a distance of twelve feet from the main tunnel (and still working through solid ore) they broke through into a cavern. Hollow echoes came back from the cavity, and rocks thrown into the cave were heard to roll a considerable distance.

"Taking a candle in his hand one of the men descended into darkness and found himself in an immense natural chamber, the flickering ray of the light showing him the vaulted roof far above seamed with bright streaks of galena and interspersed with masses of soft carbonates, chlorides and pure white talc. On different sides of this remarkable chamber were small openings leading to other rooms or chambers, showing the same wonderful rich formation." Leading away from this big chamber was "an immense natural tunnel, running above and across the route of the present working drift a distance of some 100 feet [with] great boulders of pure galena and mounds of soft gray carbonates."

Going through another opening off the main chamber was a cave some forty feet in length, similar to the first and showing the same wonderful display of ores. Several other similar but smaller caves or natural tunnels led off the main chamber. "It would seem as though nature had gathered her choice treasures from her inexhaustible storehouse, and wrought these tunnels, natural stopping places and chambers studded with glittering crystals and bright mineral to dazzle the eyes of man in after ages, and lure him on to other treasures hidden deeper in the bowels of the earth. To estimate the amount of mineral in sight would be almost an impossibility, but an estimate of the entire length of cavities which have been explored, is given at close on 300 feet. The owners, Messrs. Pye, Abrams, Hovey, Wood, Journey and Read, will proceed to more thoroughly develop the different mineral openings at once, and explore them more thoroughly, especially one leading to a chamber which they suppose to be much larger than any of the others, as it runs deeper into the hill. A large body of soft mineral which fell during the night effectively seals up the entrance for the present. The news of the discovery spread like wildfire, and crowds came to see the sight, and to many of them, it was one never to be forgotten."[16]

This scene depicts the discovery of the treasure cave at the National Belle Mine in July 1883. "It would seem as though nature had gathered her choice treasures from her inexhaustible storehouse . . . to dazzle the eyes of man in after ages and lure him on to other treasures . . ." *Drawing by Ingersoll, 1890; courtesy Tom Rosemeyer collection)*

As an indication of the intense promotion that was being done at all the local mines, the same article announced that "the [National Belle] will be closed for a day or two while timbers are being put in and the different entrances made easy of access. Then the chambers and tunnels will be lighted up and thrown open to visitors. This mine alone can produce 100 tons a day of ore which will mill from $100 to $400 per ton. A mill run of sixteen tons of their black copper ore gave 45.9 per cent copper, twenty-six ounces of silver and seven dollars in gold. Fifty tons of what looked like soft yellow dirt, and was at first considered worthless, netted $30 per ton." The soft ores of the National Belle didn't even need to be blasted. Workmen simply shoveled the valuable metals into sacks. This meant that the original owners could mine the rich ore without having to buy expensive machinery, and the National Belle therefore became the exception to the rule that a Red Mountain mine had to be sold to investors in order to be properly worked.

On July 21, another large cavity was opened at the National Belle. It also overflowed with rich ores. The public was again admitted to look at the caves. By the next week, the *Red Mountain Pilot* was eager to report that people were coming from miles around to gawk at the treasure cave. "Nowhere in the world is there such a large body of mineral as there is in the National Belle and no one knows the extent of the mineral; there is at least one million tons in sight and no one can estimate the value . . . One of the best features about this rich discovery is that the present owners were the original locators and they will reap the fruits of their toil instead of some tin-horn capitalist."[17] Pretty strong words of praise from the *Red Mountain Pilot,* since the National Belle was located near the center of the competing Red Mountain Town.

The next week, yet another big cave was discovered at the National Belle, and it was even larger than the other discoveries. Dozens of large and small cavities were later added to the list. Workmen began to timber the caves with heavy square sets and cribbing so that the ore could be removed safely from the ceilings and walls. Eight men were employed just drying, selecting, and sacking the rich ore. Soon the work force at the National Belle was expanded to a total of fifteen men, and a large boardinghouse was built within a few hundred feet of the main tunnel so that the National Belle miners could live on the site all winter.

The entire Red Mountain Mining District appeared to be one large mass of ore. It seemed that there were literally mountains of silver ore in sight. In late June and early July, many new strikes of large amounts of low-grade ore were made in the extreme northern part of the Red Mountain district, on Brown and Hayden mountains. The new discoveries included the Full Moon, Guadalupe, Maud S., Saratoga, and the Carbonate King mines. Back near the center of the district, the Grand Exchange and the Treasure Trove were being earnestly worked just outside the city limits of Red Mountain Town. The workers at the former mine struck galena containing up to eighty ounces of silver. The latter hit three caves similar to those of the National Belle, although on a smaller scale. Even at the Salem Mine, near Congress (its thirty-foot shaft was discouraging in production and its forty-foot tunnel wasn't much better), a workman who was shoveling what was thought to be plain dirt discovered a small vein of copper ore near the main shaft. Although limited in quantity, selected portions of this ore were reported to contain twenty-five ounces of gold and two thousand ounces of silver.

The Genessee had been one of the first mines located in the Red Mountain district, but it was only now coming into its own as a great mine. It was located about a half-mile north of Red Mountain Town "up a footpath from the main trail" at the base of a perpendicular cliff. Its ore was basically composed of a relatively low-grade cube-type galena that averaged twenty-five ounces of silver and seventy percent lead. "A shaft of twenty feet is the development here, and forty or fifty tons of ore are now on the dump . . . leaving on each side a tall column of solid ore rising up some thirty feet against the perpendicular cliff, their jagged edges glittering in the sunlight and giving them the appearance of two diamond studded towers."[18] The original locators, J. W. Pierce, Jasper Brown, and Adelbert "Dell" Parsell (the Ouray County Sheriff), sold the mine in late August 1883 for twenty thousand dollars to P. D. Mallory of Baltimore. The Vanderbilt was discovered close by and officially located on October 23, 1883, by Perry Terpenny, a local saloonkeeper and miner who would remain prominent in the Red Mountain district for several decades.

By the end of August, the Yankee Girl had increased its work force to twenty men. Not all of the workers were drilling and blasting. Nearly half of the men were reported to be merely sacking and sorting ore, although it was reported that very little sorting was actually needed. The new wagon road to Ouray had recently been finished, and the Yankee Girl now shipped twenty-five to thirty tons of high-grade ore per day.

At the extreme southern end of the district, in the thriving settlement of Chattanooga, work was started August 7 on the foundation of the Mineral Creek Concentrating and Sampling Company's thirty-ton concentrator. The mill building was a large structure — forty-two feet by fifty-four and a half feet — that used a thirty-two-inch turbine waterwheel for power. The mill contained a Blake crusher, two sets of Cornish rolls, and four jig and slime tables. The owners announced that ore that contained as little as ten ounces of silver and ten percent lead could be milled by them at a profit. By November, the concentrating mill was complete but, unfortunately, could not begin to operate. Its machinery was driven by water power and couldn't be activated because the cold winter temperatures had frozen the nearby stream.

The purpose of the Chattanooga mill wasn't to extract precious metals from the ore. Refining the Red Mountain silver from the local ore wasn't a simple matter because many of the ores were complex and could not be treated with ordinary refining methods. A partial and relatively inexpensive solution to the problem was the concentrating mill like that at Chattanooga. The mill simply rid the ore of most of the waste rock, thereby concentrating the minerals for shipment. A smelter, on the other hand, used heat to try to refine the rich minerals from the ore. At the time of the Red Mountain discoveries, the early smelters in nearby Silverton or Ouray were small lead-based operations. Since most of the Red Mountain ore was copper-based, shipments quite often had to be sent over long distances to get to the proper smelters.

The produce of the concentrating mill looked like sand but was eighty to ninety percent mineral as a result of the removal of the waste rock. Thus, transport to the smelters was made much more economical. *(Colorado Historical Society; George Wagner Collection)*

Whether lead- or copper-oriented, none of the small 1880s smelters or concentrating mills were particularly efficient. Most smelting processes were just beginning to be perfected at the time, and a lot of trial and error went into any operation. A process that could capture seventy or eighty percent of the rich minerals was considered to be extremely satisfactory, and better results could usually be obtained only at the big smelters at Pueblo or Denver. This meant that twenty to thirty percent of the gold and silver was being lost in the milling process. This loss, and the high transportation costs to Denver and Pueblo, were the greatest expenses of the Red Mountain mine owner. The cost of getting the ore out of the ground was actually one of the lesser expenses.

The National Belle (the easiest of all the Red Mountain mines from which to extract ore) remained the sweetheart of the Red Mountain district. Most work at the mine continued to center not on drilling or blasting, as in most mines, but on timbering to eliminate the possibility of falling rocks and cave-ins. Mine rail also needed to be laid throughout the maze of caves that branched off the main tunnel. About fifteen to twenty tons of ore were sacked and shipped from "The Belle" each day during the summer. Each ton of its ore averaged fifty to fifty-five ounces of silver, seventeen percent lead, and contained seven to ten dollars in gold.[19]

During September 1883, it was reported that the Grand Exchange hit a quality of ore that entitled it to join the ranks of the foremost mines of the Red Mountain district. Although it never produced the volume of ore originally estimated, the mine certainly showed some of the most varied mineral formations of any on Red Mountain. It produced iron, copper, and galena – sometimes separate and pure, and sometimes molded into "fantastic shaped boulders and nuggets with bright rainbow colors peeping from numerous pockets and crevices."[20] A black and yellow copper ore from the mine contained 20 to 60 ounces of silver, a white talc averaged 20 to 30 ounces of silver, and a dark-colored sand carbonate in wavy seams averaged up to 282 ounces of silver. The Guston Mine shipped three tons of ore daily to Ouray during the summer and fall of 1883. The Congress worked fifteen men and shipped about twenty tons of rich ore daily. Enough activity was going on in the Red Mountain district that by September the *Red Mountain Review* could boast that "Red Mountain already has forty producing mines and prospects, fifteen of them shipping. How's that for a camp scarcely one year old. Oh! we're a gitten thar."[21]

Once again the newspapers let their optimism get the best of them. Only a month later it was obvious that, because of adverse weather conditions, the Red Mountain mines would have to shut down or at least severely curtail production for the winter. The Senate announced it would buck the trend and attempt to work three men all winter. The Hudson stopped mining but made the decision to continue to ship its stockpiled ore for as long as possible into the winter. The owners of the Congress concentrated on bringing in lumber and timber to be used later to build additions to its boardinghouse and to construct ore sheds and a new hoisting apparatus. In an attempt to get ahead of the winter snows, the Congress shipped 850 tons of ore in August and September. The Yankee Girl announced that twenty-one men would work all winter and that ore would be shipped, even though transportation costs had been extremely high the previous winter. In an effort to beat the winter snows, the mine shipped thirty-two tons of very high grade ore in September, together with seven hundred tons of lower-grade material in August and September. Even low-grade Yankee Girl ore ran one hundred to three hundred dollars per ton. In preparation for winter, the owners built a large two-story boarding house that could hold a hundred men. Construction also began on a new forty-foot by eighty-foot shed that could store the ore being held for shipment. The National Belle shipped 570 tons of ore in August and September, but in October the mine was forced to shut down temporarily due to water in its shaft. In November and December, more mineral caves were found in the National Belle. Sixteen men were employed during the winter, and its ore continued to be shipped (when possible) without sorting. The Guston's force was substantially reduced, but a large new boardinghouse was to be built to allow most workers to live on the site during the winter. Even in the face of all the mines shutting down for the winter, the *Red Mountain Review* still optimistically proclaimed that certain Iowa and Nebraska capitalists who had visited Red Mountain that fall had returned home to gather five million dollars to develop various Red Mountain claims the next spring.

All together, it was estimated that the Red Mountain mines produced fifty-five hundred tons of very rich ore in August and September alone. In its wrap-up for the year 1883, Ouray's *Solid Muldoon* figured that the Yankee Girl had shipped 3,000 tons of ore worth $450,000; the National Belle 980 tons worth $69,600; and the Congress 2,500 tons worth $220,000. "There is certainly no camp on the continent that is compelled to rely on burros, sleds and wagons to market their output, that can exhibit such an envious showing."[22] The editor of the *Red Mountain Review* announced that he would keep the newspaper open all winter and estimated that three hundred men were prepared to stay up on the divide until spring. As usual, the paper was overly optimistic. By mid-December, less than a hundred men were actually working as miners in the Red Mountain district because it was so hard, and therefore expensive, to ship the ore. But the sounds of the hammer, saw, and plane were heard everywhere. Red Mountain's residents eagerly prepared for the activity that they knew would come with the spring thaws.

As the year drew to a close, the editor of the *Red Mountain Review* wrote an article on the National Belle that could have applied equally as well to the region as a whole: "It can fitly be called a storehouse of wealth, for the heavy expenses of the present season in the way of good wagon roads to the mine, ore houses, boarding houses, bunk houses, machinery and other necessary appliances have been paid for from the proceeds of the ore sold and the owners have realized a handsome dividend over and above all."[23]

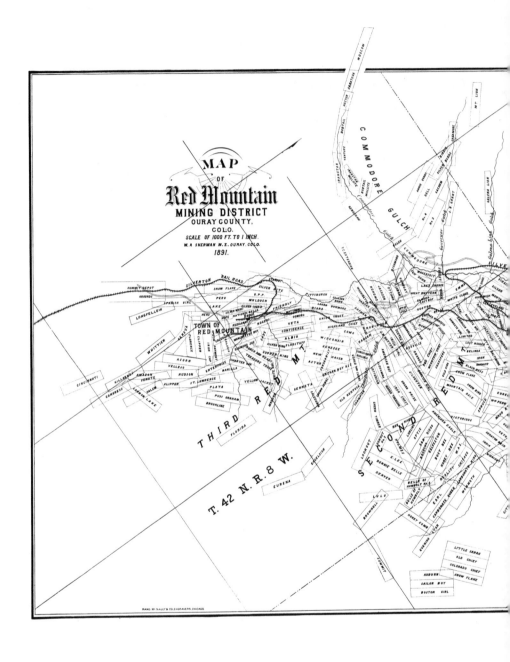

MAP
OF
Red Mountain
MINING DISTRICT
OURAY COUNTY,
COLO.
SCALE OF 1000 FT. TO 1 INCH.
W. A. SHERMAN M. E. OURAY. COLO.
1891.

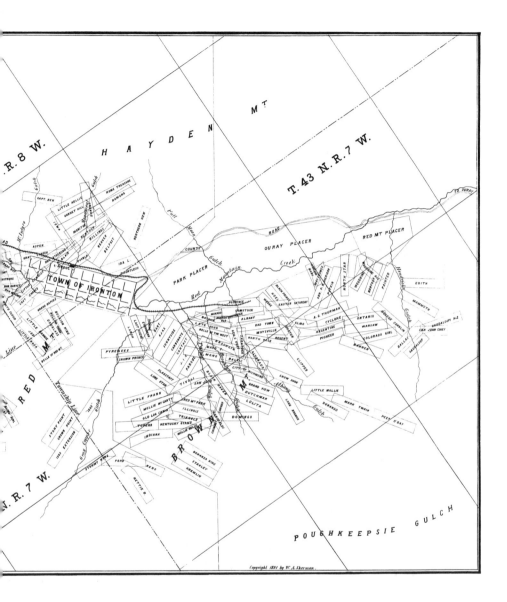

As can be seen by this map, the entire Red Mountain district was eventually covered with mining claims. Although this claim map was made in 1891, ninety percent of these claims had been filed by the end of 1883. Many overlapped one another, in which case the earlier filing predominated. (*Author's collection*)

FOUR

===∞∞∞◎◎◎∞∞===

THE TOWNS

In 1882, hundreds of newcomers, all seeking their fortunes, poured into the Red Mountains; the early "pioneer" prospectors were soon greatly outnumbered by the "greenhorns." Unlike their predecessors, most of the recent arrivals were a long way from being self-sufficient. They needed nearby merchants to supply their food, clothing, and equipment. They had little time or desire to hunt, gather food, make their shelters, or sew new clothes. Many loved to drink, gamble, and visit with the loose women that quickly followed them. Most of the older prospectors soon left either because they couldn't stand the crowds or because they had sold their claims to the speculators and capitalists or investors that were pouring into the new district. The speculators were only waiting to resell their property at a quick but large profit. The capitalists brought in miners and machinery with which to work their new claims.

When the first wave of greenhorn prospectors and much-needed miners began to flow into the Red Mountain Mining District, it was an absolute certainty that the merchants, the lawyers, and the mining speculators wouldn't be far behind. The saloonkeepers and prostitutes also arrived early, as did hotel owners, grocers, and restaurateurs. So many support personnel were needed on the divide that eventually there was at least one businessman or his employee for every miner or prospector in the Red Mountain Mining

In this 1883 photograph it is evident that the settlement of Chattanooga is booming; however, in another year's time it would already have reached its peak. As soon as wagon roads were available, many of its residents moved up to the Red Mountain divide. Most of Chattanooga's structures were layer destroyed by an avalanche. (*Joseph Collier photo; Denver Public Library, Western History Department*)

District. Bringing in goods and commodities for the merchants and freighting out the ore on the way back home also became a major business. All of the Red Mountain entrepreneurs had a simple goal – to establish some permanence on the divide, perhaps even a town, and thereby put as much as possible of the prospectors' new riches into their own pockets.

When the extent of the Red Mountain discoveries became evident, the only settlements that already existed anywhere near the district were the small camps of Sweetville (later called Chattanooga) and Poughkeepsie. Although Poughkeepsie, located high above timberline at the head of the gulch by the same name, had boomed in 1878 and 1879, by 1880 it was merely a collection of a few hard-to-reach cabins. Sweetville was located at the far south end of the district at an elevation of 10,400 feet on the extreme northern end of the gently sloping Mineral Creek valley. The small camp quickly became the main staging area for supplies being sent to the Red Mountain mines, especially for those coming in from San Juan County. As the community expanded, one key man soon appeared. Jim Sheridan ran the hotel, livery, and, most important, the saloon. For a while he so dominated the settlement that it was called Sheridan Junction. Later he switched locations and ran the Sheridan Hotel at the railroad station at Summit, which was at the very top of Red Mountain Pass; but the Sheridan Saloon remained a landmark in Chattanooga for almost two decades.

The first hint of what might possibly be thought of as a true "town" was mentioned in Silverton's *La Plata Miner* of December 30, 1882. The editor wrote of the importance of the Red Mountain Mining District having a centrally located town and reported that such a place was being considered high on the south-facing slopes of Red Mountain No. 3. The editor mentioned, quite properly, that "no mining camp can exist and prosper without its mining town. And certainly a point, from which the country around within a radius of three miles $10,000 per day can be produced in gold, silver, lead and copper is a good place to locate a town, and a town there is bound to prosper." The site mentioned was where Red Mountain City was eventually built.

The same article went on to verify, however, that "two or three points have been talked of for town purposes. The most prominent point, and the one to which attention is now most generally directed, is the ground located three-fourths of a mile north of the divide, at the head of Mineral Creek." A geographical mix-up seemed to exist at the newspaper, because Mineral Creek runs south toward Silverton and most certainly could not have its headwaters three-quarters of a mile north of the divide. Furthermore, the editor of Silverton's *La Plata Miner* would not have been purposely promoting an Ouray County settlement. More than likely, the editor mistakenly thought that the new settlement was located in San Juan County. It was an easy mistake because the county line was on the top of the divide and there were many small hills and depressions in the vicinity. The article pointed out that Oliver Matthews, Jack Rodgers, B. P. Renstrom, and Samuel Houghton had staked several claims near the settlement to which it was referring, and that a town site had been laid out and surveyed. The new settlement was to be called Rodgersville "in honor of our worthy and enterprising citizen, John Rodgers, who was one of the first to prospect and locate property in the now famous camp."

Rodgersville was, in fact, located at the northern edge of the same large bowl situated at 10,800 feet elevation that eventually was filled with the buildings of Red Mountain Town. The use of the name "Rodgersville" disappeared quickly after its founding, in part because the Ouray papers always considered those cabins located at Rodgersville to be a part of Red Mountain Town, but also because the location of Red Mountain Town shifted slightly so as to take over the former location of Rodgersville. In 1882 and 1883, the Silverton papers reported Rodgersville as one settlement and Red Mountain Town as a totally different town, although only a few hundred yards separated the two locations. By the end of the year 1882, D. F. Watson had opened a store on Red Mountain Divide and, even though he was operating in deep snow, he quickly expanded his operation to include lodging accommodations for the traveling public and their animals. The snow was now deep enough that Watson announced that he could run a sleigh daily to the mouth of Mill Creek, two and one-half miles south of his establishment. B. P. Renstrom commenced building a hotel near Watson's store, and Oliver Matthews started construction on his residence on West Lake Street (probably each was building on his own mining claim).[1] Exactly where the store, hotel, and residence were located is unknown, but since Renstrom and Matthews were known to be in the vicinity of Rodgersville, it is likely that they were forming the nucleus of what later came to be known as Red Mountain Town.

January 1883 turned out to be a very busy month for the Red Mountain district, even though it was smack in the middle of a cold and harsh winter. Not only were many more prospectors and miners moving into the Red Mountains, but the merchants of both Ouray and Silverton were anxious to open businesses in the Red Mountain Mining District. Those who built the earliest structures were not interested in looks. The important thing was simply to become established. At eleven thousand feet elevation in the middle of winter it was not just economically profitable to act quickly, it was a practical necessity to provide protection from the elements. As events were to show, the first merchants and prospectors were lucky, because the winter of 1882–1883 was not a very harsh one. Otherwise, it would have been impossible for the new arrivals to start their fledgling settlements on the Red Mountain Divide.

Ouray and Silverton were both anxious to "annex" the Red Mountain Mining District; each wanted its town to be the main source of supplies for the flourishing mines on the divide. Silverton definitely had the early advantage because a very rough wagon road already existed from that town to Sweetville (later called Chattanooga). Silverton's *La Plata Miner* of January 6, 1883, reported that John L. Haines (later called both "Hines" and "Harris" in the papers) had announced he would build a hotel in the Red Mountain district and that he would ship in four thousand pounds of freight a day from Silverton. His route would take him to Chattanooga and then up the steep divide. The paper also announced that a post office would soon be established at the same site. The very day that the Silverton paper was published, Haines's location was officially named Red Mountain City. John Haines did, in fact, get his first shipment of supplies on Sunday, January 7, and the next day Deputy Mineral Surveyor John J. Seymour laid out Red Mountain City's First Street in more than three feet of snow. The fact that they couldn't see the land they were buying didn't deter the real estate customers. Ten business lots were sold the next day, and contracts were let for the construction of six buildings, including the home of the town's new newspaper, the *Red Mountain Pilot*. The businessmen and citizens of the new town met the evening of January 9 to establish building regulations. Evidently lots continued to sell well, because on January 10, 1883, an additional fifty lots were surveyed on Red Mountain Avenue and Congress Street. By the next day all of the additional lots were reported sold, and contracts had been let for the construction of a dozen additional buildings.[2]

Heavy January snows and cold weather that always prevailed in the winter at an elevation of eleven thousand feet slowed down the local optimism only slightly. On January 29, 1883, the first post office was established in the Red Mountain Mining District at the settlement of Red Mountain Town. No more than a few tents existed at the site, which was in a clearing several hundred yards south of the town's eventual location near the National Belle Mine.

A small community had also been established about an equal distance between Red Mountain City and Red Mountain Town, at the Hudson Mine. Although it lay on the original route over the divide, Hudson never had a very large population because it lay on a steep – almost impassable – slope between the two towns. Most travelers found it much easier to travel around the steep mountainside by passing to the west, and the town never contained any permanent inhabitants other than the employees at the Hudson Mine.

By late January, permanent construction had also started at "Copper Glen" (later to be known as the town of Ironton), which was located at the north end of the Red Mountain Mining District. A hundred or so men were already living in the vicinity of the new settlement; but most of the early arrivals slept in tents – sometimes lined up wall-to-wall on the dirt floor and paying a dollar or two a night for the privilege. When logs were readily available, a slightly better type of construction for protection from the elements was a structure with log walls and a canvas roof; and one further improvement was a rough cabin (including a wooden plank roof) that was then covered with canvas to make it weather-tight.

Exactly what construction actually occurred in the Red Mountain Mining District is now difficult to discern because the early boom days were a time of intense exaggeration. Everyone said that Red Mountain was the new Leadville, or at least everyone wanted it to be. One way to be successful was to bring more people to the Red Mountains by whatever means necessary. The number of jobs available was consequently exaggerated. The end justified the means. As a result, it was often impossible to tell whether a project was truly planned, started, or finished by the way it was reported. A tent was reported as a house. Each miner's cabin seemed to take on the aura of a settlement. Two or three cabins close together made a town.

Regardless of the truth of the reports, prospectors continued to pour into the Red Mountain district in February 1883, even though the deep snow made it impossible for them to see the ground to prospect for new claims. The newcomers just wanted to be sure to be on the divide when the very first spring thaws allowed them to look for new discoveries. The investors who had recently acquired existing mining claims also wanted to begin their development work immediately, regardless of the conditions. Trees were cut for cabins, mine timbers, or fuel when the snow was so deep that five to ten feet of the trunk was discovered to be still standing in the spring. The men could travel about only on snowshoes, and it was necessary to dig deep holes into the snow to build foundations for cabins. Some of the buildings turned out to be totally lopsided when the snow melted and the frozen ground thawed out. Nevertheless, "clouds of prospectors" were reported to be drifting into the Red Mountain district, staking their claims in up to ten feet of snow. Carpenters and loggers were reported to be as thick as the miners and prospectors.

In early February, there were two locations on Red Mountain Divide proper that seemed to be drawing all the action. One area of activity centered around the settlements of Congress and Red Mountain City, which were both near the Congress Mine. The other lively region was at Red Mountain Town, Rodgersville, and the National Belle Mine. The latter were basically only tent cities at this time, while substantial building had been accomplished at Congress and Red Mountain City. In great part this was due to the sun melting the snow from the south-facing slope of "the City," while Red Mountain Town was located in a heavily wooded north-facing depression. Congress was recognized by the Silverton papers as the most permanent settlement on the divide; Red Mountain City and Rodgersville were acknowledged as struggling for a start. At this time, the Silverton papers made no mention of Red Mountain Town. The first logs for Red Mountain Town cabins were not laid until February 18, 1883,[3] while development had progressed enough on the San Juan County side of the divide that the February 22, 1883 *Red Mountain Pilot* announced "the telephone office will be opened at L. W. Patterson's store at Congress the coming week." The Congress Hotel (John L. Haines, proprietor) was optimistically named Red Mountain City's "official stage stop," even though construction on the hotel hadn't even been started, and there would be no wagon road to the settlement for several years.

Haines's Congress Hotel is one good example of the extreme optimism and overstatement of the local papers. The March 3, 1883 *Red Mountain Pilot*

This is the only known photograph of the town of Congress. In 1883, when this picture was taken, it was already a very substantial settlement. But within months it would be almost a ghost town at the same time Red Mountain Town flourished. The reason: The main highway through the district moved to another location. *(Joseph Collier photo; Denver Public Library, Western History Department)*

announced that John L. Haines had let the contract for a huge two-story, eighty- by sixty-foot hotel. It was anticipated that the building would hold seventy-five very crowded people. On March 17, the paper predicted that the hotel would be totally finished and open in three weeks. On April 7 it was reported that Haines was two weeks away from completion, yet on April 28 the papers announced that Haines was still working on the building. The hotel didn't actually open until late June, and its size had shrunk to only sixty by thirty feet. The Congress Hotel was said to have cost four thousand dollars, not counting an additional two thousand dollars that had been spent on its furnishings. Although scaled down, the finished structure was still impressive—two and one-half stories tall with a seventeen- by twenty-six-foot office, twelve- by twenty-foot barroom, ten- by ten-foot "private room," seventeen- by thirty-six-foot dining room, twelve- by twenty-four-foot kitchen, and sixteen bedrooms, each ten by fourteen feet.

All the participants on Red Mountain Divide were extremely optimistic, but the editors of the newspapers in Ouray and Silverton were outright boastful of the settlements that were located on their respective sides of the divide. It was considered their duty to inflate the status of their county's settlements, mines, and towns, and Ouray and Silverton both had hopes of capturing whatever resulting business might come their way. The *Red Mountain Pilot* of March 10, 1883 reported that there were many more buildings in Red Mountain City in San Juan County than at "the town at the Hudson Mine." Later the paper bragged that "About the last of January there was one tent where Red Mountain City now stands. Now there are twenty-five creditable cabins, seven good and substantial business buildings occupied, and six more ready for occupancy in less than a week. Therre are two large tents occupied as places of business. Four large business buildings will be begun the later part of this week."[4] Red Mountain City already boasted a hotel, general store, meat market, saloon, several other small businesses, and the *Red Mountain Pilot* newspaper.

But while Red Mountain City was experiencing good growth during March 1883, Red Mountain Town seemed to have suddenly leaped to the front of all the Red Mountain settlements. Dozens of businesses had been opened in the town: Alling & Co. Hardware, Red Mountain Saloon, Rollins and Stanton Butchers, several realtors, the Miner's Meat Market (fresh meat brought in by pack train daily from Ouray), the Excelsior boardinghouse, the Hudson House, Dr. J. J. Stoll, M.D., a barber, the Red Mountain Hotel, Diamond F. Drugstore, Park Street Lodging House, Yankee Girl Saloon, Red Mountain Billiard Hall, Bon Ton Saloon, Forsyth and Valiant Saloon, The Assembly Club, several mining agents, Loring Hardware, an attorney, Fish Boot Repair, and a laundry. Mail was being received three times a week. Red Mountain Town also had its own newspaper – the *Red Mountain Review* – that wasted no time promoting local real estate – "the town below the Hudson got in some good licks this week. Only $1,060 worth of lots sold on Thursday."[5]

Nearby Rodgersville was awarded a post office on March 19, 1883. The editor of Red Mountain Town's *Red Mountain Review* was furious that the second Red Mountain post office was being established within five hundred feet of the post office at Red Mountain Town and that it would be called Rodgersville. "Upon what representations it was secured we were not informed. It will be within the city limits of Red Mountain Town." The presence of a post office didn't really mean much in the 1880s. Since the United States Postal Service couldn't tell which settlements would last, its policy was to set up offices at every little cabin, closing those that didn't make it.[6] The editor of the *Red Mountain Pilot* pointed out in his June 16 issue that "Red Mountain is well supplied with mail facilities. There are five post offices in the district, viz.: Chattanooga, Congress, Red Mountain, Rodgersville and Ironton. Post offices will also be established at Burro Bridge, Butte City, Gladstone and Del Mino, which will swell the total to nine." The editor need not have worried. Many of the post offices were soon shut down. The Rodgersville post office was closed the next week, less than three months after it opened.

The original Red Mountain Town in 1883 was located in a very swampy area, as is indicated by the wooden "corduroy" road leading into town in this photograph. This, plus the discovery of the National Belle Mine a few hundred yards away and a change in the route of the toll road, resulted in the entire town being moved to what had been the site of Rodgersville. (*Joseph Collier photo; Denver Public Library, Western History Department*)

By late March 1883, the editor of the *Red Mountain Review* (located in Red Mountain Town) had, unfortunately, begun to refer to his town solely as "Red Mountain." It was probably an attempt on his part to snub Red Mountain City, but the arrogance caused great confusion for later historians. He boasted that "Red Mountain is today the best mining camp in the world, taking everything into consideration . . . Red Mountain has made more progress in the development of her mines in the short space of six months than Leadville did in two years . . . The town is full of prospectors and the hills are black with men searching for the indications of the ore bodies which may have been overlooked by previous prospectors . . . Town property is rapidly advancing in value. Lots with no improvements are selling all the way from $100 to $1,000. There are not at present sufficient accommodations for those who visit our camp . . . Red Mountain will be a town of 5,000 people by July 1, 1883."[7]

Dave Day, editor of Ouray's *Solid Muldoon*, carried on the audacious tradition by referring to "The Town" simply as Red Mountain and boasted that "five weeks ago the site where Red Mt. now stands was woodland mesa covered with heavy spruce timber. Today, hotels, printing offices, groceries, meat markets . . . a telephone office, saloons, dance houses are up and booming; the blast is heard on every side and prospectors can be seen snowshoeing in every direction. Everything has been packed or sledded over or under three feet of snow . . . We predict that by September 1, Red Mountain will have a population of ten thousand and a daily output surpassed by Leadville only."[8]

With all the boasting and self-congratulation, it might have been suspected that Red Mountain Town and Red Mountain City were the only locations of importance in the district, but by March 1883, two other settlements had begun to blossom on either side of Red Mountain Divide. Both communities owed their existence to being situated in locations that were logical freighting and transportation terminals. On the south side was Sweetville (later named Chattanooga), and on the north Copper Glen (later called Ironton). Both settlements had the advantage of lying at a substantially lower elevation than the new towns on top of Red Mountain Divide: Copper Glen at 9,800 feet and Sweetville at 10,400 feet in elevation. Both locations were within a mile or two of the rich Red Mountain mines but were conveniently situated at the end of long, narrow, nearly treeless valleys that contained plenty of flat ground for expansion. Sweetville allowed for easy access up the Mineral Creek valley from Silverton; however, Ironton was cut off from Ouray by the "impassable" Uncompahgre Canyon. Spring came earlier to these towns than to those located up on the divide, and winter was put off for a few precious weeks in the fall. Life in general was easier at Copper Glen and Sweetville, and yet they still had the advantage of being very close to the heart of the Red Mountain district.

Copper Glen was surveyed on Sunday, March 4, 1883, and laid out directly adjacent to Corkscrew Gulch. Ouray's Dave Day wrote in the March 9 *Solid Muldoon* that in only five days of existence, thirty-two cabins were being built and "the every ready lot jumpers were on hand." Within three weeks of its founding, a hundred buildings were reported to be in some stage of construction at or near Copper Glen. Most of these buildings were of a substantial character, even if built of logs or green timber. The main problem faced by the new settlement was that lumber could not be brought to the site fast enough to keep up with the amount of building taking place. The answer to the problem was soon provided when several sawmills were set up nearby. Trees were not only being cut for lumber at the sawmills but were also cut whole for log cabins, cribbing, mine timbers, and, later, railroad ties. The local trees were also used as fuel for the mines' boilers and burned for heat to keep the miners warm in the winter. Soon the dense forests of Red Mountain began to look as if they had been hit by a hurricane.

By April there wasn't a vacant lot to be found for sale in the town of

Although this photograph was taken in September 1888, the town of Ironton hadn't changed much since 1883. It was preparing to boom, however, in anticipation of the arrival of the Silverton Railroad. Ironton would be, for all practical purposes, the northern terminus of the railroad. *(Colorado Historical Society)*

Copper Glen. The townspeople decided to drop the name Copper Glen in favor of "Ironton." The new name was suggested by the large iron deposits in the nearby Red Mountains. Down in Ouray, Dave Day wrote that the "outlook for business is enough in Ironton to cause several Silverton residents to abandon that village and move to the new Eldorado. Each day brings scores from the outside, notwithstanding two feet of snow."[9] Many of those newcomers stayed in Calvin Strayer's Hotel, which was one of the first in the Red Mountain district. Ironton's post office opened May 2, 1883. Soon the town had the first church services in the Red Mountain district. It was a sure sign of prominence and respectability.

To the south of the divide, Sweetville had also become a thriving town. Even the *Red Mountain Review,* on the Ouray County side of the pass, had a few good things to say about the new town, explaining that Chattanooga and Sweetville were the same place. The only difference between the two sites, according to the paper, was that Chattanooga was located on a placer claim and Sweetville was situated next to it on a mill site. The town had a lively appearance in the spring of 1883. "It seems almost incredible the amount of lumber and supplies which is here unloaded for the mines and camps embraced in our district."[10] By March 30, the construction of many of its commercial buildings had been completed, including the Walker House, a two-story hotel. Like Ironton, Chattanooga's growth was stymied for a while by lack of lumber, yet by mid-April it had grown enough to include four groceries, two bakeries, a restaurant, clothier, drugstore, two butchers, three boardinghouses, and three saloons.

Even as Red Mountain Town, Rodgersville, Congress, Red Mountain City, Ironton, and Chattanooga boomed, other towns continued to sprout on the divide as fast as the spring flowers. For example, the March 17, 1883 *Red Mountain Review* boasted "another new town has been started near the Yankee Girl which will be called Missouri City. Of the beginning of towns there is no end." Nothing more was ever heard of "Missouri City," but it may well have been the early beginnings of what eventually became the town of Guston.

So many towns were formed in the hope of making money from the sale of lots that no one seemed to know whether or not a town really existed. For example, a town that went by the name of "Butte City" was supposedly built in the spring of 1883, but its location is unknown. This led the *La Plata Miner* to exclaim that "a great number of towns in these days of enlightenment are born for speculative purposes."[11] It listed the settlements of Chattanooga, Red Mountain City, Red Mountain Town, Rodgersville, and Ironton as the only important ones in the Red Mountain district. It mentioned yet another town, called by various sources "Del Mino," "Del Mine," or "Dela Mino," as having been started on the east side of the Red Mountains in the Cement Creek drainage.

The actual existence of a real "town" at Del Mino is somewhat in doubt, but a post office of that name was open from June 22, 1883 to May 19, 1884. As best as can be determined, it was located near Prospect Gulch and Cement Creek in San Juan County on the eastern slope of Red Mountain No. 3. The May 5, 1883 *Red Mountain Review* was of the opinion that the town existed only on paper, but three weeks later the same newspaper reported that the town had been surveyed and platted. By June 2 the *Review* even mentioned that Del Mino was growing rapidly. In 1884, Del Mino was documented as containing a population of forty by the Colorado State Business Directory. Undoubtedly, the "town" of Del Mino was established as another transfer point. Like Chattanooga or Ironton, it was a location where freight bound for Red Mountain was unloaded from wagons onto pack mules or burros; but unlike the other two locations, Del Mino never consisted of more than a few cabins.

In April 1883, with the first of the spring thaws the mountain was a frenzy of activity. Close to two thousand prospectors now crowded into the Red Mountain Mining District. Even though the divide hummed with activity and Red Mountain City had grown into one of the largest towns on the divide, the first signs were appearing that "The City" was faltering. There were two very logical causes for its decline. Most of the really large and valuable mines were now found on the Ouray side of the Red Mountain Divide, much closer to Red Mountain Town, and Red Mountain City was quite a distance off the newer and more efficient trail from Chattanooga to those mines.

The confusion over the status of Red Mountain Town, Red Mountain City, and Congress was great enough that, in early April, a large group of Silverton residents made a special trip up the mountain to survey the situation for themselves. They wanted to see what was fact and what was fiction. Upon their return they reported optimistically that Red Mountain City (now often called Congress) had grown to an estimated population of 150 people and contained three hotels, a confectionary, drugstore, hardware store, newspaper, and meat market. The twenty-room Conley House had opened and was reported to be first class. The "gulch addition" had also been added to Red Mountain City and was reported to have forty substantial log cabins—all full of men who occupied every available square foot of space.[12]

However, just weeks later, Silverton's *La Plata Miner* changed its primary allegiance from Red Mountain City to Chattanooga. On April 2, a post office was established in Red Mountain City, but it did not take that settlement's name—it was called Congress. The editor of the *Red Mountain Pilot* headed a column:

CONGRESS

CONGRESS

CONGRESS

CONGRESS is our address.

He complained that "a large number of our exchanges continue to address us as Red Mountain City and are carried to Red Mountain Town and frequently lay there a week before the thick-headed postmaster sends them back . . . All our exchanges will please change their addresses to 'Congress, San Juan County' and thus avoid delays."[13] By June 30, the *Pilot's* editor conceded that Red Mountain City would have to officially change its name to that of the post office, Congress.

In reply to the tirade in the *Red Mountain Pilot,* the editor of the *Red*

Rodgersville is in the process of becoming Red Mountain Town in this 1884 photograph. The arrangement of the streets hadn't yet been worked out; the buildings face every which way, no road is evident, and wooden sidewalks haven't been built. The saloon on the right looks worn and may have been moved to this site from either Red Mountain City or the original site of Red Mountain Town. *(Colorado Historical Society)*

Mountain Review postulated that Washington, D.C., had decided that "The City" had no right to the name "Red Mountain" but "The Town" did. One of the deciding factors in the post office battle must have been that Red Mountain Town already had a post office using the title "Red Mountain." Another factor may well have been that Red Mountain Town was in fact rapidly progressing toward becoming an "official" town. The April 14, 1883 *Red Mountain Review* carried the notice of election for incorporation of the Town of Red Mountain, to be held on April 30.

Actually, both "Red Mountain" communities were still in a primitive state. An unbiased source reported: "Could it be that (Red Mountain Town) was built in from two to six feet of snow? It was and Congress also . . . The architecture of the buildings is not attractive. Many of them stand on uncertain footing, are wapple-jawed or bias and one of the grand hotels of Congress looks cross-eyed out of many a miss-set window frame. Red Mountain Town has an unsteady look after the boom, but there is still a healthy glow."[14]

Spring 1883 was a time of great excitement and intense speculation in the Red Mountain Mining District. Everyone hoped to make a fortune, if not by mining then by real estate speculation or development. Every day brought reports of even greater riches being found in the mines. Just how big would the towns grow? Just how many people would move to Red Mountain and buy lots? As one man wrote: "I understand there is a grand lady living at Red Mountain and her name is prosperity."[15] Workers were needed everywhere and wages were high. Never mind that the cost of living was astronomical. The expenses would decrease as soon as new roads, and perhaps even a railroad, were built to the new towns.

In May 1883, Red Mountain City's editor bragged that its population included six women, but in that same month, Red Mountain Town became an officially incorporated town. Not surprisingly, 115 out of 117 voters had voted to incorporate. Ironton soon followed suit, holding its incorporation election in mid-May. The *Red Mountain Review* reported that Ironton continued growing rapidly, although "they have only one street two miles long."[16] One of the first orders of business for both town councils was to establish law and order and to provide fire protection. City marshals and fire chiefs were appointed and a volunteer fire department established at each town. Sanitary conditions, liquor laws, and the regulation of prostitutes were all matters on the early council agendas.

The new officials of Red Mountain Town admitted that, at one time, their settlement had had a problem with the quality of its water, but with the spring thaws they had discovered that two previously unknown streams were flowing right through the middle of town. The streams had been covered with the winter snow and ice but "good water in abundance year round is now an established fact."[17] What had actually happened was that the location of Red Mountain Town had shifted slightly to the north so that it occupied the spot formerly held by Rodgersville. The town officials then bragged that "the quality of our water cannot be excelled in the State." Water lines and even fire hydrants spread throughout the entire town. The local paper did admit, however, that there was still at least one problem: "our streets are paved with silver and stumps; a small quantity of the former and a large quantity of the latter."[18]

In June, J. D. Rollins was elected the first mayor of Red Mountain Town, and it was announced that regular mail service to Ouray and Silverton would start in July (up to this time the mail had been carried in by a private carrier). The improvement of local streets was also given top priority. An ordinance was passed that provided for a poll tax, or its equivalent in labor, to be used for improving the streets and cleaning up vacant lots. All owners of lots on Hudson, Main, and First streets were to remove stumps to the middle of the road or be assessed for such. A bridge was built over the creek on Main Street, and grading of all of the town's streets was begun. Fully two blocks of Red Mountain Town's Main Street were completely filled with business establishments, and to the east and south of town were well-developed residential sections.

Chattanooga also continued to grow quickly. By mid-May it was reported that fifty buildings had been completed and were occupied. An estimated

It was a busy day in Ironton in 1889 when this pack train arrived with supplies from Ouray. Several locals turned out to greet the arrival, including the man on the bicycle to the right. The Saratoga Mill and Mine can be seen on the hillside behind Main Street. (*Author's collection*)

twenty-five more were under construction. Since March, the town had added a considerable number of businesses to its commercial district, including several general stores, another drugstore, a blacksmith shop, a hotel, a restaurant, and at least one more saloon. Many other local businesses centered their work around freighting, packing, or acting as forwarding agents. Perhaps even more important for the morale of the town, a post office had been established on April 4, 1883, and F. M. Carroll was appointed the first postmaster.

By midsummer, the *Red Mountain Review* reported that Ironton had grown into the largest community in the Red Mountain district. Among many other business establishments, it had twelve saloons, four restaurants, and even a bookstore that sold cigars and included a newsstand. "[Ironton] lies in one of the most beautiful parks peculiar to the Red Mountain district, and presents a picturesque appearance when viewed from the rocky bluffs surrounding it . . . the mountains present a more busy appearance than the town itself."[19] There were estimated to be two hundred to three hundred houses, tents, or cabins at or near Ironton, and in the summer the population was estimated at "probably a thousand in and about the place and prospecting on the mountains in the vicinity."[20] Grading of its one-mile-long street was given top priority by the Ironton trustees.

Red Mountain Town, in late summer of 1883, continued to bust at its seams, especially after the rich discoveries at the National Belle Mine, located within the town's new city limits. Postmaster Leslie moved into a large new building on Main Street. The *Red Mountain Review* touted that "The Town" had no rivals, and boasted that "Ironton and Chattanooga are simply transfer points and feeders to this great center."[21] Real estate agents, surveyors, and attorneys were abundantly represented in the town. Further signs of civilization were the many new ordinances that were being passed. A single fire ordinance provided for construction standards, inspections, and disposal of ashes. Much of the building activity centered on the upgrading of existing structures. For example, it was quite common for rough log cabins to be finished off with sawn lumber, better windows, and perhaps even Victorian detailing. The new materials went right over the top of the old. The Red Mountain Saw Mill (Hawthorn and Airey, proprietors) continued to operate near the town, turning out rough green lumber for use throughout the district. Because of high transportation costs, the local sawmill, although crude, could turn out lumber considerably cheaper than its competitors in Ouray or Silverton, and it was to carry on a successful business for years to come.

By August 1883, the editor of Congress's *Red Mountain Pilot* had closed his newspaper office and left what he described as a dying town. The settlement seemed to lose its population as quickly as it had boomed a few months earlier. However, on the other side of the divide, Red Mountain Town continued to grow rapidly. With his usual optimism, its editor wrote in September 1883 that "the spring of '84 will see [Red Mountain Town] the liveliest camp in Colorado."[22] At the same time, a reporter from the *Omaha Commercial Record* wrote a more unbiased account: "Red Mountain is in the rough, but time will polish it and make all things even. Wherever nature has planted her richest treasures, neither heights or depths can withhold them from the grasp of men. All over these Red Mountains are the footprints of miners, and their tents and cabins are set above the clouds. It is a rugged and desolate region but delicate flowers nestle in the very borders of eternal snowbanks . . . The district wears the richest surface coat we have ever seen. Pay begins, as the miners say, at the grass roots. Whether it will ever make a second Leadville, as some have prophesied, remains to be seen. It will not be this year . . . ."[23]

By December 1, 1883, the "town" of Congress was all but dead. Its boom and decline had come in less than one year. The Colorado State Business Directory of 1884 listed the population of Red Mountain Town at between five hundred and eight hundred and that of Congress at forty. No mention was even made of Red Mountain City. By January 7, 1884, even the post office at Congress had closed. The December 1, 1883 *Red Mountain Review* reported that all of Red Mountain Town's rivals had soon died a natural death. Red Mountain Town, on the other hand, "enjoyed a steady growth and has obtained a foothold and recognition as the leading camp in the district. It is the direct geometrical center of the richest mining district in the world."

There was still plenty of snow on the ground at Red Mountain Town in the early summer of 1887 or 1888. The National Belle Mine, at left, watches over the town. Half a dozen men are lounging in front of their hotels on the west side of Main Street, enjoying the early morning sun after a long, cold winter. Red Mountain Town was reported to be the liveliest camp on the divide. *(Denver Public Library, Western History Department)*

At the end of the year, in the town's second election, Abbott Lorring was elected mayor. W. E. Leslie was made sheriff, and two constables were hired to support him in his efforts to keep law and order. The town now also had its own justice of the peace.

What had happened to what was left of the original town of Red Mountain? The author of a "special" to the *Rocky Mountain News* gave the answer. "The Town of Red Mountain will be moved from its present location to a point on the Silverton and Red Mountain toll road near the National Belle Mine. L. Dahl has the contract to remove the large and substantial buildings belonging to Slover and Wright, and has been spoken to by other parties in reference to the removal of a number of other buildings. The work of moving the town will be commenced inside of ten days. As is generally known, the town of Red Mountain is situated on a bench some distance beyond and considerably higher than Red Mountain Pass. The removal to the point contemplated will put the town directly on the new wagon road and make it a more desirable stopping point in every respect."[24] About a month later, the July 6 issue of the same paper announced the job complete.

FIVE

———∞∞∞∞◯∞∞∞———

THE NEWSPAPERS

In the 1880s, a newspaper did a lot more than just collect and report the news: The local paper was expected to be a strong advocate of the town or settlement it served. It was through newspaper exchanges that outsiders might learn of new discoveries at the nearby mines and keep themselves posted on day-to-day occurrences. The newspaper was an important and essential economic tool for producing optimistic mining publicity for would-be investors and speculators.

The local newspaper was often a badly needed source of humor in a world that was full of tragedy. It was in the newspaper columns that the local citizens learned of sickness, found out about deaths and births, and even got free medical and legal advice.[1] The newspaper was a town's main contact with the outside world. Every small-town editor relied strongly on outside newspapers to send free copies of their publications so that local readers might remain informed about what was happening elsewhere. Most editors resembled a present-day chamber of commerce and did not hesitate to boldly proclaim the virtues of their towns, the riches of the local mines, and the economies of the local businesses.

In the case of Red Mountain, its geographic location and the normal newspaper promotion assured controversy. The dividing line between Ouray and San Juan counties was the ridge at the top of Red Mountain Pass.

Those mines and settlements to the north of the divide were in Ouray County, with the city of Ouray as the county seat; those mines and settlements to the south of the divide were in San Juan County, with the town of Silverton as the county seat. Ouray and Silverton were an almost equal distance from Red Mountain, and both hoped to become the main provisioner for the booming Red Mountain Mining District. Each county vigorously promoted the outlay of its mines and wished to add the rich ores from the Red Mountain district to their local production totals.

In their efforts to outdo one another and to extol their own benefits and attributes, the local papers didn't hesitate to print articles that became more and more outrageous. The best mines, the best roads, the best towns were all on their side of Red Mountain Divide. The exaggerations (and sometimes just outright lies) came so often and were so overdone that it became an almost impossible task to discern the truth of any particular article in any one of the local papers. There was only one exception to the rule. If one of the Red Mountain papers said anything good about a mine or settlement on the other side of the divide, then it was undoubtedly true! Accurate reports generally came only from outside reporters who might be traveling through the Red Mountain Mining District, but even these reports were sometimes tainted. The Denver papers were, in particular, often chastised for their overstatements. It was like the pot calling the kettle black, but Dave Day, editor of Ouray's *Solid Muldoon,* noted that "some of the largest strikes in Ouray County are found in the columns of the Denver papers. It pays to be truthful in matters and 'special correspondents' should cease to blow up assays."[2]

The *La Plata Miner* and the *San Juan Herald* were both located in Silverton, and they championed the settlements of Congress, Red Mountain City, and Chattanooga, all located in San Juan County. And, of course, they claimed that San Juan County had all the biggest and best mines of the Red Mountain Mining District. In the city of Ouray there were also two papers, the *Ouray Times* and the *Solid Muldoon,* which bragged about Ironton, Red Mountain Town, and the mines located to the north of Red Mountain Divide in Ouray County. In terms of color and controversy, all of the other papers were totally outmatched by Ouray's *Solid Muldoon,* whose liberal democratic editor, Colonel David Frakes Day, was known nationwide for his caustic wit and biting sarcasm. Day relentlessly poked fun at rival towns, newspapers, and persons that did not agree with him. But Dave Day was also responsible for bringing many speculative mining or business scams to light.

David Day was a Civil War hero who moved to Ouray in 1878 and immediately took up odd jobs (his specialty was cutting wood) to make a living. He was sometimes called "Colonel," but the term was merely an honorary title, since Day had been only a private during his army days. Gerald Letcher, a friend who had come with Day to Ouray, told him of a newspaper press that was for sale in Lake City, Colorado. Letcher, who was an Ouray lawyer, raised the money for the venture by soliciting funds from local Democrats, and Day walked twenty-eight miles over Engineer Pass to arrange for the purchase of the press. Day and Letcher printed the *Solid Muldoon* as a weekly Ouray newspaper, and the first issue appeared September 5, 1879. For a while Day made the *Solid Muldoon* a daily paper, which meant that he had seven times the chance to take potshots at his weekly adversaries.

Day never did reveal why he had chosen the strange-sounding name for the paper or what the word "muldoon" meant, other than the implausible explanation that it meant "virgin" in the Zulu language. However, when trying to think of a name for the paper, Day said he wanted it to stand for something

"solid," and William Muldoon was a nationally recognized promoter of prizefights in the 1870s, widely known for his honesty and fair play. Although Day never did mention it, it is highly probable that the name was derived from a famous hoax that occurred in 1877 near Pueblo, Colorado. A "petrified" man, later named the "Solid Muldoon," was discovered near that town and was touted as Darwin's "missing link," because its spine included a short tail. The statue turned out to be made of Portland cement with various human bones mixed in to add authenticity.

At one time, later in his career, Day was rumored to have had forty-seven libel suits pending against him. He seemed to thrive on the attention and used the lawsuits simply as an addition to the mystique with which he surrounded himself. Day prided himself on his honesty, and it is important to note that he never lost a single libel suit. He was, however,

David F. Day was the editor of Ouray's *Solid Muldoon* for over a decade. He was known far and wide for his caustic humor and biting sarcasm. Day was a staunch Democrat and was highly respected throughout Colorado, even though his wit often caused him so much trouble that he was forced to carry a gun. (*Denver Public Library, Western History Department*) once jailed for contempt of court for making comments in his paper about a judge to the effect that it took a liar to know one. The *Solid Muldoon* was supposedly "snatched hot from the press by locals and read among roars of laughter."[3] Day's reputation as a humorist and philosopher gained him such a wide reputation that even England's Queen Victoria was said to have read his paper for many years. He was well respected among most other newspaper men. "But for Dave Day's brains the *Solid Muldoon* would never be heard of outside of Ouray County. He is a very much bigger man than the paper and it cannot get along without him" (*Denver Tribune*, July 28, 1881). "The *Muldoon* sticks to the mind, indelible and fixed, like a plaster to a poor man's ribs . . . This paper is a success in name as well as form" (*Dolores News*, September 23, 1879).

Day was never afraid to make a blistering attack against anyone or anything that he perceived to be fraudulent or contrary to the best interests of Ouray and the state of Colorado. His wit was coarse but genuine, and he was instantly perceived as an equal who could be trusted. He was particularly quick to attack any mining venture that he felt might be a mere scheme to make money through the sale of stock. He noted, quite correctly, that many capitalists relied on the information contained in his newspaper to make their investments, and one or two bad schemes could badly hurt the valid mining ventures that desperately needed capital for development. It was sometimes extremely unpopular for Day to take such a stand, but the mining news in his newspaper could be trusted to be the truth. Almost every week someone was trying to fight Day over a comment that had been made in his paper. Day's life was often threatened when he refused to go along with some of these hoaxes. As a result, Day always carried a pistol and usually kept a rifle or shotgun at the *Muldoon*'s office. Supposedly, Day was actually only fired upon once, by an old friend who was upset at one of the articles.

The *Solid Muldoon* was actually Ouray's second newspaper, the *Ouray Times* having been started several years earlier by Henry and William Ripley— on June 16, 1877—just a few years after the establishment of the town of Ouray. Their press was freighted in some three hundred miles by wagon from Cañon City over terrible roads, at the time just pack trails. The Ripley brothers bought the entire production plant of the *Cañon City Times,* which they had helped operate for five years, and then moved the whole operation to Ouray over Otto Mears's rough toll road. Henry Ripley later wrote that "there was supposed to be a toll road between Saguache and Lake City—at least at frequent intervals we were held up for toll . . ." He swore the only road from Lake City to Ouray was the faint trail made by United States Army wagons when they transferred the Ute Indians from the Los

This scene is obviously staged. The blacksmith to the right of the portal wears his good hat and tie, and even the "ore" is too uniform. It looks as if the winter's snow has just been shoveled away from the Beaver Mine, located just outside the town of Ironton. Owners of some mines tried to use the newspapers to promote fraudulent mining schemes, but most editors attempted to keep their mining news factual. *(Denver Public Library, Western History Department)*

Piños I agency near Cochetopa Pass to the Los Piños II agency on the Uncompahgre River.

Ripley wrote of what "a great day it was when the first paper was printed. All day long, men came to the office to see how things were progressing. The first paper, as was usual in such cases, was put up for auction and sold for ten dollars . . . The first paper was made as much of as the advent of the first baby, and well it might, for its travail in getting there had been long and hard."[4] Although it was Ouray's first newspaper, the *Ouray Times* went out of business in 1886, in large part because of competition from Dave Day's paper.

Silverton's *La Plata Miner* was started by John R. Curry of Iowa. Curry and his hand-operated equipment came into Baker's Park from Del Norte over Stony Pass. He quickly set up shop in Silverton and published his first paper on July 10, 1875. The first newsprint for his paper was brought in during the winter on the backs of two men on snowshoes who received a dollar a pound for their labor. For several years Curry went back to his native Iowa during the harsh winter months, leaving his paper to be run by an assistant. It wasn't until 1877 that he actually moved his family to Silverton. He was well respected and seemed to enjoy starting papers in the small mining communities. Newspaper editors, publishers, and printers changed jobs often in the San Juans, but Curry lasted eight years in Silverton, leaving the paper on June 16, 1883. A quick succession of publishers and editors then took over the *La Plata Miner*. Curry later became the editor of the *Red Mountain Pilot*, the *Telluride Times,* and half a dozen other Western Slope newspapers.

The *San Juan Herald* printed its first issue on June 23, 1881. It was started by G. N. Raymond and James Everingham. The *Ouray Times,* also Republican, complimented the *Herald* for being "a sound Republican paper and a valuable organ for our party." Raymond had been in the San Juans for a while and was known as a good man and a fine printer. Everingham was new to the San Juans but had been a printer and assistant editor in Peekskill, New York, before moving to Silverton. Gid Propper took over as editor in November 1883, after Raymond left to become editor and publisher of the *Red Mountain Review.*

Until January 1883, it had been left to the newspapers in the towns of Ouray and Silverton to harass one another over their towns' claim to the Red Mountain Mining District. However, in that month two new papers were started on the divide, one at Red Mountain Town and the other at Red Mountain City. Each paper backed its own Red Mountain community and added fuel to the barrage of boasts or even outright lies that were being printed. The Red Mountain editors arrived at their respective towns almost as quickly as the first lots were laid out in the snow. In fact, it is quite likely that they both were tempted to move to their respective settlements by the promise of free land in exchange for good publicity.

In January and February 1883, John Curry, who at the time was still publishing the *La Plata Miner,* printed the first seven issues of Red Mountain City's *Red Mountain Pilot* from his offices in Silverton. Of course, he showed a definite bias toward the San Juan County settlement of Red Mountain City. The town's founders were evidently partners of Curry in the newspaper business. The *Red Mountain Pilot,* in its very first issue of January 12, 1883, announced that its settlement had been located on Sunday, January 7, 1883, and by Monday, January 8, "ten business lots were selected and contracts let for six houses." One of the ten lots was to be used by editor Curry for his newspaper office. On January 13, 1883, Curry, through the *La Plata Miner,* pronounced that "every mine in the district that is a producing mine today is in San Juan County. The line between San Juan County and Ouray County

In the early 1880s, freight was shipped by railroad to Silverton, where it was transferred onto wagons headed to Chattanooga and then onto burros or mules for the final trip to Red Mountain Divide. All this kept a small army of merchants, freighters, and packers busy. The newspapers were one weapon in the battle to make sure business came through Silverton and not Ouray. (*Reprinted from* Harper's Weekly, *June 9, 1883; author's collection*)

actually runs north of the Yankee Girl mine." The statement was a total false-hood. The editor admitted in the article itself that Red Mountain Divide was the county line but went on to announce that it had been the obvious intention of the Colorado legislature to put the county line north of the Yankee Girl Mine (which, of course, didn't even exist at the time Ouray County was formed out of San Juan County). The editor wasn't sure exactly how it had happened, but San Juan County had definitely been cheated! Curry even made the outrageous claim that the Red Mountain Mining District bordered on the northwestern city limits of the town of Silverton.

Of all the editors in the district, it was perhaps Curry who most consis-tently exaggerated his articles. On New Year's Eve 1882, in a detailed account of the Red Mountain Mining District, Curry mentioned not a word about Red Mountain City; yet just two weeks later, the editor announced that construc-tion of more than twenty buildings there had been started or finished. Curry proclaimed that Red Mountain City was "beautifully situated at the junction of the Congress, Yankee Girl, Telluride, Bridal Veil, Ophir, Marshall Basin, and Sneffels [sic] trails." Once again the newspaper's account was at least partially fictional. Some of the trails were nowhere near the town, the trails did not come together in one spot, and a couple of the trails were situated miles apart at their closest points.

Originally, Dave Day had nothing good to say about the *Red Mountain Pilot* or George N. Raymond's *Red Mountain Review*. Raymond's mistake was that he printed his paper in Silverton! "The *Red Mountain Pilot* and *Red Mountain Review* are both published in Silverton and are a tissue of Falsehood. There is but one tent and three bunches of shingles in Red Mountain City, they blow so much about, and the miners of Red Mountain refuse to patronize and tolerate such frauds. Both the enterprising editors have been ordered out of camp. Red Mountain needs neither gush nor exaggeration. We have enough ore in sight to attract capitalists and insure permanency and do not desire the services of journalists who are willing to do an unlimited amount of lying for a certain number of town lots. Curry and Raymond would kill any camp."[5]

Even when the *Red Mountain Review* was later printed at Red Mountain Town in Ouray County, Day did not warm to Raymond, and week after week Day exchanged insults with Curry, who continued as the editor of the *Red Mountain Pilot,* located in San Juan County. Day seemed to have absolutely no respect for Curry because of Curry's exaggeration and his San Juan County location. Day's attitude toward Raymond stemmed in great part from Day being a staunch Democrat and Raymond being a solid Republican. Day also disliked Raymond because of the latter's attitude toward Otto Mears, "the Pathfinder of the San Juans." Mears and Raymond did not get along well at all, while Dave Day and Otto Mears were good friends and mutual supporters. Mears disliked Raymond so much that he eventually convinced Dave Day to move his paper to Durango. At the time, Raymond had left Red Mountain and started a paper there, and Mears was determined to drive him out of business.

There is little doubt that both Red Mountain Town and Red Mountain City were grossly overpraised by their respective editors. Curry's tendency to exaggerate could be seen every week on the masthead of the *Pilot,* which carried a statement that the paper was "Published in the Richest Mineral Belt in the World." The *Review* was a little more realistic. It was "Published in the Leadville of the San Juans." The practices did not go unnoticed by the outside community. The *Denver Times* carried an article admitting that the Red Mountain Mining District "is thought to be the richest in this part of the State—if not the United States and the wealth and probabilities of the country have generally not been overestimated, though some of the local newspapers have printed very inconsistent and unfounded statements about it.

The people of the region are especially to be commended for their desire to be written up on their merits. They discountenance exaggeration of any kind . . . There are, of course, a few men who overestimate the production of the country, thinking that time will prove the truth of their statements, even though the facts at present do not. They believe they are aiding their camp and encouraging immigration by this course. Any level-headed mining man will tell you they are doing just the contrary. The worst enemy a mining region can have is the man who lies about it simply to bring people to it."[6]

Since it was usually impossible to rely on the truthfulness of any statement concerning its own town that was printed in either Red Mountain paper, it was much more reliable to look for articles from the newspapers of other towns. Sometimes this led to some heated exchanges, because the local editors weren't hesitant to lock horns with even their big-city brothers. For example, on January 15, 1883 a reporter for the *Denver Republican* visited Red Mountain City and later published a seemingly unbiased if not complimentary article. He called the settlement a paper city, built in a bad location and vastly exaggerated by the Silverton papers. Curry, through the *La Plata Miner,* responded that the Denver correspondent was unfortunately printing a lie because he had been in Red Mountain City only nine days after the settlement was founded and hadn't given the town a fair chance. Curry ignored the fact that he himself had printed an article claiming that eighteen buildings were under construction on January 11, 1883 – four days after its founding. The Silverton editor admitted that perhaps the location of Red Mountain City was not the best for scenery but was adamant that action had been taken to make sure that the settlement was centrally located so as to be near the heart of the district.[7] In fact, the scenery was pretty spectacular. Red Mountain City's problem was that it had been located outside the mainstream of activity on the divide.

Even though Raymond printed the *Red Mountain Review* in Silverton, Curry, through the *La Plata Miner,* began to take potshots at him for setting up his office in Ouray County: "The only reason Mr. Raymond located his ten cent printing office at the Hudson mine was because they put up a cabin for him and without an investment of $100 he seeks to start a newspaper in opposition of the interests of the business men of Silverton and San Juan county. The facts are that a greater number of paying mines are nearer to Red Mountain City than any other point in the district. Red Mountain City is on the south side of the mountain while Hudson Town is on the north side. Red Mountain City has pure water. The water at Hudson Town is poisonous with mineral, and will not fail to result in the sickness and death of a large percentage of the people who are compelled to drink it."[8] Hudson

A. W. Begole and Gordon Kimball of Ouray outfitted many a prospector in the Red Mountain area. Each store was reported to be grossing over $200,000 in sales each year during the 1880s. It was important to both the Ouray and Silverton merchants that their towns capture Red Mountain's business. The newspaper was one way to obtain that goal. *(Denver Public Library, Western History Department)*

was located on a north-facing slope in a dark and forested spot, but its water was undoubtedly not poisonous; in fact, it was probably some of the best water on the divide. Curry also had problems with his geography. Raymond's paper was not located at the Hudson Mine but rather at the original location of Red Mountain Town—a good quarter of a mile down the north side of the divide from the Hudson.

On March 3, 1883, Dave Day buried the hatchet with the *Red Mountain Review* because George Raymond had left to go to work at the *San Juan Herald* in Silverton. Charles S. York had assumed the position of editor, and Day actually praised the paper and its new editor for being intelligent enough to locate in Ouray County's Red Mountain Town. The editor of the *Red Mountain Review* reciprocated by listing on his masthead that the paper was located in Ouray County and by issuing his statement that the *Review* was "Ouray Mountain Town's" newspaper.[9] Day in return predicted that "by September 1, 1883, Red Mountain Town will have a population of nearly ten thousand and a daily output surpassed by Leadville only."[10] A week later, York made his own prediction that was only slightly less optimistic—five thousand people would be in Red Mountain Town by July 1, 1883. Unfortunately, these predictions were later used by several historians to establish as fact that Red Mountain Town had grown to a population of five thousand to ten thousand inhabitants. Such was never the case. In fact, there were never more than two or three thousand people in the entire Red Mountain Mining District at any one time.

After a few months, Silverton's John Curry had backed off his previous statement that all of Red Mountain's mines were in San Juan County—although he did so in a very reluctant and diminutive way. His revised estimate placed four-fifths of the Red Mountain mines in San Juan County. Curry used the same article to make the point that he was very upset at a "neutral" Pueblo newspaper that had estimated that four-fifths of Red Mountain's mines were located in Ouray County.[11] Curry adamantly noted (as he had in every issue since the boom had started) that the *only* way to get to the Red Mountain Mining District was from Silverton and that the district was not accessible from Ouray. In this case, the editor of the *La Plata Miner* might be credited with at least printing a half-truth, because a very rough wagon road did run all the way from Silverton to Chattanooga at the base of Red Mountain Divide, while a much longer and very dangerous pack trail was available for travel from Ouray.

Curry soon decided to begin publication of yet another newspaper. In the April 7, 1883 *La Plata Miner*, he announced that "the first number of the *Chattanooga Enterprise* will be issued at Chattanooga, San Juan County, in the Red Mountain Mining District, on Saturday, April 21st." The same article noted that Chattanooga was "reached by four or five stages per day from Silverton in a very pleasant two hour ride. It is now by far the liveliest business point in the district." The fact that the seven-mile trip from Silverton was an easy grade yet was estimated to take two hours to traverse is, in itself, proof of just how bad the road must have been. It was also very doubtful that four or five stages were running daily to Chattanooga, because a regular stage route had yet to be established from Silverton.

Curry, through his newspaper, continued to take potshots at everyone and everything located in Ouray County – the city of Ouray, Red Mountain Town, and even the newly founded town of Ironton. "The town or sprouting known as Ironton does not properly belong to the Red Mountain District, but on account of its proximity to the best mines in Ouray County might injure the growth of the Town of Ouray were [Ironton] not located in a miserable iron bog marsh."[12] In the same issue Curry again blasted Red Mountain Town (which he continued to call Hudson), stating "lots have been sold over and over so often in Hudson Town that property is held too high there today . . . The life of the town is mainly C. S. York's *Review* newspaper." Curry reprinted the article almost verbatim in the *Red Mountain Pilot* of the same date but added that the town of Red Mountain "is said to be in a boggy place and not so centrally located in the heart of Red Mountain and older and adjoining districts, as is Red Mountain City." He predicted that the new wagon road from Chattanooga would pass right through the heart of Red Mountain City but would be built a good distance to the west of Red Mountain Town. In fact, by the time the road was actually constructed, Red Mountain Town had relocated to the National Belle Mine, and the road passed right through the middle of town. The new road bypassed Red Mountain City by half a mile and sealed the fate of the new settlement.

The *Red Mountain Review* reciprocated against Curry's attacks by blasting the *La Plata Miner* for publishing legal notices for patent applications on mines that were located in Ouray County. It notified its readers that, in its opinion, the patents for such mines would not be legal. "The applicant should have more sense, the editor more honor."[13] The *La Plata Miner* responded that Colorado law only required that the owner file the legal notice in the nearest paper, with no mention made of the county in which to file. The debate continued for some months, but evidently the reasoning of the *Red Mountain Review* was correct.

Instead of spotlighting their neighbors, the Red Mountain newspapers continued for months to snipe at one another. The April 28 *Red Mountain Review* called Red Mountain City "Lookout City" and noted that it was unfavorably located on the side of a steep hill. The *La Plata Miner* of April 24 claimed Red Mountain City to be the greatest city on the divide, "high and dry with an abundance of pure water." Again, only an outside paper, the Lake City *Silver World,* seemed capable of giving an accurate and non-hostile account of prominence on the divide. It reported that, as far as it could tell, Red Mountain Town "seems to be the great [sic] of the Red Mountain mining region."[14]

Some indication of the status of the two towns could also be gleaned from the *Pilot*'s ads, which were mainly taken up by builders looking for work. Only the Haines Hotel and Patterson and Frink, General Merchants, advertised consistently in the Red Mountain City newspaper. On the other hand, the Rodgersville Supply and Hotel, the Excelsior House, the Red Mountain Saloon, the Miner's Meat Market, the Red Mountain Billiard Hall, Ailing and Co. Hardware, the Red Mountain Hotel, and the Assembly Club all regularly advertised in Red Mountain Town's *Review*. There were also a dozen other occasional advertisers. The Assembly Club advertised billiard tables and boasted that it carried "the Best of Imported Wines, Liquors, Cigars, etc."

As the first full winter on the divide came to a close (spring didn't come until late May or June at such high altitude), everyone's spirits seemed to pick up. Even the ads in the two Red Mountain papers veered toward the humorous. The May 26, 1883 edition of the *Red Mountain Review* reported that the snow was fast disappearing, and the paper carried an advertisement that "June First is near at hand when it will be everybody's duty to celebrate by changing their socks. Three pairs seamless at the Spot Cash Store in Silverton." The Spot Cash store also advertised in the *Red Mountain Pilot* that it had "just received . . . a fresh stock of boots, California underwear, etc. These goods must be sold cheap for cash to defend our Eastern agent, who, by the way, stole them."[15]

In May 1883, several columns of the *Red Mountain Review* were devoted to its editor's favorite pastime – blasting the newspaper at Red Mountain City. He referred to the *Red Mountain Pilot* variously as "The Lookout Mountain Orphan" and "The Lookout City Pilot" and further reported that a burro had drowned in the middle of Red Mountain City's main street and lamented that "unfortunately for that community, it was not the idiot that runs the *Pilot*."[16]

In June, the Lake City *Silver World* reported that the original location of Red Mountain Town was now all but deserted – in part because the surrounding heavy forest was supposed to have blocked the sunlight and kept the settlement in two to four feet of snow. The area was also very swampy in the summer, and the new toll road would run by the National Belle, which had made major new discoveries of ore. Red Mountain Town was booming, but it was now located at the site of what had been Rodgersville, a name that was no longer mentioned in the papers. By July 1883, John Curry announced that he was shutting down the *Red Mountain Pilot* to work full time on the *Silverton Democrat*. He couldn't resist one last parting shot at what had been the old Red Mountain Town (which he continued to call Hudson). "The citizens of Hudson Town are now wrestling with the question of whether it would be cheaper to move the town or move the bog iron marsh."[17]

At only six months of age, the *Red Mountain Pilot* and Red Mountain City were dying. The editor quit the *Pilot,* the printer left, and the paper was reduced to two pages of length. Charles Pattisson, who admitted that he had so little newspaper experience that he couldn't properly be called an editor, ran the paper the last few months to "make a lot of money running legal notices." Pattisson later claimed that a big strike in Telluride sucked off the citizens of Red Mountain City. "They were followed by the merchants, saloon men, gamblers, dance hall people and all. Within a week there was no one left there but postmaster, James Edwards and myself . . . I was certain to get my money for the notices as soon as they had run the required length of time, so I could not leave. We had everything our own way. I would help him run the post office and he would help me write 'hot stuff,' set up and pull the lever on our old Washington hand press. The post office business was confined wholly to handling the circulation of my paper – the *Red Mountain Pilot* – about fifty copies." As soon as the legal notices were finished, Pattisson reported that he and Edwards "locked up the town" and left.[18] Now only the *Red Mountain Review* remained to print its rival's epitaph. "The *Red Mountain*

Pilot has ceased to exist; turned up its toes to the daisies after a brief existence of less than eight months . . . none to mourn its loss."[19]

Although Red Mountain City may not have been as much of a ghost town as Charles Pattisson made it sound, there was no doubt that the new Red Mountain Town had established itself as the predominant town at the top of Red Mountain Divide. Now the newspaper battles were to be fought between Ouray and Silverton, each of which was courting the Red Mountain district for its business. Since it was the major settlement on the divide, Red Mountain Town could play the bigger towns of Ouray and Silverton to its advantage. The *Red Mountain Review* reported in its December 22, 1883 issue that the Ouray merchants were trying to get the Red Mountain paper to feature the importance of Ouray to the town. York responded that Ouray's *Solid Muldoon* talked only of the town of Ironton, and if that paper were to write more and better articles about Red Mountain Town, then the favor might be returned. The *Red Mountain Review* was, itself, out of business just a few issues thereafter but was quickly replaced by the *Red Mountain Miner,* which carried on the printing of the local paper until 1885.

Over in Ouray, Dave Day didn't care who was running the papers in the other towns. He was more than willing to criticize any of the nearby editors or their settlements. The town of Telluride had been founded just a few years earlier, and Day reported that "Telluride has seven lawyers and two dance halls, 0 churches and 000 school houses. Mercy, what a wicked village."[20] In September 1884, Day took a particularly savage shot at Silverton, commenting that masked balls were a favorite pastime of that city as "the average Silverton woman never appears half so attractive as when masked. The majority of them are so dumpy they have to stand on a chair to scratch their backs, and the remainder are so lofty that the average masher would have to hook his toes in the kilt on their basques to get a good bite. It's in Ouray you find symmetry in human architecture."[21]

In early 1884, Curry left Silverton's *La Plata Miner,* and Iles and Coleman took it over. What had been a bitter feud seemed to now turn into a friendly rivalry. Dave Day took the opportunity to push the "balmy weather" of Ouray as compared to Silverton, and most of the winter of 1884–1885 was spent with the two papers debating the climate of Ouray and Silverton. Iles and Coleman were quick to jump on Day when he claimed the barometer fell below zero in Ouray for the first time that winter. They reported that freezing weather had indeed come to Ouray and "the beautiful Magnolia trees, of which so much has been said, have been blighted."[22] Later in December, the *La Plata Miner* reported that "the car load of bananas from Ouray to Denver and destined for the holidays, were caught on top of Marshall Pass in the snowstorm of

By the late 1880s, Ouray had become a fairly sophisticated town. This six-horse Concord stage is ready to pull out for Red Mountain with a full load (thirteen passengers and a driver) this fine fall morning. The famous Beaumont Hotel is in the background. Its first floor housed Thatcher Brothers Bank. (*Denver Public Library, Western History Department*

Sunday and Monday. It is hoped that the blockade of the Magnolia route has been raised and that the fruit can reach its destination before Christmas."[23]

In mid-January 1885, the *Red Mountain Miner* was forced to shut down. Dave Day reported that "the *Red Mountain Miner* followed in the footsteps of its predecessors, cashed in its checks on the 17th. Of illegitimate conception, born and raised in adversity, and a disgrace to the district, it died unhonored, unmourned."[24] For a while there was no local paper in the Red Mountain Mining District. After the newspapers on the divide proper had all folded, the *Solid Muldoon* started a special Red Mountain mining column to help fill the void. But the Red Mountain district was pretty well taken for granted, and Dave Day soon dropped any special preferences. Less and less was written about the Red Mountain mines, even though the district produced eighty percent of Ouray County's ore in 1885. The *Solid Muldoon* even felt it necessary to print a small article every now and then that would apologize for the lack of news about the district and perhaps point out that "because nothing is said about our own Yankee Girl, the outside world need not think she is under the weather. The fact is that the great mine was never in better spirits than at present."[25] Every now and then Day would publicize for a Red Mountain correspondent, and he commented that he trusted "someone of the intelligent number will respond,"[26] but no great amount of space was given to the Red Mountain Mining District – certainly nothing like in the boom period of 1883–1884.

In 1887, the *Red Mountain Mining Journal* was started by Gid R. Propper, who had worked for the *La Plata Miner* in Silverton and then became the editor of the *Animas Forks Pioneer*. Propper also had experience as a writer and editor for half a dozen other San Juan newspapers. He had worked so many places and moved so often that the Rico newspaper called him "the rolling stone of San Juan journalists, who yanks the lever, wields the scissors and is the brains of the concern."[27] Propper's time on Red Mountain was longer than his successors' and just as exciting. A newspaper was also published in Ironton in 1888 and 1889, but it just didn't seem to have the same type of lively spirit as the papers that had been published on the divide proper. The name of the *Red Mountain Mining Journal* was shortened to the *Red Mountain Journal* in 1889, and the paper continued to publish until the building in which it was located burned to the ground in the big fire at Red Mountain Town in 1893. At that time, the Red Mountain paper merged with Silverton's paper (the *Silverton Standard*) and ceased to exist. It was only when the story of the Red Mountain Mining District was almost complete that the last of the editors gave up hope and newspapers ceased to exist on Red Mountain Divide.

SIX

∞∞∞∞◎◎◎∞∞∞

THE ROAD

At first all supplies were shipped into the Red Mountain Mining District by large pack trains composed of burros or mules. All mineral production was taken out the same way. Today, it is difficult to conceive just how huge this job was. Thousands of tons of ore were shipped each month. Each burro carried about a 150-pound load, while a mule could carry an average of 300 pounds. A packer normally led the mules, tied together with ropes, in a long line. The burros were usually driven like sheep. Dozens of men and hundreds of animals were needed for the task.

A massive support system was also necessary to meet the needs of the packers, the teamsters, and their animals. Otto Mears once said that "wherever there were people, there were ten times as many stock [without counting cattle on the range] which means barns, corrals, blacksmith shops, livery stables and flies innumerable, flies everywhere."[1] Mears himself owned a freighting company that used well over a hundred burros and sixty mules to pack ore into Silverton from the nearby mines. His charge ran from $2.50 to $5.00 per animal for a round trip, but only if it could be made in one day.

The pack-train system proved to be satisfactory for the early prospectors, who were basically only trying to ship a little ore out to the smelters to be assayed. However, the capitalists needed to send out vast quantities of ore and bring in large amounts of heavy equipment if they intended to do serious

88

LUMBER AND PROVISION TRAIN.

A train of burros carrying lumber and provisions is driven through the deep snow on its way to Red Mountain. Burros were driven like cattle; mules were led in long strings. Winter trails packed down hard and filled in ruts, making travel easier. (*Reprinted from* Harper's Weekly, *June 9, 1883; author's collection*)

mining. Boilers, crushers, cables, ore cars, pumps, and many more heavy, bulky items could only be brought into the district by substantial freight wagons that traveled over true wagon roads. It was much too expensive to continue to pack the ore out and supplies in by mules or burros. All of the potential profit of a mine could be eaten up by high costs of shipping the ore to the smelters, which sometimes ran as much as eighty dollars per ton. In order to help defray development costs, some mines hand-sorted the ore and shipped only their highest grades; the low-grade ore usually piled up on the mine dump or, better yet, was left in place in the mine until the arrival of a good wagon road or a railroad made it economical to ship.

At the time of the dramatic Red Mountain discoveries, several pack trails existed in the district, such as the route from Lake City to Mineral Point to Del Mino. A relatively good wagon road had also been completed in 1879 from Silverton up Cement Creek to Del Mino, but travel from that point into the heart of the Red Mountain district was on foot or by horseback. At the north end of the district the terrain of the Uncompahgre River canyon was too steep for any type of freighting to be done directly to Ouray. The easiest, most direct, and most used route was from Silverton to Chattanooga. This "road" was merely a rough path over which only a brave soul would dare to take a wagon, and a very steep pack trail existed from Chattanooga up the last mile or two to the top of Red Mountain Divide.

Soon after the rich Yankee Girl strike, that mine joined with the Congress Mine and offered the sum of two thousand dollars to help defray expenses to anyone who wished to build a road to a mine. The La Plata Miner pronounced that the San Juan County commissioners should match that amount.[2] It was obvious that roads were desperately needed, but in the 1880s there was very little in the way of state money available for such purposes, and absolutely no federal funds could be obtained. It was up to the local counties to build their own public roads, or in the absence of public funds, a private company might be organized to construct a toll road.

In the winter, snow and ice filled in the gullies and covered the stumps so as to make the routes up to the Red Mountain mines much more passable. D. F. Watson, who ran a store, hotel, and stable at Rodgersville, was therefore able to run a sleigh daily during the winter of 1882–1883 from that settlement down the snow-covered trail to the mouth of Mill Creek near Chattanooga. The La Plata Miner proclaimed that the two-and-one-half-mile route was "a first class trail over which sixty animals pass each way daily,"[3] but it was only a trail and not a road.

The merchants of Chattanooga quickly went to work to upgrade the trail from Silverton and soon managed to make it into a pretty decent wagon road. However, travel from Chattanooga up to the Red Mountain district on the "first class trail" continued to be by horseback or on foot. When the railroad arrived at Silverton in July 1882, most Red Mountain ores were shipped in that direction to be milled, and the concentrates were economically shipped out from that point by rail to the smelters. Ouray wasn't able to obtain a railroad until 1887, although in the fall of 1882 the D&RG railroad had been extended thirty-two miles farther north to the town of Montrose. Ouray merchants did their best to encourage the Red Mountain mines to ship in their direction, but only a few mines actually did so because it took five days for the freighters to make the round trip from Montrose to Ouray.

It was common in the 1880s for freight rates to vary depending on the value of the item being shipped. For example, charges were $15.00 per ton for supplies being shipped from Montrose to Ouray, yet only $7.50 per ton for the return trip when the wagons were loaded with ore. There were additional charges for the pack-trail route from Ouray to Red Mountain – a trip that could be made only by a very circuitous route. It therefore wasn't surprising that, after the arrival of the railroad at Silverton, ninety-five

When freight could be moved in the wintertime, wagon wheels were often replaced with runners. Larger and heavier loads could then be hauled, and the ride was usually much smoother. This wagon/sled has just been unloaded at a bunkhouse at Red Mountain, and everyone is enjoying some sociality. *(Author's collection)*

percent of the Red Mountain ore went to that town. Ouray merchants weren't pleased that the ore wagons came back up the divide loaded with supplies that had been purchased from Silverton merchants.

With the arrival of the D&RG railroad at Silverton, low-grade ores from all of its nearby mines could be economically shipped to market. Haulage rates that had been as high as fifty or sixty dollars per ton from Silverton to the smelters now dropped to twelve dollars per ton for the several-hundred-mile railroad trip. The results of the lower fares were astonishing. Less than one million dollars in ore had been shipped to market from Ouray and San Juan counties combined in all the years prior to 1882; with the arrival of the railroad at Silverton, the amount of ore being shipped each year from the Red Mountain Mining District alone exceeded that amount. Because of Red Mountain's rugged and remote location, cheap transportation was the main factor that opened up the region's mines. With the railroad close by, miners, capitalists, and merchants all began to turn their attention to "the new Leadville."

In the winter of 1882–1883, thoughts of a good wagon road from Ouray to Red Mountain began to formulate in the minds of the Ouray merchants.

The teamster in this photograph is doing double duty by driving a group of burros before him while leading a string of mules behind his mount. The burros' pack saddles are empty because they are not being used to help carry ore down from the mine. *(Walker Arts Studio photo; author's collection)*

The people of Silverton scoffed at the idea: "The people in Ouray say they will build a wagon road to Red Mountain. How absurd and ridiculous. The people of Ouray began seven years ago to build a road to Mineral City and have not got it completed yet."[4]

The last statement was the truth. A road company had been formed by Ouray merchants in 1877 to build a road up the Uncompahgre River to Mineral Point. The Ouray, Mineral City and Animas Forks Toll Road Company failed within a year, having done little to change the condition of the miserable, unsafe pack trail. Then on April 1, 1880, the Ouray and San Juan Wagon Toll Road Company was formed to upgrade the same route up the Uncompahgre River to Poughkeepsie Gulch. At that point the proposed road forked: The main road headed to Mineral Point, Animas Forks, and then Silverton, and a branch road was to extend to the headwaters of Poughkeepsie Gulch. No part of the route would be easy to construct, and in three years' time the development of the road was very slow. Progress was particularly difficult at a section that crossed the steep quartz cliffs south of Bear Creek Falls. There the road had to be blasted inch by inch from high up on the mountain cliffs. When the valuable ores of Red Mountain were first "discovered" in 1882, other investors for the road were quickly found. Work advanced a little more rapidly, but it was still obvious that it could take years to finish the road.

Eventually, the Ouray County commissioners had to step in and take over the toll company.[5] The rich Red Mountain strikes made a branch road to the booming mining district not only profitable but almost an economic necessity for the merchants of Ouray. The commissioners devised a new plan to convert the Poughkeepsie Gulch branch road into the main route and to extend the road from the top of Poughkeepsie down Corkscrew Gulch into the Red Mountain Mining District. Additional men were immediately put to work, but even after an expenditure of forty-two thousand dollars the Ouray commissioners weren't close to completing the road. At the established rate of construction, it could take many more years to reach the Red Mountain Mining District. The Ouray County commissioners decided to contract with Otto Mears to finish the job.

Otto Mears has always been somewhat of an enigma to historians. On the one hand, he is known and honored as "the Pathfinder of the San Juans." He was responsible for the construction of a dozen wagon roads and railroads in Colorado, which brought riches and benefits to the local populations. He seemed at times to have been gracious, charitable, generous, and a genuine humanitarian. Yet, typical of the capitalists of his time, Mears made great personal profit from his efforts – usually at the expense of others – and although most of his gains were reinvested, it was always with the hope of making an even more valuable return on his money. His tolls were very high, and his railroad rates were even higher. He seemed to be perfectly willing to take advantage of someone else's misfortune but could also be extremely sympathetic and thoughtful. Mears has rightfully been honored for his achievements, and yet, as is so often true, a very human side of his personality has probably been ignored.

When the Ouray County commissioners asked Mears to help complete the road from Ouray to the Red Mountain district, it didn't seem to bother him at all that the route had great obstacles to overcome and would therefore involve a much greater than normal cost. Mears and the people of Ouray came up with a new idea – continue to blast the road out of solid rock in the Uncompahgre canyon and then go directly up the "impassable" Red Mountain Creek. The new course would be very expensive but would save ten miles and avoid a steep climb and descent. The *Red Mountain Review* of March 31, 1883 announced that this time the people of Ouray were earnest in their labor and that the new route was a good one. Even though work on the new section of road hadn't yet begun, the paper predicted that at least a trail would be built up Red Mountain Creek canyon by the first of June.[6]

In the meantime, the San Juan County commissioners had developed their own plan, which was to build a road east from Red Mountain that would

connect with the newly built road
from Silverton to Gladstone. A rough
and steep trail was, in fact, constructed
in 1883 from Gladstone over the
12,217-foot divide between Red
Mountain No. 1 and Red Mountain
No. 2 and down Corkscrew Gulch.
The route was basically the same as
the present Corkscrew jeep trail.

To the south of the Red Mountain
district, the new wagon road from Silverton to Chattanooga got smoother
and easier to travel during the winter
of 1883–1884 because the snow and
ice packed in the potholes and covered
the stumps. The new-fallen snow
sometimes piled up so deep along the
route that it had to be shoveled by
work gangs of hundreds of men.
Boilers, pumps, and other heavy machinery were able to start moving
toward the Red Mountain district on
large sleds pulled by six- and eight-
horse teams. Issue after issue of the
Silverton paper proclaimed that the
only way into Red Mountain was
through Silverton. It was perhaps true
for sleighs in the winter, but men on

Chief Ouray and Otto Mears were fairly
good friends for almost two decades.
Each played an important part in the development of western Colorado. Ouray
was famous for his peacekeeping skills,
Mears for his toll roads and railroads.
This photograph was taken at the peace
treaty negotiations in 1868, at which the
Utes deeded most of the eastern Colorado
mountains to the United States government. (*Denver Public Library, Western
History Department*)

foot or on horseback could come into the booming district by using any one
of half a dozen routes. However, the pack routes were treacherous, especially
in the winter. The *Red Mountain Pilot* exaggerated the dangers only slightly
when a reporter wrote that the road to Ouray "is down a fearful grade, so
that in the most favorable seasons of the year the mountain sheep pause and
tremble to walk the precipitous trail, and in winter, it is practically impassable
except for the most daring and heroic mountaineers."[7]

One example of the dangers along the trails was an incident that occurred
in February 1883. Two men and a pack train of fifteen mules started from
the Yankee Girl Mine to Silverton. When near the Genessee Mine, one of
the mules slipped off the trail, and while it was wallowing in the snow a slide
started and swept the whole group down the mountain. One of the men and

eight of the mules were killed. Such incidents made it obvious to those living on the divide that no matter how good the road, only limited travel could be counted on during the winter months.

Work on the new wagon roads continued frantically all winter. By March, the *Red Mountain Review* announced that the toll road from Ouray had been blasted in many places and would be ready some time in the spring. The *Red Mountain Pilot* countered that a free wagon road was being surveyed from Silverton. That Ouray had made substantial progress was evident in a Denver *Rocky Mountain Mining Review* article that proclaimed "[Red Mountain] is presently accessible only by precipitous and dangerous trails. Every ounce of food, pound of mining implements and foot of lumber were transported by jacks [burros] through shine and storm. Today, the camp is reached from Ouray by what will, in a few weeks, be the grandest highway in the Rocky Mountains – covering a distance of seven miles and costing $10,000 to the mile."[8] By the first of May, Sanderson and Co. reported that it had added two extra daily stages to its regular route from Montrose to Ouray in order to handle the increased traffic coming into the Red Mountain Mining District from that direction.

On April 28, 1883, the *Red Mountain Review* carried a short story mentioning that the wagon road from Ouray had reached Ironton Park, where the road still had to skirt many ponds, swamps, and boggy places by switching to the west side of what was then called Red Mountain Park, or simply "The Park." In fact, the route was at this time just a rough path and was only passable to those on horseback or foot. In 1883, with the road issue so critical, the Silverton and Ouray papers continued their outrageous exaggerations. Ouray's *Solid Muldoon* started the spring exchange by claiming that "the wagon road from Silverton to Chattanooga is dangerous even to pedestrians . . . The average depth of mud is three feet . . . The grade is four parts vertical and one part perpendicular."[9] The *La Plata Miner* retorted that "the five men working on the road between Ouray and Red Mountain were congratulating themselves the other day upon their good fortune in getting employment for life."[10] The Silverton article went on to claim that work on the Ouray–Red Mountain road had been basically abandoned and that even the town of Ironton would have to look to Silverton for supplies.

By summer 1883, the new "road" from Ouray was still little more than a rough trail, and it was at this point that Otto Mears became totally involved. On June 14, 1883, he was given controlling interest in a new toll road company. His contribution to the project was enough capital to allow hundreds of men to be hired to work on the road, thereby moving completion forward to a date that was perhaps years earlier than what Ouray County would have been able to meet alone. The need for the road was desperate. The *Red Mountain Pilot* announced that "fully twenty mines badly needed a wagon road to ship their ore."[11]

Whether due to an unhealthy anticipation or a desire to exaggerate the progress of the road so as to attract outsiders, the papers consistently overestimated the status of the roads. The June 16, 1883 *Red Mountain Review* announced that the wagon road from Ouray was anticipated to be in the town of Ironton in two weeks, yet it would be months before it actually arrived. The June 23 *Red Mountain Pilot* claimed that the wagon road had been completed that day from Chattanooga to Red Mountain City, although, as events were to prove, that road would not be passable to wagons for many months to come. On June 30, the *Red Mountain Review* announced that the wagon road from Ouray had "at last been completed to Red Mountain Town, the richest district in Colorado."[12] In fact, only the pack trail had arrived. However, with the summer snowmelt and the construction of the new trails from Silverton and Ouray, the Red Mountain mines were finally able to begin shipping large quantities of ore to both of those towns, although the transportation was by pack animals and not by wagons.

Otto Mears's new toll road from Ouray to Red Mountain was steep and narrow and often blasted out of solid rock. This section south of Bear Creek Trail was actually nearly finished by the time Mears became involved in the project. (*W. H. Jackson photo; author's collection*)

In July, another new trail was built to connect Red Mountain City "over the divide above the city" to Rodgersville and "by the National Belle" to the Yankee Girl. Not a word was mentioned of Red Mountain Town, although the trail must have passed right by the rival settlement. It was a very steep and rough trail, but the *Red Mountain Pilot* announced that "this is the natural route for the road."[13] The same issue also mentioned that Otto Mears was still at work upgrading the pack trail from Ouray in an attempt to turn it into a good wagon road.

Lack of an adequate wagon road didn't slow the rush of activity in the Red Mountain Mining District in the summer of 1883. The *Solid Muldoon* noted that "Red Mountain Town presented a lively appearance Sunday. There were over 400 burros loaded with ore, lumber and supplies in the village at one time, and business was brisk."[14] The same issue reported that the stage would run daily from Ouray to Red Mountain as soon as the trail was upgraded. Plenty of ore continued to be shipped daily off the divide. The Congress Mine sent a large pack train daily to Silverton via Del Mino. The Yankee Girl's pack train was reported as running daily to Ouray, carrying a small fortune in ore each trip – the latest hand-picked ore contained up to four thousand ounces of silver per ton.

By the end of summer 1883, the wagon road from Ouray still was not finished; but it was reported as fast approaching completion, with the total cost having reached $190,000. The August 25, 1883, *Red Mountain Review* carried an article that read: "We are assured the road will be kept open for travel this winter, no matter what the expense may be. The Ouray County Commissioners have a large force of men at work extending the road to Red Mountain Town, and we may soon expect to see Concord coaches roll into our town daily from both Silverton and Ouray." It is interesting to note that Ouray County, not Otto Mears, was finishing the road into Red Mountain. In the same issue, the editor predicted: "There is every prospect that Red Mountain will be far more lively as a winter camp than it has so far this season. A large number of mines will be worked, and ore sledded to shipping points as soon as sufficient snow has fallen." The September 14, 1883 *Solid Muldoon* announced that the wagon road had been finally finished at a cost of nearly ten thousand dollars per mile, but the road had in fact been completed only to the town of Ironton and had yet to reach the majority of the Red Mountain mines.

In the late summer of 1883, Otto Mears promoted the idea of building railroad tracks along the side of the new wagon road to the Red Mountain district. The idea was to have empty cars hauled up to the mines by mules. Gravity would pull them back down loaded with ore, and men on board would operate their brakes. The *Montrose Messenger* announced that the funding for the scheme was secure and suggested that the idea would "completely revolutionize mining in Ouray County. All of the ore of the great Red Mountain mining camp will be delivered to Ouray at a very low figure, and from there to Montrose it will be hauled for a few dollars per ton. With the Mears' railroad in operation, the production of Ouray County will be quadrupled the present season."[15]

Yet the wagon road itself (little less "the railroad") was not complete on September 22, 1883, when the *Red Mountain Review* reported that the bridge over the Uncompahgre River (at the present-day Engineer jeep road turnoff) had just been finished and the wagon road was progressing rapidly. "All the larger rocks still need to be removed and the smaller ones covered with dirt." Again, in October, the *Red Mountain Review* complained that work on the wagon road from Ironton to Red Mountain was not complete as promised. Freighter Dave Wood vowed that if the road were finished, he'd freight all winter. He only asked that the mines contract to ship ten or twelve wagon loads of ore per day.[16] The next week's paper reported that Mears's road was complete to within a few miles of Red Mountain Town, with spur roads finished to the Yankee Girl, National Belle, and Congress mines.

Although Mears's toll gate (which consisted of a long log that blocked the traveler's way until the fee was paid) was installed at Bear Creek Falls, his part of the construction work had basically consisted of blasting the narrow wagon road from the present-day Engineer jeep road cutoff to Ironton Park. How Mears got away with making those going up the Engineer road pay tolls is unknown. To give credit where credit is due, Mears had completed quite a feat. It had eventually cost almost forty thousand dollars per mile to blast his section of the road into the quartzite cliffs that rose up to eight hundred feet above the canyon floor. Even with the enormous cost, the new road was so narrow that, in most places, two wagons couldn't pass each other.

Meanwhile, the "road" from Silverton wasn't progressing. The *Omaha Commercial Record* declared "a passable wagon road has been opened to Silverton (from Red Mountain City) and conveyances for carrying passengers and mail make daily rounds between the two places."[17] The emphasis should have been on the word "passable." The actual status of the road can be determined from an announcement in the same article that the owners of the Congress Mine were talking of building a tram all the way to Silverton in order to reduce their transportation costs. They finally decided that it would be cheaper to build their own wagon road to a point about a mile south of Chattanooga, where it would connect with the good wagon road that ran to Silverton.

In late fall 1883, Otto Mears shifted his attention from the basically finished Ouray–Red Mountain road and began to negotiate with the San Juan County commissioners for work on a wagon road to Red Mountain from the Silverton side of the divide. In September, he agreed verbally to remake the Silverton–Red Mountain trail into a toll road if the commissioners would pay him twenty-five thousand dollars. Many of the Silverton merchants wanted a public highway instead, and for weeks to come they were very vocal (through the local paper) about their feelings. They didn't want Mears to continue his monopoly of the toll roads in the San Juans, for they believed that control of so many local roads by a single person was bound to mean higher tolls. Others felt

Almost every nineteenth-century mode of travel is represented in this scene at Mears's Bear Creek Falls toll gate. From left to right are a stage, a pedestrian, a carriage, a rider on horseback, burros, and a surrey. The gatekeeper lived in the cabin at the toll gate; the log gate to the right of the cabin has been swung open. (*Author's collection*)

that San Juan County could not afford to pay for such an expensive project. Many stressed the fact that the best solution was not even a road but rather a railroad. Most Silverton merchants had already made a valiant attempt to convince the Denver and Rio Grande Railroad to continue its tracks from Silverton on to Red Mountain, but the D&RG had announced that such construction would be much too expensive to be feasible.

The Silverton merchants knew they had to do something quickly to offset the advantage that the city of Ouray had taken with its new road. If they didn't, their town would be facing a major economic hardship. Instead of being intimidated by the publicity, Mears increased his requested payment for construction of the road to fifty thousand dollars, payable in Silverton and San Juan county bonds. The proposed agreement also provided that Mears would have complete control over the project. The parties agreed in principal, but it would be almost a year before the entire agreement was committed to print and work actually began.[18]

In the meantime, the citizens of Silverton still hoped that the narrow-gauge railroad would be extended from Silverton. The *Omaha Commercial Record* predicted "a few more mines opened and the baby railroad will be in their midst. This narrow gauge system will penetrate every rich nook of these mountains."[19] But the same newspaper article admitted that, at least at the present, burros were the main mode of transportation for the ore coming to Silverton. "At any time of the day hundreds of these little fellows may be seen winding up and down the mountains by the narrow trails that look like pencil marks on the yawning declevities [*sic*]." In late October, the editor of the

Red Mountain Review pointed out that only the completion of a really good wagon road through the Red Mountain Mining District would enable the mines to ship out their second-class ore. Since the Ouray road was already basically finished, the editor must have been referring to potential access by wagon to the railroad at Silverton.[20]

In fall 1883, the owners of the Congress Mine finished their rough road to a point just outside of Chattanooga and announced that during the winter they hoped to sled ore all the way to Silverton. The citizens of Silverton, by a vote of eighty-one to twenty-one in November 1883, authorized the issuance of bonds on the Silverton–Red Mountain road, with work to begin as early as possible in the spring. By late November, the road from Ouray was finished to the Yankee Girl, and its stockpiled ore was immediately taken out on sleds—fifty sacks per skid.

However, the road to Ouray didn't stay open continuously that winter, nor was it to stay open without interruption in any of the years to come. At the time, no one realized that the "Million Dollar Highway" crossed some of the most avalanche-prone mountains in the United States. The Riverside Slide would run often, sometimes covering the road with sixty feet of snow and eventually killing many people. Although not so deep, the Mother Cline Slide proved especially dangerous, killing or trapping dozens of people over the years. The snow was simply too deep and the slides too dangerous to allow extensive winter travel between Ouray and the Red Mountain Mining District.

When the spring of 1884 arrived, Otto Mears still was not ready to begin work on the new road from Silverton to Red Mountain. Silverton's *La Plata Miner* ran a lengthy piece warning the public that Mears would rip them off with high charges if allowed to make the Silverton-to-Red Mountain route into a toll road. The paper merely needed to look to the other side of the divide for an example. Mears was receiving five dollars for each team and wagon and a dollar apiece for each pack animal that passed along the Red Mountain-to-Ouray toll road. Then, in addition to the payment of fifty thousand dollars in bonds and his proposed high tolls on the Silverton-to-Red Mountain road, Mears had the gall to ask for a "donation" of twelve thousand dollars from San Juan County.[21]

By the end of the summer of 1884, the papers were full of talk about Mears and his toll road, and the tone was not good. Dave Day felt compelled to defend his friend: "Mears is the San Juan 'Pathfinder,' and if there is any one individual or corporation in all this section that had done one-fourth as much toward developing this country as Otto Mears we are ignorant of the fact."[22] The very next week Day again wrote that Mears had done much

The two gentlemen in this photograph are on the toll road to Ouray in 1886 or 1887. The Silver Bell Mine is to the left of center, the Paymaster is on the right. Construction of the Silverton Railroad is still a few years away. Red Mountain No. 1 dominates the background to the left and Red Mountain No. 2 is almost denuded of trees. (*W. H. Jackson photo; Colorado Historical Society.*

more "than those who engage in perpetual kicking . . . Otto Mears is entitled to liberal toll rates; to the good will and patronage of this people . . . What the *Muldoon* desires is more gratitude and less gall." Finally, in exasperation, Day wrote a tongue-in-cheek article on October 31. In question-and-answer format he asked a dozen questions in which he listed Mears's achievements (such as who helped build the Colorado capitol building, who built the most roads in the San Juans, and so on), but instead of Mears's name he put in the names of other locals as the answers. The final question – "Who killed Christ? Ans. Dave Day and Otto Mears." Later, the *Solid Muldoon* carried an article in which Day claimed that "Otto Mears and the *Solid Muldoon* are the recipients of more abuse than any two other industrial institutions in the San Juan country."[23] Mears's high tolls brought him little gratitude, but, in his defense, he did the construction quickly (which must have added to his expense), and the heavy snows and flash floods did keep maintenance costs high.

On June 28, 1884, the San Juan County commissioners and Otto Mears finally came to a written agreement for the construction of the Red Mountain–Silverton road. That same week the *Silverton Democrat* commented that Mears had continuously tried to avoid a binding agreement. "Mr. Mear's forte is in having contracts that will shrink or swell as the weather is wet or dry, and that seem one way by the sun and another way by the moon." When the contract was finally signed, it contained a clause that the grade should be continuously downhill toward Silverton at no more of a drop than 350 feet to the mile (a seven percent grade). The road was also to be wide enough to allow teams to pass one another and could contain no curves so sharp as to prevent six animals from exerting their entire force at all points. Ample provision was also to be made for winter traffic and for water drainage.

The July 5, 1884 issue of the *La Plata Miner* reported that Mears had received his requested "contribution" of twelve thousand dollars from the county. The editor knew the entire toll road to be a cheat, because Mears "will just redo existing roads and not much more." Mears began construction (or reconstruction, as the case might be) of the Silverton-to-Red Mountain toll road on July 8. With more than 350 men working to upgrade the route, the work went quickly, and only the last mile or two of road near the top of Red Mountain Divide required any real effort. Much of the final portion of the road had to be blasted from the sheer cliffs. While blasting in August, Mears's workmen hit a large body of carbonate ore. Then a second body was discovered just seven feet farther along the road. Even when workers weren't looking for ore, valuable mineral discoveries were being made on the divide! The Silverton merchants had another type of riches in mind and predicted that their road would be open by late November. The road actually did open in December 1884, but the problem of winter travel to the Red Mountain district is indicated by the fact that the stage did not start its regular route until the next summer. Although there was no regular passenger transportation, the Mears Transportation Company was announced as having obtained the contracts to haul ore from the Yankee Girl, the National Belle, and several other mines during the winter.

The June 6, 1885 *La Plata Miner* reported: "The first stage ever to arrive at Silverton will come through from Montrose in the course of a few days, and there is every reason to believe that it will be loaded with passengers. The stage will be decorated, drawn by six white horses. An effort will be made to drive over from Ouray, a distance of twenty miles, in about three hours." The Pioneer Stage Company's regular route left Silverton at 7:00 A.M., arriving at Red Mountain at noon (where lunch was eaten), and then pushed on to Ouray by 5:00 P.M. Another stage left Ouray for Silverton at 7:00 A.M., mirroring the route in the opposite direction. The Concord coaches were drawn by either four or six horses and carried six passengers inside, usually with one or two more "up top" with the driver. Baggage and mail were carried in the boot on the back.

It was Red Mountain's ore, fuel, and supplies – not passengers – that made the freighter his money. A typical freight team was made up of three pairs of mules or horses. The freight wagon itself had extremely heavy large wheels and usually could carry five to ten tons of ore. Heavy brake locks were a necessity, and long poles gave the driver necessary increased leverage. Sometimes the freighters even dragged anchors or logs behind them to act as brakes on the extremely steep hills. Until the wagon roads were built, the packers received up to eighty dollars per ton for hauling ore. Since most of the Red Mountain mines were producing good low- to middle-grade ore worth fifty to one hundred dollars per ton, it was obvious that a lot of ore wasn't shipped before the building of the wagon roads. The exception was the hand-sorted ore at the Yankee Girl (assaying up to eighteen hundred dollars per ton) and the National Belle (valued at up to seven hundred dollars per ton). The owners of the Yankee Girl Mine complained that they had spent forty thousand dollars in 1883 to ship their ore. Although the cost of packing was extreme, the Yankee Girl still could ship its ore at a profit. There weren't half a dozen other mines on the divide that could afford the expense. When the toll road was fully passable, the cost of shipping the Yankee Girl ore was reported to have fallen as low as $4.30 per ton, which even included Mears's toll charge.[24] This low rate may have been exaggerated by the papers, but actual transportation costs had fallen drastically.

By the end of 1884 Mears's famous highway was finished, but it was a much tougher route than today's version. The original road started out of Ouray near the Milk Ranch (today's Highway Barn), went up at an eighteen percent grade to the old town dump, down almost to the river, and then up an incredibly steep twenty-one percent grade to the top of Bear Creek Falls. The stretch of road from the falls to the Engineer cutoff pretty much followed today's highway route, but then dropped back almost to river level at the Riverside Slide. It followed Red Mountain Creek straight up to Ironton Park (there were no switchbacks) and went along the western edge of Red Mountain Park until eventually becoming Ironton's main street (called Ouray Street). It switched over to the east side of the canyon and went through the Guston workings and passed by the Yankee Girl Mine on its way up the hill to Red Mountain. The route down to Silverton was almost the same as the present-day road.

J. J. Gibbons, who came to the Ouray and Silverton area as a Roman Catholic priest in August 1888, often traveled the Red Mountain road. He later wrote that "the novice is so alarmed at the sight of the abysses around him that even in the summer, when the roads are good and the danger is remote, he alights from the coach and prefers to walk, not trusting himself to the best vehicle and driver . . . The road follows the circuitous canon and it tested all the genius of Otto Mears, the pathmaker of the West, to construct it; it went east, and it went west, it twisted and turned and boxed the compass, and on a dark night it would perplex the most wide-awake traveler to know what to do on this road."[25]

As dangerous as it might be, the towns and mines at Red Mountain were pleased as punch that the new road had been opened. Editor Curry, at the *Red Mountain Pilot,* wrote that "it should be the policy of the various counties throughout the state to build and own their own roads, but when they are without the means to build them, it is nothing short of commendable judgement on the part of the people to prevail on those having the means to build toll roads. A toll road is a long way better than a burro trail, and even if the rates of toll are rather high, shipping over a wagon road is always much cheaper than packing on mules and burros. The advantage that Silverton will receive from the road just completed to Ouray, will not be alone in increased ore shipments, but in an increased number of visitors as well."[26] Dave Day agreed and wrote: "The ride is one that America cannot duplicate, and the road the most grandest and expensive ever inaugurated and completed in the land of pluck and nerve – the Great American West."[27]

The *Red Mountain Pilot* reported that the eleven miles of road from Silverton to the Yankee Girl had cost $56,937, the three miles from the Yankee Girl to Ironton $9,800, and the eight miles from Ironton to Ouray $143,200 (but this figure also included a one-mile section of road from the Engineer cutoff toward Poughkeepsie Gulch). The expenses for the entire twenty-two miles of road from Ouray to Silverton came to about two hundred thousand dollars. The route eventually came to be known as the Million Dollar Highway, but it certainly did not get its name from its original cost. However, many millions of dollars of precious ore were to be shipped over the road in the future.

SEVEN

———≫○○○○◯○○○○≪———

LIFE ON RED MOUNTAIN

Everyday life for the inhabitants of Red Mountain was an incredible mixture of the harsh and the beautiful. The first frenzied prospectors who came to the divide spent every waking moment searching for their pot of gold (or silver, in the case of Red Mountain) at the end of the rainbow, and quite a few of them were not disappointed. But the footloose, eternally optimistic prospectors either "hit pay dirt" or soon moved on to a more promising district. They were followed by the hard-working miners, some of whom were disillusioned prospectors–men who, finally, had given up on the big strike and settled down to a more routine, but less harsh, life. Many of the miners were foreigners who had always made their livings in mining and had been attracted to the United States by the "high" wages.

A miner's life was a hard one in the 1880s. He followed a regular and grinding daily routine. Most of the men worked twelve-hour shifts for six or even seven days a week. A miner might work for weeks and weeks without a day off, especially when high up in the mountains during the winter. He usually toiled in dimly lit surroundings, his only light a candle or two mounted in an iron holder stuck into the timbers or a crack in the rocks. Each miner was allocated three or four candles for his ten- to twelve-hour shift. If a man was willing to take a chance with fire, he might light an oil lamp. Breathing was almost impossible in the mines because the ventilation was poor and the

This postcard depicts men working in a mine. Several candles light the scene. The type of drill pictured used no water, which accounted for its nickname, "the widow maker," so called because the fine dust it produced soon clogged a miner's lungs. These drills also exploded on occasion, causing even more havoc than a dynamite blast. (*Author's collection*)

black powder and dynamite used for blasting kept dust and fumes in the air for hours after the explosion. The nitroglycerin from exploded dynamite often caused splitting migraine headaches. Although touted as one of the healthiest spots in Colorado, the combination of dust, fumes, high altitude, and cold often gave the Red Mountain miners pneumonia. In the winter, almost every issue of the paper carried an article such as "J. Stewart, a miner from Red Mountain, was brought to the hospital in Ouray last week with pneumonia and died yesterday morning at 5 o'clock."[1]

Whether one was a driller or a mucker, the work was backbreaking. In the smaller mines, the driller stood for hours pounding a drill steel (a long chisel) with a four-pound hammer. Such work was "single-jacking." If two men were involved in the operation, they took turns swinging the eight-pound "double jack" and holding the drill steel. Twenty strokes a minute was the norm. Miners would pick up a bundle of newly sharpened bits at the blacksmith's shop when they went to work. Different sizes and lengths of drills would be in the bundle, since the miners used progressively longer but smaller-diameter steel as the hole got deeper. In the big mines, the miners might use the new reciprocating steam drills, but early-day automated equipment wasn't very safe. Scalding was a major danger, the drills often exploded, and the machines produced a fine but sharp dust that settled into the miners' lungs, causing miner's consumption. Only at the turn of the century were some of the problems solved when water was used to cool the steel, flush the hole, and eliminate the dust.

Muckers were the men who carried the blasted rock to the buckets, where the ore was winched up the shafts to the surface. All day long they shoveled or carried rock. The men who operated the buckets, or cages, in the shafts were called "cagers." Young boys were often used in the mines to pick up the dulled drills and deliver them to the company blacksmith. Usually boys or men who had been injured were used to sort the ore. Powder men stored and sometimes distributed the powder. Engineers ran the steam boilers and steam engines. Pump men ran the huge bronze pumps that ran continuously to keep the shafts from filling with water. Carpenters and timber men built shaft houses and boardinghouses and placed timbers in the mines. As opposed to prospectors, the men working in the mines were extremely specialized, and a large mine could easily employ one hundred or more men.

Mining was a very hazardous profession. The most common cause of death, involved in about half of all fatal accidents, was a premature explosion. Dynamite could blow a man into small pieces or, if left unexploded in a drill hole, the explosion could make the new drill a hurtling spear crashing through a man's chest. The newspapers were full of reports such as: "On last Saturday about 4 o'clock a Swede by the name of Andy Miller was badly shattered by a premature blast in the Silver Ledge Mine in Chattanooga."[2] The most common causes of injury were huge slabs of rock that fell from a roof, crushing a man or his limbs in seconds. Many a miner had an arm or a leg amputated because of such an accident. Heavy machinery could run loose and crush a man or tear off his limbs. Men could fall hundreds of feet down shafts or watch helplessly from the bottom as a two-thousand-pound bucket full of ore fell from above. There were hundreds of ways a man might be killed in a mine: the cage he was riding in could wind onto the drum; the cable could break when he was riding in a bucket; he might accidentally drop a candle into a box of detonators; or he might succumb to more "common" causes, such as a rupture that didn't heal or the act of working his heart too much.

Red Mountain prospectors and miners were typically of a ferocious and independent nature, but they were also bighearted individuals. They tended to be young and not married, probably because of the hazards and hardships they endured. Federal and state census records show us that the typical San Juaner would have been in his early thirties, white, American-born, and single. Most were literate. About a quarter were married, but many of these chose not to bring their families to the harsh San Juan frontier.

The first miners in the Red Mountain Mining District were very well paid—usually five dollars or more a day. Later, during harder times, pay dropped to as low as $3.50 per day. Although these were good wages for the time, a miner's cost of living was high. A good home-cooked meal might cost a dollar, and a hotel room with a bed could run two dollars a night. Two blocks of businesses lined Red Mountain Town, and most were very successful in providing goods and entertainment to the miners. But when many of the men did get a day off, they were often too tired to spend their money and would simply rest.

The blacksmith's shop was usually located right next to the shaft house because miners needed a freshly sharpened bundle of drills every day. Most of the men in this photo are miners, not blacksmiths. There certainly seems to be more than a few characters among the group. *(Ouray Historical Museum)*

The miners on Red Mountain liked to eat—at least in quantity if not quality. Room and board were supplied by many, but not all, mines. The food wasn't fancy, but it usually was plentiful. Meat and potatoes were the standard fare. Bacon, eggs, and pancakes were normal for breakfast. Fruits and vegetables were harder to come by but, in season, were often brought in fresh from Durango or the Uncompahgre Valley near Ouray. Strawberries, melons, and peaches were readily available at inexpensive prices in the summer. Many of the local women would cook pies and breads and sell them to the miners for extra spending money. The local restaurants usually carried more exotic meals and did a booming business.

There was good reason why the miners were well paid at Red Mountain. The lives of all miners were punctuated by moments of terror and death, but in the San Juans the miner faced danger in and out of the mines. Life in the mountains was dangerous, especially in the winter. "Snowslides come down the mountainside, bearing many to death . . . pneumonia affects the young and strong, or the premature blast opens the day of eternity to the most careful and virtuous."[3] At an elevation of eleven thousand feet, winter could last from early September to late June. One local joke held that at Red Mountain there were only two seasons in the year—winter and the Fourth of July.

The newspapers were full of reports such as "Charles Hanson's body was found after having been lost in a snowslide since Christmas. He was recognized only by the clothing that he was wearing,"[4] or "the remains of Swan Nelson the mail carrier who was buried in a snowslide on December 22, 1883 (a year and a half earlier) was found last week. The mail bag was found still strapped to him and was distributed a few days ago at Telluride."[5]

Whether living or traveling in the mountains, there was a special code that grew out of necessity. The miners and prospectors had to stick together and watch out for one another's safety. A man had made a deadly mistake if he hadn't brought in adequate food or fuel for the winter. His only hope was to obtain what he needed from those who lived nearby. Prospectors watched for smoke coming from the neighbors' tents or cabins. Its absence usually meant trouble. If traveling and caught out in the open in a blinding blizzard, a man could freeze to death in less than an hour. Another miner's cabin and food could always be used in an emergency. Strangers were always welcome, whether the occupants were home or not. "The prospector's cabin on the mountain trail was left unlocked. You might step in, cook your dinner and go on, or if tired, unroll your blankets and rest to your heart's content. If the owner was home it was all right; if not, the conditions of hospitality were the same, and these were, 'come in, help yourself, and go rejoicing on your way,'—a striking contrast to great cities, where a selfish opulence drives the needy from the door. The owner of the mountain cabin, free with his money, bacon or bunk, deemed it an honor to entertain his caller, however poor."[6]

With deadly dangers lurking around every corner, and with prospectors sometimes isolated from social contact for months, it was no wonder that the *Red Mountain Review* reported "only six saloons in (Red Mountain Town) and three restaurants. Verily, bread is not the staff of life in the mountains."[7] The miners worked hard, and they liked to play hard, too. They needed to relax after long, hard, sweaty shifts in the mines, and their favorite pastime was to visit the saloons. An amazing amount of beer and hard liquor was shipped to Red Mountain. Drinking, gambling, prostitution, and a dozen other vices ran rampant in the hills. "The lights never went out in the camp, unless when coal oil failed, or a stray cowboy shot up the town. The men worked night and day, shift and shift about, and the people were happy. The gambling halls were never closed, the restaurants did a profitable business, and no one could lay his weary bones on a bed for less than a dollar. Whiskey was as plentiful as the limpid water that gushed from the hills behind the town, sparkling in the sunlight. In those days it never cost a stranger anything for drinks; he was welcome to eat, drink and be merry; indeed, it was deemed an insult to refuse to partake of anything that was going."[8]

If they couldn't find the kind of entertainment they wanted on the divide, the Red Mountain miners thought nothing of walking all the way to Ouray or Silverton for a night of fun. There they could take their choice of dozens of saloons, prostitutes, and gambling halls. They would often rent a horse for the uphill climb, tying the reins to the saddle horn when they reached their destination and letting the animal make its way back to town riderless.

The saloon wasn't always a safe haven. Trouble could happen—especially when liquor was involved. Most of these events were not the heroic gunfights that we see on television. Many were simple and mundane affairs, such as when Perry Terpenny, who owned a saloon near the Yankee Girl and later owned the famous Vanderbilt Mine, came to Red Mountain Town and shot it up; he was quickly fined fifty dollars and sentenced to twenty days in the Ouray jail. Other "shoot-outs" took a grisly or macabre turn. On June 29, 1886, a miner who had recently been fired came to find his ex-boss, a Red Mountain saloonkeeper. He threw a beer keg through the front door and went in and sat down. The meek but terrified saloonkeeper hit his ex-employee in the head with a pick, the point of which went through the skull and out an eye socket. The frightened saloonkeeper fled into the woods and eventually committed suicide rather than face what he thought would be a lynch mob. The unfortunate businessman left a wife and two children behind. The ex-employee lived. Or there was the incident in which an unidentified man was insulting ladies and shooting into the crowd at a Red Mountain saloon in November 1890. When several men approached to stop him, he fled, fell, and shot himself in the stomach, dying of the injury.

Dave Day tells the story of September 1891 of "one Mr. Cowan who shot Mr. Newton through the side of the head with a 44 calibur pop Saturday last. The row took place in the blooming village of Red Mountain, the occasion being the rivalry over the attentions—not to say smiles—of a swamp angel of the vintage of 1832 . . . Moral, if you don't see what you want, ask for it."[9] Such events prompted Dave Day to write: "Gun-plays are entirely too numerous in Ironton and the *Muldoon* advises the belligerents to lay aside their artillery and unload that thirst for gore induced by over-indulgence in an article of whiskey."[10]

As much as we like to think of the typical miner as someone who liked "to raise hell," just how little hard-core trouble miners did in fact cause is testified to by the one very small jail at Red Mountain Town. It was ten by fifteen feet, built out of four-inch-thick planks, and contained a narrow hallway between the two cells, which were five by ten feet. The jail had no provisions for heat or any other comforts that would allow more than a summer's over-night stay. The few "long-term" prisoners were "boarded out" in Ouray or Silverton.

Especially during the early part of the Red Mountain boom, the "devil's" saloons often did double or triple duty, sometimes serving as courtrooms, churches, or theaters. Before an abundance of hotels and boardinghouses were built on the divide, saloons were often used as such by many of the local prospectors, who simply slept on the floor. Later, more civilized functions such as plays or orations frequently occurred in the saloons, which were usually just one large easy-to-clear room. The Florence Hayden Dramatic Club performed a temperance play, "Ten Nights In A Bar-Room," in a Red Moun-tain saloon in 1891. No one had a second thought of putting on the temperance drama in a saloon, although a curtain hid the whiskey bottles in deference to the women present. A reporter for the *Denver Times* was present and sent a wonderful "special" back to Denver. He not only chronicled the drama but did a good job of explaining the importance of the saloon to a mining town.

"Red Mountain has saloons – every mining town has saloons. The saloon is one of the most important institutions of every mining camp; but Red Moun-tain has no theater . . . Almost everybody goes to the saloon in Red Moun-tain. The town justice held court in the same saloon a short time ago. It is where all matters of public interest are discussed; there were some decidedly emphatic debates on the silver question there last winter. It is where the miners meet and drink and gamble and read the daily papers. It was therefore very properly and quite naturally selected as a place where a dramatic company could perform. In this quiet town, the announcement that a dramatic company was coming to town was received with public rejoicing. You see, Red Moun-tain is not a theatrical center, it is out of line of the theatrical circuit, and the people are not critical; they are very thankful for the efforts of the most ordinary dramatic talents . . . The manager was a little timid about a saloon at first, but the best people in the town came to him and urged him to give his performance, assuring him that though Red Mountain was not exactly a temperance town, he could be assured of a crowded house every night . . . The bartender served a few glasses of water during the performance, but everything more stimulating was kept behind a curtain . . . At the close of each performance the chairs were cleared away and the bar was open for business. As the company became pretty thirsty during the long presentation of the temperance drama, the bar did a thriving business after the performance. The manager of the company declared, when he came to leave town that Red Mountain was the best 'show town' of its size that he had ever visited."[11]

Red Mountain wasn't on the regular theatrical circuit, and the citizens therefore quite often produced their own entertainment or relied on volunteer groups to come up from Silverton or Ouray. Sometimes this did not work out well. For example, in April 1890, the Rainbow Cornet Band from Silverton "arrived with the intent of showing the Red Mountain dagos the talent of Silverton." Admission was high, one dollar for adults and fifty cents for children. "The most interesting item of the performance was an impromptu dog fight, which pleased the men of snow even more than the performance of 'The Toodles.'" A ball followed the performance, and since there were no beds available, the Silverton band was forced to sleep on the saloon's pool tables.

As Red Mountain Town grew, it took on the rosy-sounding nicknames of "The Sky City" or "High Line Camp." The town's inhabitants welcomed any evidence of civilization as a sign to the rest of the world of the town's prosperity. Red Mountain Town had a music group and several clubs like the Odd Fellows and the Knights of Labor. The Sky City Miner's Club, the Knights of Pythias, and the Free Coinage Saloon Dancing Club all gave frequent balls. Even debate and literary societies were welcomed recreational activities. As an example of the variety of entertainment present on the divide, on February 8, 1888, the Red Mountain Lyceum and Dramatic Association gave its first performance. Among other songs, the club sang "Dipped in the Golden Sea," a member gave a guitar solo, O. K. Franklin presented the soliloquy from Shakespeare's *King Richard III*, and, for the finale, the group debated the question of "whether the land should be a free heritage to all mankind."

Red Mountain Town even found itself in the unusual position, for a mining town, of being a summer tourist attraction! The Red Mountain district became an important link in two different circular routes that the railroads promoted intensively as Colorado tourist attractions. One was a trip by train, called "Around the Circle," which ran from Denver to Ouray, then by stagecoach to Silverton, and back to Denver via the Denver and Rio Grande Railroad. Another later and shorter route, called "The Loop," ran from Durango to Silverton, then by stage to Ouray, train to Ridgway, and back to Durango via the Rio Grande Southern Railroad. When it was built, the Silverton Railroad handled the part of the trip from Silverton to either Red Mountain Town or Ironton, and the stage carried the passengers the rest of the way to Ouray. There was spectacular beauty along the route, but a big part of the lure for the tourist was the travel through what the D&RG called "one of the greatest mining regions in the world; the fame of Red Mountain is well deserved both from the number and richness of its mines."[12]

The *Red Mountain Pilot* bragged that "the wonderful scenery along this road surpasses in wilderness and grandeur anything in the State."[13] The

The toll road from Ouray to Silverton was narrow and dangerous, but it passed through the heart of some of the most beautiful scenery in the world. Tourists who discovered the area were an extra boost to the local economy. In this photograph, the Circle Route stage has stopped to allow its photographer-passenger a chance to record the awesome scene. *(W. H. Jackson photo; author's collection)*

La Plata Miner echoed the statement: "The Silverton and Ouray wagon road is destined to bring thousands of people into this section who would never have thought of coming."[14] The citizens of Ouray even dug the snow tunnel in the Riverside Slide, in large part because it fascinated the tourists. Sections of the roof would periodically fall in during the summer, causing a delay in the stage trip; Dave Day, throughout the summer, gave reports of the current tunnel length. It was always a sad day (usually in late July or early August) when the last part of the roof caved in. Travel could get a little scary along the road. In August 1888, under a column labeled "Reckless Driving," Day chastised the driver of the King and Company stage for his driving. He evidently was going too fast, hit a rock, and threw Mrs. L. P. Berry out of the stage somewhere between the Yankee Girl and Ironton. She broke three ribs and had other injuries. "Tourists don't need to have their nerves unstrung and bones broken by negligence and incompetency."[15]

Most of the Red Mountain inhabitants recognized the beauty of their surroundings. They often took hikes or went out in the mountains to pick flowers. Even the miners loved it when a visiting journalist might write in glowing terms of the beauty of Red Mountain. For example, this article from the *Omaha*

Record was often quoted: "Overhead the clouds, out of which the rain falls as if trickling from a sieve, while underfoot waters glisten everywhere and dance and sing. Ground hogs sport among the rocks above the line of vegetation, and the delicate birds chirp at us as we mount skyward. The heart thumps like a stamp mill and the blood tingles the fingertips at this altitude. It is 14,000 feet above the ocean, and there is a deadlike stillness all around. The sky is hazy and clouds fleck the mountains beneath us."[16] Red Mountain citizens would often send reports to Ouray and Silverton that the wildflowers were near their peak or mention that bighorn sheep had been spotted just outside town. Some miners even wrote poetry about the beauty surrounding them.

There was also a seedier side to the lure of Red Mountain. The men were, of course, starved for female companionship. Because of the severe shortage of women, a large number of

The Riverside Slide had left debris as high as forty feet for a distance of four hundred feet before this photograph was taken, and the tourists were out in full force to see the snow tunnel. The stage has just driven through the tunnel, and another group of sightseers has stopped on the winter trail atop the slide. (*Moore photo; author's collection*)

prostitutes soon followed the miners to the Red Mountain district. The prostitutes provided not only sex but companionship, and in some cases the women became business partners with the men. There was no attempt to hide the presence of the prostitutes. For example, in March 1883, the editor of the *Red Mountain Pilot* proudly announced that "three female devines, 'Long Annie' of Silverton, 'Molly Folly' and Lizzie Gaylor of Durango were among the distinguished arrivals this morning." Obviously many of the prostitutes liked the use of assumed names. The newspaper editor almost got himself hung, however, when he announced, in the same article, that " 'Deaf Mat,' " a Silverton dame, was on her way to Hudson – "the first female in that camp." The woman, who claimed she was not a prostitute or a madam, later threatened to kill him.

The supply of prostitutes always increased in the Red Mountain district in the summer. The *Solid Muldoon* of July 24, 1885 announced that "the rainy season is here. A profusion of flowers and soiled doves hereabouts." And the next week the same paper noted the Red Mountain "dance hall is kept in full blast night and day – some days. Whoop her up boys, the season will not last long." In the winter, many of the prostitutes returned to Ouray or Silverton – the latter town being reported as having 130 "ladies of the night"in the winter of 1885. It was not an easy life for the Red Mountain prostitutes. For example, on September 15, 1886, Willard Donnehauer assaulted Lulu Waters, better known as Indian Lou, and pounded her over the head with a gun while another man watched. Both men were arrested and charged with assault with intent to murder. As more and more men brought their wives and children to the camps, the prostitutes dwindled in number.

The August 2, 1889, *Solid Muldoon* reported that the Ouray County commissioners had been presented with a petition, signed by eighty-five Red Mountain citizens, which requested the closure of the Hiscock Saloon near Guston because it was frequented "by disorderly, disreputable characters" who used foul language, often discharged their pistols, and usually frequented the house of prostitution next door. The citizens claimed the county road, which ran directly in front of the saloon, had become dangerous because of the actions of the rowdies, and the *Muldoon* wanted quick action to declare the saloon a public nuisance. Note that the citizens wanted the saloon, not the house of prostitution next door, closed; however, as a camp began to mature and take on airs, the prostitutes were usually encouraged to leave.

As early as June 1883, the population of Red Mountain City had included six "respectable" women, and both the Congress Hotel and the Conley House (both large lodging establishments) had opened with women managers. Refined parties were often held on Red Mountain Divide with dignified women invited from both Ouray and Silverton. Red Mountain Town was very sociable, with balls and dances especially popular. The papers often carried announcements of dances, such as: "A social party will be given at the Yankee Girl boarding house next Saturday evening. The house is a large one and will serve nicely as a place to 'trip the light fantastic.'"[17]

The December 28, 1888 *Solid Muldoon* described "Christmas in the Hills" as celebrated by employees of the Yankee Girl and Guston mines at the latter's boardinghouse. The party included a huge Christmas tree and was attended by 125 people. The Yankee Girl band played, manager T. E. Schwartz talked on the meaning of Christmas, five-year-old Miss Cummings recited "A Christmas Stocking," the Yankee Girl quartet and John Jones sang, and "Kris Kringle himself appeared with presents for everyone – from the sturdiest miner to the smallest babe." The management of the Guston Mine apologized for not inviting the general public, but there wasn't any possible way to squeeze more people into the boardinghouse.

The Fourth of July, Christmas, and just about any other justifiable event were times of great festivity. The opening of the road from Ouray, for example, was an occasion for jubilation, with gourmet food, orchestras, and all-night dances. Later, when the Silverton leg of the road was opened, a large group traveled from Ouray to Red Mountain Town and then over to Silverton for speeches and a dance. With the opening of the Mears toll road, luxuries, such as special food and entertainment, were regularly brought to Red Mountain Divide.

On the quieter side, letters and newspapers from home were a prime form of relaxation. By June 1883 there were five post offices on the divide at the settlements of Chattanooga, Congress, Red Mountain Town, Rodgersville, and Ironton. The mail was not dependable, but most letters eventually reached their destinations. It is hard to remember today, but there was a time when letter-writing was an art form. The beautiful handwriting of the time had great style, and letters were written as a leisure activity as well as to pass on the news.

Many of the miners were married, and a few lived with their families in the Red Mountain camps. Most married men tried to spend every waking hour they were not working with their families, or they could be found writing or reading letters if their loved ones didn't live nearby. Some men even commuted from Silverton or Ouray, where they lived in comfortable, sometimes even luxurious, surroundings. For those who could afford to do so, it was a common practice for married men to bring their families to the Red Mountain district for the summer and then move them to the lower altitudes of Silverton, Ouray, or even Denver for the winter. The practice provoked the paper to note that "quite a large number of families are residing in camp this summer, and the presence of a goodly number of ladies gives this place a more civilized appearance than usual."[18]

Single men usually were looking for female companionship, and that didn't necessarily mean prostitutes. It was reported by the *Telluride Republican* that Red Mountain Town had an abundance of weddings. "It is a lonesome place to live in and the young people are not to be blamed for doubling up. A man who will sleep alone during a winter in Red Mountain has no affection for the fair sex or they have none for him. Besides, Red Mountain needs an increased population."[19]

In the summer, relaxation could include hiking, picking wildflowers, or picnicking. Hunting and fishing were also available just a short distance from the mines. The local Catholic priest, the Reverend Gibbons, recognized the miner as "nature's student: his special delight is to examine the various rocks and discuss the different formations . . . It would seem that the lofty peaks

This domestic scene was photographed in Ironton on September 8, 1886. Some of the women seem quite young, but they often married at an early age in those days. And the ever-present dog joins his master for this shot. The sign was drawn in at a later time, either by a humorist or a very dissatisfied customer. (*Thomas M. McKee photo; Denver Public Library, Western History Department*)

by which he is surrounded make him a man of broad views and noble ideals, and as the nature of his pursuit in life causes him to travel . . . he has a practical knowledge of geography and an experience which makes him quite an interesting fellow. He is possessed of a sound judgment and a critical mind which place him above the average man, though he may not understand formal logic. In short he is the embodiment of good nature and sociability."[20]

The San Juan Guide of 1877 (published by the Atchison, Topeka and Santa Fe Railroad) summed up the San Juan prospector's character when it proposed that the three things needed for success in the San Juan Mountains were courage, patience, and strength. Courage was needed to endure the hardships encountered; patience was needed to overcome the difficulties while waiting for success; and strength was needed to get the rich minerals from the mountains when they were discovered. Those same traits tended to describe the San Juaner in his approach to everyday life.

As individualistic as the miners were, it was difficult for them to join together into any type of organization; but miners did begin to form into their own labor associations in the late 1880s and early 1890s in response to attempts to cut their wages. One miner's organization at Red Mountain Town was known as the "Sky City Union." The associations were a good part social and bore little resemblance to labor unions as we know them today.

This blacksmith and machine shop is extremely tidy and clean and even includes two forges and one of the new (at the time) machine drills at the center of the shop. The fine-looking crew obviously worked for a large and well-equipped mine. *(Ouray County Museum)*

For example, the Knights of Labor often gave fancy balls with interested couples coming from as far away as Ouray and Silverton. Supper was normally included in the festivities, and confections might be brought in from the Vienna Bakery in Ouray. The usual program of twenty-four dances was often repeated a second time because dancing was so popular. Red Mountain Town even had its own miners' brass band, which often played for the dances.

Another, more somber, reason for the existence of the labor associations was to provide for burials. Mining was so dangerous and the death rates so high that many miners didn't bother to apply for life insurance. Labor union members would try to help the members of a deceased miner's family in whatever way they could. Later, labor unions on the divide performed their traditional role of helping the miners obtain better wages, increased job security, and safer working conditions. When the Western Federation of Miners was launched in the San Juans in 1893, Red Mountain was one of the first mining districts to start a local chapter. The Knights of Labor were also strong at Red Mountain Town and, as soon as they organized, they began plans for construction of a building to be used as a ballroom, library, and reading room.

The general public's attitude toward the working man was not always good. Even Dave Day, who prided himself on being the miner's friend, could write: "Friday and Saturday about 100 miners employed at the Guston became rebellious because one of their number had been given his time for gross misconduct at the supper table." Evidently the threat of a general strike had been used before successfully, but this time the management fired every one of the mine's employees. "The *Muldoon* congratulates Capt. Harvey upon the clean up, and makes to the belief that the mine would be thousands ahead had the outfit been bounced months ago."[21] One possible reason for Day's attitude was that the majority of the Red Mountain miners had voted Republican at the recent election. After blasting them for such, Day predicted that "miner's wages, with silver at $.94, cannot remain at $2.50 per day plus board. There *will* be a cut."[22]

Like the unions, the saloons also were used as social clubs. Most individuals had a particular saloon that they liked to frequent. A man's standing in society could be demonstrated by the saloon he preferred. Saloonkeepers were usually considered to be at the top of Red Mountain society. They were among the most influential men on the mountain, and their opinions were highly respected. Bartenders were among the best paid professionals on the divide.

Gambling was one of the most popular of Red Mountain activities because games of chance complemented the personalities of the men likely to have been found in the Red Mountain district. The gambling establishments were always more than ready to relieve an unwary miner of his new paycheck. Keno, faro, and twenty-one were some of the favorite gambling-hall games. All kinds of races were popular. One horse race was a "spirited contest between Ironton and Red Mountain for supremacy." Horses, mules, and even burros were raced. Red Mountain Town had a firehose cart team that competed in contests against other fire departments throughout Colorado. Foot races were often held, with one town's champion issuing an "official" challenge to another town's champion through the local papers. Hundreds of dollars were put up as a prize for the winner. As many as a thousand people showed up for some of the races. Prizefights were also popular; usually they were fought without gloves and continued until one of the fighters was knocked out. Of course, mining might be called an occupation that is a gamble in itself. The miner wagered the greatest stakes of all at work when he gambled that he would make it home safely without being maimed or killed.

The Fourth of July has always been an exciting time in Ouray. The Red Mountain miners would come down for the parades, contests, band performances, and speeches. Floats, bands, and military and fraternal organizations took major parts in the parade. There was always plenty to drink, and miners usually returned late and drunk. *(Colorado Historical Society)*

Other Red Mountain sports included occupational contests such as drilling matches—both double- and single-jacking. Drilling contests were a dangerous sport and also a source of pride at work. "In single jacking, one man held the sharp drill in one hand while pounding it with a small sledge. But, the real test came with double jacking. One man held the drill turning it a quarter of a turn after each blow from the heavy sledge held by the other. One slip and a man's hand was crushed. An even greater challenge was switching to a longer drill as the hole got deeper. Good teams could do it without missing a beat. Teams practiced for weeks as thousands of dollars could change hands at a large contest. A good team could drill twenty inches into solid granite in the fifteen-minute contest."[23]

The celebration of the Fourth of July always included drilling contests, and the day was observed in a big way in Silverton and Ouray. Most of the Red Mountain locals came down from the divide for the events, which always included much more than just occupational contests. Ouray's July 4 celebration in 1888 spread out over two days and included a parade, pigeon-shoot, horse races, baseball games, burro races, tugs-of-war, fireworks, children's games, and a balloon ascension. Prizes ran from a minimum of $10 all the way up to $150 for the tug-of-war contest. Drinking was always popular on July 4 and was usually done to excess. "The Fourth was observed tamely at Red Mountain. Quite

OTIS. SNOW SHOE BRIGADE

The Red Mountain miners not only used "snowshoes" (what we now call skis) for winter travel, they also often held sporting contests with them. The long pole was used to steer, balance, and brake. Several children and a dog have decided to join in this day's activities. (*W. H. Jackson photo; Colorado Historical Society*)

a few of the boys went to Silverton and Ouray to celebrate the one hundred tenth anniversary of the nation's birth. Though pretty badly demoralized, all say they had a good time. They are a pretty tough gang away from home."[24]

Baseball was played by semi-pro teams in both Ouray and Silverton in the summer. Even Ironton had a team that "mopped up" Ouray and won the one-hundred-dollar prize on July 4, 1889. Ouray had its hot-water caves to help take the soreness out of a miner's muscles. In fact, the *Solid Muldoon* of October 19, 1883 advertised Ouray as a "most desirable place for all who appreciate the beauties of nature."

In the winter, sports changed to snow-oriented activities. Skiing was done on twelve-foot-long boards (called snowshoes in those days). In the winter, skis or "netting" (today's snowshoes) were often needed in the Red Mountain district to travel from one spot to another. Different Colorado towns sent teams to compete with one another. Aspen, for example, issued a skiing challenge to Ouray and Silverton in 1887. "Snowshoeing" could be dangerous. In January 1886, a miner skiing down Corkscrew Gulch hit a stump that drove his ski through his thigh. The wound wouldn't heal properly until three months later, when doctors pulled out a three-inch piece of wood that had broken off in his leg when the ski was initially removed. Sledding was also a popular and much less dangerous sport.

Although religion may not have been of top priority, many of the prospectors, miners, and mine owners held deep religious convictions. Reverend Gibbons noted that many of the miners "were not ashamed of the religion of the great heroes of history; and after crossing the ocean, continued to devote themselves to the religious practices of their childhood. When not compelled to work on Sunday, it was their want [sic] to walk to Ouray, nine or ten miles, and assist at holy mass."[25]

The church and its services reminded many of the miners of home, and the church's social functions were always welcome. Services were held on occasion in Red Mountain Town, although the only official church buildings were in Ironton and Guston. The Red Mountain churches were missions manned by missionaries—much like the overseas missionary programs of modern days. Church buildings were not common in the mining towns because of the transience of the prospectors and the very real possibility that the camp might become a ghost town at any moment. On the other hand, every town wanted a church building as a sign of maturity and respectability. The Catholic church had a parish at Ironton, and regular services were held in the little church every other week (the in-between service was held in Ridgway). Many of the mines observed the Sabbath—especially at the Yankee Girl, whose owners and managers were extremely devout religious men.

Later, a main source of pride for the town of Guston was its little church building—the only one actually on Red Mountain Divide. In 1891, the Congregational church in Denver was confident enough of Red Mountain's future to send the Reverend William Davis, an Englishman, to try to preach the Lord's word. He made several attempts to establish his church at Red Mountain Town but was actually threatened with violence if he didn't leave.[26] Davis next tried Ironton, where he established the parsonage, but the church itself was built at Guston just to the west of the Guston Mine.[27] The locals liked Davis, and the July 31, 1891 *Solid Muldoon* even printed a poem on the front page in his honor. It was entitled "The Preacher and the Miners" and read, in part, as follows:

A preacher came to Ironton from some diggins "along the line"
Along one day last summer, called the miners from their mines
To hear him talk about a "district" which he thought the very best,
That held way over Sneffles, over Uncompag and the rest.
He found lots of open country for a preacher or a priest
That hadn't been prospected for a hundred months at least
And the miners dropped their shovels, their hammers and their drills.
And they gathered from the gulches, the valley and the hills.

It's hard to imagine a more domesticated scene than this home and the Congregational church at Guston in 1893. A woman and two children are in the shadows of the log cabin, and a wagon rests in the front yard. The furnishings are rustic—slab fence, sod roof, and plank deck—but there are flowers in the window. (*Denver Public Library, Western History Department*)

The poem continued to say that the preacher's "prospecting" soon failed. The concluding verses contained the statement, "The preacher he came back again, the miners never did / And if he went to hunt them, in their tunnels they were hid."

The Congregational church was built almost single-handedly by the minister, but the local miners did donate most of the lumber and the money needed. Lieutenant Governor Story of Ouray gave the land for the church. The belfry of the church contained both a bell and a mine whistle to call in the worshippers. The former was traditional for a church, but the latter was what the miners were used to responding to on the divide. The church opened in November 1891 on Thanksgiving Day, and many miners frequently walked down the Red Mountains for the services.

Although mining was a dangerous profession, the Red Mountain Mining District was reported to be an extremely healthy place to live. The *Red Mountain Mining Journal* reported in 1887 that "[Red Mountain] Town is five years old and, as yet, there is no graveyard. Two children have died from unnatural causes. We should be contented." There never was a true cemetery anywhere in the Red Mountain Mining District; two obvious reasons being that the ground was frozen solid most of the year and it was simply too hard to get to for burials. So, as he may have done a hundred times before for relaxation, on a miner's final trip from this earth he also went downhill to Ouray or Silverton.

EIGHT

<hr />

THE SNOW

Snow was the source of more transportation and production problems for the Red Mountain Mining District than any other single factor. The district was in a unique location. Mining camps such as Leadville had existed at equal or higher elevations, but most received much less snow or were located in terrain that was not as precipitous as are the San Juans. The steep mountainsides and the large Red Mountain snowfall form the most avalanche-prone country in the United States—perhaps even in the world. Large snowslides passed across the middle of several Red Mountain mining claims, and most of the heavily populated areas on the Red Mountain Divide were susceptible to avalanches. Although it would be a while before it was discovered, a large slide ran off Red Mountain No. 3 right through the middle of Red Mountain Town. Several small avalanches ran out in the vicinity of the Genessee and Guston mines, and a huge slide came from far up in Champion Basin all the way down to the Yankee Girl Mine.

If the deadly avalanches weren't a problem, the snow still caused a lot of havoc simply because there was so much of it. The San Juan Mountains receive much of their snow from storms that travel in from the south and west, as opposed to the "northerners" that hit most of the other mountains of Colorado. Although much of the local snowfall is light and fluffy, the southern storms often carry warm Pacific moisture and can dump large amounts

This photograph gives an idea of just how high the snow could get during a bad winter at Red Mountain. It was important to have an entire winter's food and fuel supply on hand by fall. If someone was living in this cabin, it's a bad sign that no smoke is coming from the chimney. *(W. H. Jackson photo; author's collection)*

of a heavy, wet snow in a very short time. The San Juans are therefore one of the wettest parts of Colorado, and much of the precipitation comes in the winter in the form of snow. Cabins in the Red Mountain Mining District were sometimes buried to their roofs, and work often came to a standstill because tools, ore, or equipment were buried under five to ten feet of snow. It was hard and time-consuming work to shovel the snow, and often it simply couldn't be removed as fast as the new snow fell.

Travel in the winter in the Red Mountain district was often difficult, if not totally impossible, because the snow piled up so deeply. In a heavy snowstorm, visibility could be cut to a matter of feet, and all the local landmarks might quickly disappear. Travel was extremely dangerous in the months of January, February, and March, when enough snow had fallen and the temperatures were warm enough to start dozens of major snowslides. There was no heavy equipment such as today's snowplows to remove the snow, so new-fallen snow was either broken through and packed down by the first brave soul to "break trail," or travel was on the ten- to twelve-foot wooden skis or on "webbing." A man's feet were simply tied onto the boards with leather—there were no such things as bindings. Steering and braking were done with a long pole dragged in the snow. On cold nights a hard crust would usually form, and travel on foot was sometimes possible until the sun hit the snow in the morning. Trying to walk in the five- to ten-foot-deep snows was virtually impossible during the warm days without the use of skis or snowshoes because a person would continually break through the crust and sink to the waist in snow.

The original Red Mountain prospectors didn't realize it at the time, but the San Juan winters from the time of the discovery of the Red Mountain ores in 1875 through the winter of 1882–1883 were relatively easy ones. During that period it was unusual for there to be more than two or three feet of snow on the ground in the high San Juan Mountains. Quite often by March the snow was gone, except perhaps in the shade. The early-day prospectors thought the winter conditions high in the San Juans to be rough, but they hadn't encountered anything yet!

By early December 1883 a more normal snowpack had returned, and the miners and prospectors began to experience a more typical San Juan winter. By mid-December, what little work was being done on the Red Mountain Divide was only due to the fever-pitch excitement that had overtaken the Red Mountain camps; otherwise, the district would certainly have been deserted. Drifts of snow had already piled up to ten feet in the shade. The men on the divide reported that they were trying to work in "the worst possible conditions," but more snow was yet to come.

On December 19, 1883, a terrible and persistent snowstorm hit the Red Mountains. When it ended on December 26, it would be recorded as one of

Sometimes in deep snow or on steep trails, the prospector or packer had to resort to grabbing his burro's tail and following it down the slopes. The practice was called "tailing." (*Reprinted from* Harper's Weekly, *June 9, 1883; author's collection*)

the heaviest snowstorms in the memory of the white settlers. Five feet of new snow had fallen on Red Mountain Town in one week. Work on the Red Mountain Divide came to a virtual standstill. Cabins were swept away in avalanches, several lives were lost, and communications ceased throughout the entire San Juan region. At the town of Congress, the roof of the Haines Hotel collapsed from the weight of the snow. At Chattanooga, an avalanche claimed one life and injured two miners at the Silver Crown Mine. It was the first slide death in the Red Mountain Mining District, and there would be many more to come.

After the bad December storm there was a temporary lull during January, and then winter struck again with full force on February 3, 1884. It snowed three feet in five days, stopped for a few days, and then commenced snowing again. That January, Mr. Patterson of Chattanooga reported that he somehow managed to haul 450 tons of ore from the Congress Mine to the Walsh Smelter in Silverton, even though there was at least five feet of snow on the ground. In February, he reported that "at Chattanooga, the snow was twelve feet deep; we measured it. It got so deep we could no longer shovel the trail, so we dug a tunnel under the snow from our cabin to the barn in order to take care of the stock."[1]

By the end of February 1884 there was already four times as much snow on the ground at Red Mountain than had been reported in any previous winter. Most of the one-story buildings were totally covered by snow. Almost every mine in the Red Mountain Mining District had been forced to shut down. Fresh food was soon gone. As the pack trains ceased to bring in supplies, the starving miners fought their way to the nearby towns to look for food. It snowed for twenty straight days at one point, and hundreds of snowslides ran. The snow piled up to fifteen feet on the level, and drifts were even deeper! Even the citizens of Silverton found themselves in real trouble, because the Durango train couldn't get to that town from February 4 to April 17, 1884 – a period of seventy-three days. All of the main trails in the San Juans were blocked by snow. Many of the San Juan residents almost starved to death; some actually did. Only a few brave men, who fought for days to bring in a long mule train of supplies, kept a real disaster from occurring at Silverton.

The winter of 1884–1885 proved that the previous winter hadn't been just a freak of nature. By Christmas, wagon travel had again come to a halt because of the deep snows. Every few weeks the papers would announce that they thought the roads would be open soon, but in fact it was late spring before there was any significant freight traffic flowing again. A few pack trains managed to get out of the Red Mountains on occasion, but they only brought out the equivalent of a wagon load or two of ore at a time. When the ore couldn't be shipped, production in the mines eventually came to a halt. As the ore piled up, there came a time when there simply was no place to put it, and without money coming in from the sale of ore, a cash-flow problem was quickly created at most mines. Without ore shipments to report in the spring of 1885, the *Solid Muldoon* was reduced to counting the number of empty ore sacks sent to each of the major mines in anticipation of their being able to ship ore. At Red Mountain Town it was June 1885 before the road was passable by freight wagons.

The heavy snow not only caused problems when it fell, it also resulted in major headaches when it melted. By the spring of 1884, the ground on the divide turned into mud three feet deep. Small creeks turned into large rivers. Travel was even more difficult than when the deep snows had covered the road, since the snow itself could at least be shoveled or packed down. There was nothing the miners could do but wait for the mud to dry out. In its review of mining for the year 1884, the *La Plata Miner* spent most of its space explaining why the production and shipment of ore hadn't been greater from the Red Mountain Mining District. All winter, the problem had been the snow blockades, followed by heavy spring thaws that washed out many of the roads and bridges. The paper pointed out that the travel problems meant not only that it was difficult to get the ore out of the district and to get the necessary supplies in, but even more important, the spring mud and floods had prevented capitalists from traveling to the Red Mountain district to look for possible investment in the local mines.

Perhaps the worst period of bad weather, at least in terms of loss of life, occurred in the winter of 1885–1886, when wet and heavy snowstorms dropped from two to four feet of snow over and over again. On January 20, 1886, slides ran heavily all over the San Juans. The heavy snow closed the road from Silverton to Ouray and again blocked the Silverton train from Durango. A major avalanche hit the Dutton Mine in Champion Gulch (above the Yankee Girl) and swept nine men down the mountain. Nearly one hundred workers responded from the Yankee Girl Mine to take part in the rescue efforts, and five of the Dutton miners were, in fact, saved. However, four men were killed at the mine, and a man also froze to death on the road trying to get to Ouray to call for additional help. Yet another man died at the Genessee Mine, which was hit three times that day by slides. As a show of their solidarity and sympathy, some seventy miners transported the six dead men to Ouray, where a relief fund was established for their families and burial expenses. The fund quickly rose to over one thousand dollars in contributions. As a result of the death of the man trying to get to Ouray for help, another fund was started to construct two shelter houses on the road

Snowslides were all too prevalent through the San Juans, not only destroying mines and mills but often claiming lives. The steep mountains and heavy snows made living in the San Juans in the winter a deadly affair. This scene depicts the remains of a mine and mill after an avalanche. *(Drawing by Charles Graham, in* Harper's Weekly, *February 17, 1883; author's collection)*

from Ouray to Ironton. Each was to be stocked with adequate firewood and food for winter travelers. However, nothing concrete ever came out of this plan.

The harsh winters of 1883–1884 and 1884–1885 had brought almost all work in the Red Mountain Mining District to a halt, but by the winter of 1885–1886, the owners of Red Mountain mines knew what to expect and had a chance to prepare for the heavy winter snows. Huge quantities of supplies had been brought to the divide during the fall. Large quantities of firewood were cut and the wood stockpiled where it could easily be reached during the winter. Plans were made to ship most of the mines' ore out during the summer. Since much of the ore couldn't be shipped during the winter, many of the men were laid off as soon as the snow got deep enough to stop traffic. For most of those left on the divide, winter became a time of development—a time to do work in the mines that could help later production. Timbers were set, drilling might be done to explore new portions of the mine, or new machinery might be installed to help reduce production costs.

Another dangerous storm of heavy, wet snow hit the San Juans in February 1886. The train from Durango to Silverton was again shut down, and supplies bound for Silverton had to be sent by pack train from Ouray. There was no other road or trail that was passable into Silverton from any other direction. The event had become common enough that Dave Day took the opportunity to begin to crow about Silverton's plight. Just a few of many barbs thrown at Silverton by the Ouray editor were "mail to Silverton should be marked 'Via Ouray,'"[2] "Silverton can boast of a tri-monthly railroad and a tobbagan club,"[3] and "Silverton's railroad is not visible to the naked eye this time of year."[4] Day did note, however, that although "the *Solid Muldoon* has joked about Silverton and her deep snows . . . when in trouble she can count on us." He promised that the offer was genuine, honest, and that "no unseemly allusions will be made to their condition."[5]

The *Solid Muldoon* predicted in April 1886 that "packing to the upper mines will be delayed until June even with the ordinary warm weather . . . One of the brightest gems in the San Juan weather is the uncertainty of it. There is only one thing certain about it, you are certain of plenty of weather."[6] Day's prediction was correct—in fact, it wasn't until late June that the roads and trails were totally passable. Until that time the Genessee, Vanderbilt, Silver Bell, and National Belle mines were all reported to be packed full of ore, which the owners were ready to ship if they could only figure out some way to get it to the mills. Shipping was available throughout most of the winter by pack train, but it was a much more expensive form of transportation than wagon. The extreme cost of "packing out" in the winter required that the ore be of a very high grade to make a profit. Only the Yankee Girl Mine could consistently meet that test, and it continued to ship regularly by whatever means necessary. If the Red Mountain mines wanted to attempt to ship by wagons or sleds in the winter, they usually had to send out their own work crews to shovel the snow from the toll road. On several occasions this was done, but as prices fell, most of the mine owners felt the best solution was not to ship ore at all but simply wait it out until the summer thaws. Although the trails were blocked in the winter, most mine owners felt that winter shipping could be done consistently from the divide if a railroad could be built to the Red Mountain district.

As bad as the winter of 1885–1886 had been, the spring was even worse. With the quick thaw of the huge snowpack, everything on the surface of the divide turned to mud or water. Bridges were washed out, mud slides occurred, and creeks overflowed their banks. Mears's fifty-foot-high bridge, which crossed Red Mountain Creek between Ironton and the Silver Bell, was washed out. Even travel by horseback became impossible, because the sharp hooves of the horses would break through the rotten snow or they would slip off the trail. Travel on foot was not attempted by most men. Later, the ruts, sinkholes, and debris left by the avalanches and floods compounded the problem. As many as a hundred men worked for months on some of the trails before they could be reopened. When the work was on the toll roads, the mines or the counties usually paid the men's wages. The money seldom came out of Otto Mears's pocket. In fact, it was reported that Mears was busy that spring trying to buy up all competing freighting and packing companies so as to monopolize freight rates.[7]

The following winter was almost as bad. There were many large snow-storms in December 1886 and January 1887, most of which included extremely high winds. The strong winds and heavy snowfall combined to bring about a high avalanche danger everywhere in the San Juans. Once again, the D&RG had trouble getting the train from Durango to Silverton. The *Solid Muldoon* reported that not only was the railroad blocked, but "a carload of ore from the Yankee Girl valued at $70,000 is lost in transit between Chattanooga and a place called Silverton. About 70,000 tons of snow is on top of it at present."[8]

It wasn't just the freighters that had trouble with the heavy snows. By stage, the trip up the mountain from Silverton or Ouray could be especially dangerous in, or immediately after, a snowstorm. The Reverend J. J. Gibbons later wrote of what he called a "typical" winter trip on the stage. "I made the trip to Silverton on Saturday morning in the usual way by stage, without any more serious inconvenience than that of finding myself obliged to shovel snow, open the road and help drag the horses from the high drifts. Napoleon's trip across the Alps may be considered pleasant when compared with the fatigue and perils of a journey away up in the clouds during one of the fierce storms which sweep through the canyons."[9]

Later, Reverend Gibbons wrote of an occasion when "the Ouray toll road was banked up with masses of snow. While passing one of the bad spots in the road the sleigh tipped over, spilling out the passengers. I happened to be on the precipice side, and was thrown down the abrupt declivity some forty feet. Here the snow proved to be a friend to me, for it saved me from bruises and perhaps death. My fellow passengers pulled me up with a long rope, and we kept on our way just as if nothing unusual had taken place."[10]

There were many tales of individuals who survived falls of hundreds of feet because the snow cushioned their fall. Reverend Gibbons tells yet another tale: "The accident happened to two miners whose names I have forgotten. They had been in Ouray overnight, and in the morning left for Red Mountain on King's stage with Ike Stephens as the driver, as good a Jehu as ever cracked a whip over a six-horse coach. Ike was a 'peach' and would stay with the horses to the last. It had been snowing a little, but it was a pretty fair morning when Ike pulled out for Red Mountain, with a big load of eggs and general merchandise, and for his live freight, the two miners who had made up their minds not to go home until morning. They occupied the back seat of the sleigh. Just as they were rounding the last dangerous point before coming by the numerous small slides that always came down when it stormed [the Mother Cline Slide], the accident to which I refer occurred. On the cliff above there were two spires of rock that shot up for many feet. The snow drifted in between these and down upon the road, forming a high bank, over which Ike had the temerity to drive. The consequence was that when the sleigh went over the ridge of snow, the box came from between the sleigh stakes and started over the precipice, the horses plunged forward, Ike held on to the reins and the now frightened leaders drew him out of the box; but the miners, the eggs and the dead pigs, together with a large amount of merchandise, went over and fell nearly 250 feet. Strange to say not a bone was broken; the two men escaped with a few scratches and a big scare, but the box was in flitters. It was no smooth slide – it was a sheer fall straight down until they came within twenty feet of the bottom, and then a tumble of about the same distance into the creek. The miners were in an india-rubber condition when they realized where they were and resolved the next time to go home before regular bed-time."[11]

Trying to work in the deep snow was just as dangerous, and perhaps even more of a hassle, as trying to travel in it. As a result, most mine managers brought their winter work indoors or into the mine itself. Many of the mines' boardinghouses connected with their shaft houses or tunnels so as to make it unnecessary for the miner to go outdoors. Boilers, pumps, and even mills were sometimes built underground. As Ernest Ingersoll, eastern travel writer, wrote: "The winter is the best of all times to work in the silver mines. The impression that the San Juan district must be abandoned for half the year is entirely wrong when any thorough system of operations is projected. Well-sheltered and abundantly fed, removed from the temptations of the bar-room (which can only be got at by a frightfully fatiguing and perilous trip on snow-shoes) and settled to the fact that a whole winter's work lies ahead, there is no season when such steady work is possible . . . ."[12]

The editor of the La Plata Miner also recognized that work shouldn't be abandoned in the winter. "There will be without a doubt more work done in the mines this winter than has been done in many past winters, for the simple reason that it is a case of absolute necessity. Mine owners must have money and the only practical way to get it is to go to work and dig it out. This summer's work has increased faith in mining more than ever before, and we know not of a single mine which has been worked this summer but which has produced ore in paying quantities, which will enable owners or lessees to lay in winter supplies and push work during the stormy days instead of laying idle like many have done before."[13]

Dave Day pointed out that, as deep as the snow might get, the business-men of Silverton didn't let it slow them down. They were greatly outdoing Ouray in rounding up year-round business from the Red Mountain district. As the snows got heavy near the end of the year, the merchants would make superhuman efforts to get supplies out to the Red Mountain mines. "There was no sitting around the stove and wishing that it would stop snowing or that the mail carrier would come and break trail or that the mine superin-tendent would come along and buy supplies and get them to their properties. They hustled out on snowshoes, sold goods to be delivered at the mines, went home, and, if need be, went out with the pack trains and helped shovel out the trails."[14]

When the mine owners realized just how bad the conditions could get, the population on the Red Mountain Divide began to decline rapidly in the winter. Almost all of the women and children left. The ranks of the freighters and packers were drastically reduced, and almost all who were doing outside work were let go for the winter. Since the ore often couldn't be shipped for months and would soon fill the ore bins, many of the miners were also let go by the middle of winter. For example, the work force at the Yankee Girl, which usually contained 125 or more men in the summer, would usually dwindle to 30 or 40 miners by January or February. Those that remained on the divide were hardy and determined. The *Red Mountain Journal* wrote at the end of 1887 that "as a class all are united and nothing intervenes to mar the happiness of all who have cast their winter lot in camp, and a silver lining and plumage of hope and prosperity are now assured. The mines are on all sides. The men have but a short walk to work and the whistle for breaks and shift times breaks the gloom of what might seem an isolated and desolate camp. It is a town of happiness unconfined the year around."[15]

Much hope continued to be put on the construction of a railroad, which most felt would allow the Red Mountain mines to work all winter. When Otto Mears began construction of his railroad to Red Mountain in the winter of 1888–1889, even the weather seemed to cooperate. It was such a mild winter that, in January 1889, Dave Day mentioned that the wagon road had been open all winter, and in the February 8, 1888 *Silverton Democrat* the editor was prompted to write "there is less snow in the mountains above Silverton at the present time than was ever before known at this season of the year." Only eight inches of snow were on the ground at Silverton at the time of the article, and when a heavy March storm dumped two feet of snow, it melted fast and did little to delay an early opening of the roads in the spring. The March 1, 1889 *Solid Muldoon* announced that the "road is in good shape between Ouray and Ironton and the stage arrives daily crowded with passengers." As light as the snows had been, the spring thaws still did considerable damage, and in May 1890 Day announced that only "two men are working the road below Ironton and a dozen more would help make the road passable."[16] Some of the problems were caused by the travelers themselves tearing up the muddy roads, because the traffic heading toward the Red Mountain Mining District at the time was described as immense and anxious.

Many of the Red Mountain inhabitants continued to hope that the heavy snowfall of the past five winters had been abnormal. Almost everyone on the divide believed Red Mountain's Silverton railroad would be little affected by the snow. When a correspondent for the *Engineering and Mining Record* wrote that the Silverton–Red Mountain railroad would be little more than a summer line, since it was in the region of heavy snows and had to cross a high divide, Dave Day shot back that "Mears' railroad is an every day enterprise and one that snow and slides cannot block."[17] Day's stand was unrealistic, because in every one of the past five winters he himself had taken particular glee in reporting the blockage of the Durango-Silverton railroad by snow and slides. The Silverton–Red Mountain railroad was thousands of feet higher in elevation than was the D&RG and was located in country just as rugged, and therefore avalanche-prone, as was the Durango-Silverton route.

After the Silverton railroad was completed to the Red Mountain Mining District, history quickly proved that, no matter how great the effort, the railroad couldn't operate without interruption in the harsh San Juan winters. One early example of the condition of winter travel was given by Adeline Gibbs, new wife of Charles W. Gibbs, the Silverton railroad's chief engineer. On their extended honeymoon, the couple left Ouray on Christmas Day of 1889 to go to Silverton. At Ironton, they learned that the Silverton railroad was blocked by heavy snows, so Mrs. Gibbs stayed behind while her husband went up on foot to determine if he could help the track crews. On New Year's Day, he sent word to his bride that it was safe to come up as far as Red Mountain Town. From there they walked toward Silverton, following a small path down the middle of the track. At hairpin turns they sometimes went

On this bright day in the early 1890s, there are over sixty men shoveling snow from the track and cars at the Red Mountain Town depot. Several wear dark glasses to protect their eyes from the bright glare coming off the snow. Most likely, there were two other gangs of men shoveling somewhere on the railroad at the same time. (*Brumfield & Gilbert photo; Denver Public Library, Western History Department*)

cross-country, sliding down the steep slopes. After a walk (and slide) of four or five miles they met the Silverton locomotive, which was snowplowing up the grade.

All of the Gibbses' effort had been expended early in the season of the relatively mild winter of 1889–1890. It had even rained all day on December 4, 1889 in Silverton – something that had never been seen before, even by the old-timers. A few major storms did occur in 1890 – the D&RG train to Silverton was blocked for four weeks in February and March – but they were followed by springlike weather that quickly melted the snow. The lack of snow in the winter of 1889–1890 actually created a new problem in the Red Mountain Mining District. The clouds of the snowstorms usually kept the temperatures from falling to extremes at night, and deep snow insulated the ground from the cold air. With the absence of a normal snowpack in the winter of 1889–1890, massive problems developed on the divide with frozen water pipes. The National Belle had been using city water from Red Mountain Town in its mine, but in the winter of 1889–1890 the mine ran short because so many people in "The Town" had kept their taps open to keep water lines from freezing. The National Belle tried to use the water it was pumping out of its own shafts, but water seeping into its mine contained so much acid that it was eating into the boilers and other machinery. The

The snow has piled up to sixty feet on the D&RG tracks to Silverton at the Saguache snowslide. Note the logs, rocks, and other debris the slide has brought down. Usually a tunnel would have been made through the snow instead of the clean cut depicted here, but it makes a great photo! (*Brumfield photo; San Juan County Historical Society, Henry M. Doud collection*)

water lines at the Yankee Girl Mine also froze several times that winter. It was usually not all that cold in the Red Mountain district, but the lowest temperature ever recorded at Red Mountain Town occurred in February 1890, when the thermometer fell to twenty below zero. The weather turned warmer in March, and by April 11 the light snowpack had melted enough that the mines were shipping heavily.

In the winter of 1890–1891, the "real" winter returned to the Red Mountain district. Two feet of snow had fallen by October 10, 1890, and the Silverton Railroad was already shut down, at least temporarily, by snow. As early as October 1890, Reverend Gibbons could tell it was going to be a harsh winter. "The rocks and mountain sides were covered with deep snow, and the tall pines, with their fleecy coat of white, looked small. The roads were blocked and often impassable. Moses Liverman, the director of the Silverton Railroad was pushed to the utmost to keep the line open until Christmas. A large number of men had been at work from October and a bank on either side of the road was so piled that no more could be thrown over. The Silverton Railroad, one of the highest in the world, connects Ironton with Silverton. I went over to Silverton in October. It was, I think, on the 3rd, and I rode part of the way to Ironton in a sleigh. I was not a party of one, but one of a party of travelers [on the train to Ironton], and it took us from 10:30 A.M. to 6:30 P.M. to reach Red Mountain, a distance of about four miles. We had only two cars, one of which was derailed at least six times that day, and all hands assisted in removing the snow and in prying on the car."[18]

The weather turned better in December, and some ore and supplies were packed over trails that normally could be used only in the summer. But the Silverton Railroad was blocked again by January 10, and the snows in the month of February were really wicked. The railroad advertised repeatedly that it would hire all the snow shovelers who would apply – pay was $2.50 per day. Snow quickly piled up to ten feet at Red Mountain Town. One miner commented that "if it stopped snowing for one minute in six weeks, I never heard of it."[19]

The snow also continued to complicate work at the mines. For example, in January 1891 the Big Elephant Slide ran off Brown Mountain, hitting a mining cabin. Two men were inside and one was killed instantly. The other was hurt badly and clawed his way through the snow to the mine's main tunnel. Rescuers later followed his bloody trail through the snow, rescued him from the tunnel, and carried him to Ironton, where they rubbed his frozen body with coal oil and snow. Amazingly, the man recovered; in fact, within a few hours he was reported to have his old zeal back. The body of his friend was kept frozen outdoors in Ironton until the road to Ouray was opened and his remains could be transported to the Ouray cemetery.[20]

By February 1891, even larger numbers of men than normal were laid off at the mines. The storage sheds of most Red Mountain mines were full, and there was no way to ship the ore. However, as it turned out, in early 1891 most of the mines were cutting back on the shipment of ore anyway. The price paid for the ore was falling, the cost of smelting was rising, and shipping rates were high. Dave Day estimated the shipment of ore to be off fifty percent by the end of 1890, and he reported that most of the big mines were storing their ore.[21] There were so many delays in the Silverton Railroad's schedule in the winter of 1891–1892 that Dave Day dubbed the route the "Silverton–Red Mountain–Rainbow Slide and Drift Trunk line."[22] The Yankee Girl continued to try to ship regularly regardless of conditions–even when a snow tunnel had to be dug on the spur through the Yankee Girl property because a slide had piled the snow up high. Instead of working in the mine, the Yankee Girl miners were often sent out during the winter to shovel the heavy snows from the spur.

Winter continued to play havoc with the light narrow-gauge cars of the Silverton Railroad. Every major snowstorm necessitated the use of large gangs of men to clear the tracks or to try to get the cars back on the rails. The common practice was to have forty or fifty men start digging at Silverton, another forty or fifty at Red Mountain Town, and another forty or fifty at Ironton. Even such a large number of men had to sometimes be supplemented by an equal number of miners. As time would show, sometime in January or February Mother Nature usually won her winter battle with Otto Mears, and the Silverton Railroad would be forced to close until late spring or early summer.

Travel didn't get any easier in the winter on the wagon roads and trails. The snow often brought the stage to a standstill. The March 1890 *Solid Muldoon* reported the southbound stage had to be totally abandoned at the Yankee Girl Mine. The passengers then trudged upward through deep snow for five hours to make it to Red Mountain Town. Tunnels or cuts through the snow had to be made at almost every point that one of the eighty major slides crossed the road from Ouray to Silverton. The Mother Cline was probably the biggest slide, the Riverside the most dangerous.

In the spring of 1891, avalanches ran constantly on the divide. The *Solid Muldoon* reported the Riverside Slide had covered the road to a 60- to 70-foot depth for a distance of 480 feet.[23] The next month the stage (actually a sled at this time of year) was swept off the road.[24] Until the snow became too soft in the spring, the sleighs would go right over the top of the avalanches because the snow was packed as hard as concrete (with trees and boulders included). When the horses and burros started breaking through the snow, a tunnel or a cut that was big enough for the stagecoach was usually dug

This view looks south down into the Chattanooga valley after the 1889 avalanche. Mineral Creek winds its way through the valley; the Silver Ledge Mill is in the foreground, next to the Silverton's tracks. After the avalanche, Chattanooga's streets were oriented east and west instead of north and south, as they had been at the time of the slide. (*W. H. Jackson photo; Colorado Historical Society*)

for the entire distance of the slide.[25] It was in the spring that conditions were the most dangerous – sometimes so bad that only the mail carrier dared to ride the trails. In March 1891, the *Solid Muldoon* reported that "the snowslides have been simply fearful, nothing of the kind had been seen for the last twelve years. The oldest timer in the district never saw anything of the kind . . . If you want to see some fine weather come to the San Juan country in the summer."[26]

Luckily, none of the heavy snowslides hit any of the Red Mountain settlements until after the mid-1890s, when most were already abandoned or at least had much smaller populations than at the time of the Red Mountain boom. The exception was Chattanooga, which was virtually wiped out by a snowslide in the late 1880s. At the time of the disaster the settlement's population was fifty-two, but not a single person was killed. Although the residents knew of the existence of the Eagle Slide, they didn't realize that in extreme circumstances it would curve to the east and head right into the middle of their town. In 1890, Reverend Gibbons reported that "Chattanooga had been dismantled by a snow-slide which a few years before swept away a part of the town . . . The ruins of the roofs and sides of houses were strewn for over half a mile over the valley, and the once flourishing hamlet had dwindled to the small number of two."[27]

This monument was erected in memory of snowplow drivers killed by the Riverside Slide. Unfortunately, the name of Eddie Imel was added in 1992. The Riverside Slide has also killed half a dozen other people over the years, and scores more have been trapped by it, some just barely escaping. (*Bill Fries III photo*)

The February 16, 1895 *Silverton Standard* reported that an avalanche ran all the way into Red Mountain Town, which, since its inception, had been thought to have no such danger. "On last Thursday, Red Mountain was visited by a terrific snowslide, starting from the apex of the great Red Mountain and coming down with such force that when it struck the flat, which is over the divide from the town, it cleared this divide and kept on across Main Street, knocking out one corner of Dan Sheehan's house and the windows of George Hessers." The same article went on to detail that "so far this winter, San Juan County has escaped a fatal or disastrous snow slide. The miners, and all who have occasion to travel, are careful not to venture out until the snow has settled." The report of little damage from the Red Mountain avalanche was somewhat misleading, because almost all of Red Mountain Town's business district had burned several years earlier. Otherwise, the avalanche would undoubtedly have done much more damage. So many of the mines had closed by the early 1900s, and there were so few miners on the divide to be caught in snowslides, that the statistics drop off sharply after that time.

Although fewer people were living in the settlements of the Red Mountain district at the turn of the century, those individuals who were on the mountain weren't any safer, and there still are many tales of deaths or near misses by avalanches. For example, the slides ran especially often at the Guadalupe Mine at the extreme northern end of Ironton Park. The main entrance to the mine and many of its buildings were built in the middle of an avalanche chute. In 1889, the papers reported that the main boardinghouse had a four-foot-thick solid wood roof so that the slides would run over the top of it. The plan worked successfully at first. In January 1899, a slide ran over the mine and the *Solid Muldoon* reported that "the only damage was the sudden breaking up of a whist game."[28] But in 1912, the same house was "sliced in two like an oyster would be split. In the grinding process of traveling a mile or so down the mountain, it was ground up so small that a careful search of the slide in the gulch revealed only . . . a little sawdust."[29] Luckily, there were no men in the boardinghouse at the time of the incident.

The deep snows and dangerous slides in the Red Mountain district have continued to be of danger right up to the present. Many experts report the Million Dollar Highway to be the most avalanche-prone stretch of highway in the world. People have been killed cross-country skiing on the Red Mountain Divide; Jim Hollis died in the Oh Boy! Slide in 1990. The Reverend Marvin Hudson and his young daughters Amelia and Pauline died in the Riverside Slide on March 3, 1963 while trying to travel from Ouray to Silverton for church services. Robert Miller was killed while plowing the road at the same avalanche on March 2, 1970, as were Terry Kishbaugh on February 10, 1978, and Eddie Imel on March 5, 1992. No matter how hard we try, no matter how far each generation feels it has progressed beyond the previous one, human beings will never succeed in harnessing nature in the rugged San Juan Mountains.

NINE

⫷∞∞∞◉∞∞∞⫸

THE SILVER SLIDE

In retrospect, it is easy to discern that the great Red Mountain strikes were made at an incredibly bad time in mining history. For hundreds of years, the secret to mining success seemed simple—find the ore, dig it out, and, if it is valuable enough, send it on to the smelters. But during the 1880s the economics of mining changed radically, and to complicate matters further, many unique production problems cropped up in the Red Mountain Mining District.

At the beginning of 1884, the Red Mountain economy was sound enough that the number of men working in the mines had begun to grow dramatically. Development work was being done as rapidly as possible, and ore of all types and values seemed to be everywhere. For example, in January 1884, the Congress Mine hit a high-grade ore in one of the few volcanic pipes on the south side of the divide. A tunnel was driven to connect with the mine's main shaft, and the workers hit good ore while still twenty feet away. The tunnel had therefore provided ventilation, drainage, and, best of all, given an indication of a large ore body in the mine. Over at the National Belle, the owners blasted tunnels that literally crisscrossed the Knob and determined the main chamber of ore to be 300 feet wide, 350 feet high, and 1,000 feet in length—the entire space filled with rich carbonates and other minerals. Boulders of rich solid galena had been found weighing as

143

Ore wagons were large, sturdy affairs, and the horses that pulled them were even larger and sturdier. Each wagon was usually pulled by a six-horse team and could hold six to eight tons of ore – the equivalent of a large burro train's capacity. It is easy to see why good wagon roads were therefore important to the mining district. *(Walker Arts Studio photo; author's collection)*

much as one thousand pounds. Then, to top all the previous discoveries, several vertical chimneys of extremely rich ore were uncovered.

However, the Yankee Girl continued to be the mine by which all others were measured. For example, in a detailed article on the Guston Mine, the *Rocky Mountain News* of July 24, 1884 mentioned the Yankee Girl Mine no less than six times. "The resemblance between the Guston ore and that of the Yankee Girl . . . is remarkable . . . On the occasion of a recent visit this reporter was unable to distinguish one from the other." The Yankee Girl's assays rose higher and higher as the mine went deeper.

Unfortunately, the overall cost of mining at Red Mountain continued to rise during 1884 at the very same time that metal prices were slowly falling. The only cost that declined was that of transportation. With the July 1884 opening of the Silverton-to-Red Mountain wagon road, one six-mule team could now pull a wagon loaded with up to eight tons of ore – the equivalent of a pack train of eighty burros! The average charge for hauling a ton of ore from the Yankee Girl to Silverton was immediately reduced by two-thirds. Even though Silverton had the train, Dave Day insisted that "via Montrose and Ouray is the shortest, quickest and cheapest route to the Red Mountains and Silverton. No danger of snow blockades or slides on the Magnolia route."[1]

By early summer 1884, rumors had begun to spread that the National Belle Mine would be sold for a large sum of money. The transaction was finalized in early October 1884. O. P. Posey and George Crawford bought

The Solid Gold and Silver Mining Company was just one early Red Mountain venture that never returned anywhere near as much money as was taken to capitalize it. The Red Mountain Mining District attracted many investors from Pittsburgh, Pennsylvania, perhaps because of the coal mining prevalent there. *(Author's collection)*

the mine from its original locators for $125,000 (the equivalent of millions in today's dollars).[2] The sale occurred concurrently with the opening of the wagon road to Silverton, and with the subsequent lowering of freight rates even the mine's lower-grade ore could be shipped at a profit. The National Belle Silver Mining Company was incorporated with total capital stock authorized at seven million dollars. Most of the stock sold quickly, but the money raised was much more than was needed to do the anticipated development work. Posey and Crawford made a quick and large profit on their sale, but there was very little hope that the stock company would ever be able to return more in dividends than had been initially invested.

By the end of October, total employment at the Yankee Girl was up to sixty men, at which level it stayed for most of the winter. Many of the workmen were involved with building the "largest ore storage bin in the San Juans." Twelve men were employed at the Guston, and the National Belle employed about forty men all winter. By January 1885, the *Solid Muldoon* reported that the Genessee, Yankee Girl, and National Belle mines were working every man they could find room for in their boardinghouses. Besides adding additional men to their payrolls, many of the bigger mines continued to bring in extensive amounts of large and expensive machinery. For example, the Yankee Girl was forced to install a large new pump in October 1884, and it put a new steam hoist into operation in January 1885. Soon, an even bigger pump was needed to keep up with the ever-larger quantities of water coming into the shaft. The old one was passed down to the National Belle, since little of its work was done in deep shafts.

It had become evident that the makeup and location of ore in the Red Mountain district was very unpredictable. "The Red Mountain country is calculated to destroy the most cherished theories of the geologist, as it has surprised the knowing ones; but as long as it continues to show up fine bodies of high-grade ore, it will make little difference to the mine owner whether the deposits are in the form of fissure or contact veins, pockets or chimneys."[3] One example of the confusion occurred at the Genessee. After the mine was purchased by capitalists, its managers consulted with their geologists and blasted shafts and adits all over the claim. In the process, the original shaft was deepened from 15 feet to 175 feet. Even with the extensive development activity, only low-grade ore had been encountered. Finally, in 1885, a new manager decided to drive tunnels north and south from the bottom of the shaft; this was done not on professional advice but just to see what might be encountered. Fifteen feet to the north, he hit a solid body of rich galena ore that was seven feet wide and averaged two hundred ounces of silver per ton.

The details of Red Mountain ore distribution were so complex that even in 1890, when T. E. Schwartz, manager of the Yankee Girl and Guston mines, read a paper to the American Institute of Mining Engineers, he is quoted as saying: "To the practical mining man, as well as the theorist, mineralogist and geologist, [the Red Mountain district] is a most interesting one. Chemical and structural geology here have a brilliant field for study. Many new and rare mineral combinations may here be brought to light. The miner is interested in a district which presents more difficulties in following one's ore body than almost any others, and requires the most careful study of rock faces."[4] In other words, when mining in the Red Mountain district, no one knew what was going to happen next.

Not only finding but also refining the Red Mountain ore was a problem. Although the initial discoveries at Red Mountain were lead-based ores, the majority of the local ores were copper-based. Since most San Juan ore was lead-based, the Silverton and Durango smelters were not set up to inexpensively or effectively treat copper ores. As a result, much of the Red Mountain ore was shipped through Ouray or Silverton to be forwarded all the way to smelters in Denver or Pueblo. In November 1884, Durango reported the successful "blowing in" of a smelter that could reduce copper-based ores. The announcement was met with hopeful caution. "If the smelter at Animas City [a suburb of Durango] proves it can treat these copper ores at greatly reduced figures . . . at that moment the Red Mountain mining industry will receive a stimulus based on something tangible, a stimulus that will remain."[5] The smelter, unfortunately, proved to be only marginally efficient, and the *La Plata Miner* lamented that "if smelters could be built in Durango to treat the Red Mountain ores successfully, not a ton of them would be marketed north of the divide."[6]

The only reason any ore came through Ouray was that the distance by railroad was much shorter (and the rates cheaper) from Montrose to the Denver or Pueblo smelters than from Silverton. Enough ore was being shipped through Ouray to Montrose that the total ore shipped from San Juan County actually fell by about one thousand tons in 1884. With an adequate smelter in Durango, virtually all Red Mountain production would come out through Silverton.

Both the Ouray and Silverton papers were unhappy with the D&RG railroad. The editor in Silverton wanted that town's rates to be competitive with Montrose. "What is now of the most vital importance to every businessman, every mine owner and every miner in the country is cheap railroad transportation of the ores we send out of the country and upon the supplies we bring in to it."[7] Five weeks later, John Curry headlined a column "Railroad Extortion." He claimed that anywhere from one-third to three-fourths of the final price of goods shipped to Silverton was the cost of freight. On the other side of the divide, Dave Day was upset because the D&RG had cancelled its plans to extend the line from Montrose to Ouray. The railroad was now in the hands of a receiver and could not afford the expense. Again and again Day pointed out that low-grade Red Mountain ore wasn't worth shipping. He predicted that the amount of ore shipped through Ouray would double if only the D&RG would extend its line to his town.

Although transportation costs fell, most of the Red Mountain mines were experiencing increases with almost all other costs of production. For example, the Yankee Girl and the Guston seemed to have an ever-increasing need for newer and larger pumps because of water filling their shafts. Besides increased capacity, the need was also caused by acids in the water that could eat out the pumps' inner workings in a month or less. Candlesticks, picks, and other iron and steel tools were quickly coated with corrosive copper. Other items, like hoist cables, seemed to simply disintegrate. Miners covered everything possible with a thick heavy grease. The only permanent solution for pumping the acidic waters seemed to be expensive bronze-lined pumps. Some of the pumps cost up to thirty thousand dollars – a small fortune in the 1880s. Other expenses necessitated by the acids included replacing water lines with wooden troughs, using wood for mine rails, and replacing iron shaft cages with wooden ones.

Perhaps the greatest threat to the well-being of the Red Mountain Mining District was the slow and continuous fall in the price of silver. Before the year 1873, prices had never fallen below $1.29, but silver was quoted at $1.10 per ounce in early October 1884, and then dropped to $1.07 by the end of the year. The reason for the decline was simple economics – all the new silver discoveries throughout the United States produced too great a supply for the demand. The problem was often ignored in the San Juans, and on the rare occasions when it was recognized it was often minimized. In Silverton, for example, the *La Plata Miner* verified that a lot of new silver was being produced, but claimed that world demand should easily absorb the new production.

Even a small drop in the price of silver could have a disastrous effect on silver mining, since a mere five-cent-per-ounce decline in the value of silver could equal the entire cost of sending a high-grade ore to the smelters. Luckily, in 1884 the fall in silver didn't affect the Red Mountain district greatly because the value of lead was rising. As the *Ouray Times* pointed out: "Counting the decline of silver at eight cents, the depreciation of a car load of 150 ounce ore would amount to $120, but if the ore carried forty percent lead, the gain on that metal would be $100, reducing the absolute depreciation to $20.00."[8] However, this offsetting advantage was soon lost because the price of lead began to decrease, and the local ore changed from lead-based to copper-based.

At the very time that the supply of silver was increasing dramatically, demand for the metal was falling because the biggest purchasers of silver were trying to get out of the market. In 1873 the United States, as well as many European countries, had abandoned the bimetallist standard (the use of silver and gold, at a 16 to 1 ratio, to back their currency) in favor of the gold standard. By 1884, the United States government had cut back sharply on the minting of silver dollars in favor of using paper silver certificates. In the meantime, Colorado gold and silver mining had done a complete turnaround. As late as 1868, in terms of dollars the Territory of Colorado had produced four times as much gold as silver. Just twenty years later, Colorado produced four times as much silver as gold, even though the price of silver had fallen by thirty-five percent.

In 1878, in an effort to help the silver-mining industry, the Bland-Allison Act provided for the federal government's purchase of two to four million dollars of silver per year. This action supported the price of silver for a time, but the government decided to keep its purchases near the minimum. All of the Colorado communities pushed for a return to the bimetallist standard, or at the very least that both gold and silver be allowed as legal tender for paying the debts of the United States. The silver-producing states also desired unlimited coinage of silver at the old ratio of sixteen to one.

In the 1880s, Ouray, Silverton, and Red Mountain politics were totally dominated by the silver issue, and each of the towns had their own bimetallist associations. Dave Day devoted the front page of issue after issue of his paper to an attempt to reinstate the bimetallist standard and the fight against further actions that might devalue silver. "The fierce war that is being waged against the silver industry calls for liberal contributions and prompt action on the part of Ouray County."[9] Day insisted that a dollar of silver needed to be in every silver dollar. He pushed for the election to public office of only those who believed in the bimetal standard, and he suggested that the government should pay all foreign debts in silver. He noted that the United States, by value, held only half the amount of silver as gold and suggested the government should even up the situation. Day even suggested that the price for silver should remain high since, if silver mines closed, the United States would lose fifteen to twenty million dollars a year in gold that was recovered as a by-product of the silver mines.

As many and unique as the problems had been as the year 1884 drew to a close, most of the Red Mountain population had good reason to be optimistic. Silverton residents ended the year by inviting all of those on the divide to a giant celebration of the certain boom of the Red Mountain district. In what had become a local New Year's custom, the Ouray and Silverton papers took turns estimating how much ore had been shipped from the Red Mountain district in the past year. The *Solid Muldoon* put total production at $951,000, with just the Yankee Girl's share at $635,000. For some reason, the *La Plata Miner* placed the total production figure at only $300,000 but later revised the figure upward to $400,000, of which $340,000 was allocated to the Yankee Girl and National Belle mines. "The remaining $60,000 was produced from between thirty to forty properties."[10] Day, in response, declared that his figures were correct.

The National Belle and the Yankee Girl continued to be the premier mines on the divide during 1885. Each mine produced and shipped five to seven tons of very rich ore each day. Select ore often assayed up to five thousand ounces of silver per ton, and none of the Yankee Girl ore was worth less than two hundred dollars per ton. The *Solid Muldoon* felt that "as a sample of what the mine is capable of producing we will cite one instance of a lot of twelve tons being shipped this year which comes within $11,000 of paying the entire expense of the mine [for 1885], which with an average of fifty men at work is not inconsiderable."[11] After the Yankee Girl and National Belle, the best of the Red Mountain mines were the Genessee, Vanderbilt, Guston, and Silver Bell. The Yankee Girl and National Belle often hit rich pockets of concentrated, valuable ore. The other mines had to depend on larger deposits of lower-grade ores to show a profit.

As they went deeper, most of the Red Mountain mines were making richer discoveries. It became so common that new strikes received little, if any, attention. The *Solid Muldoon,* for example, would include only occasional small articles that stated in a few short sentences that "the high-grade ore recently encountered at the National Belle holds true. Assays of over $1,000 [per ton] have been had . . . Yankee Girl ore is averaging up to $2,700 per ton."[12]

Day reported that he suspected he was being used to exaggerate the values of some of the mines, and he maintained that it was his duty to keep up the credibility of the Red Mountain district. "The sooner such parties abandon the country or get down to legitimate work, the earlier they will get the help of the *Muldoon* and aid those of our citizens who prefer legitimate to wild-cat mining." Day felt that the sale of stock in bogus mines in the early 1880s had set Colorado mining back a decade, and he was bound and determined it would not happen again.

In 1885, George Crofutt visited Red Mountain to get information for

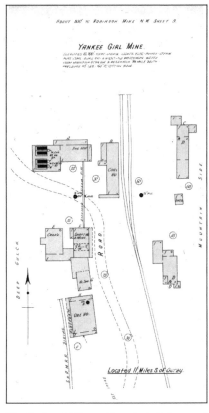

The Yankee Girl's workings included several railroad sidings of the Silverton and Red Mountain Railroad – the upper right for the delivery of coal and the lower left for the shipment of ore. There was an engine room for electrical power, steam heat, and electric lights that was reported to run night and day. *(Sanborn Map Company; author's collection)*

his Colorado guidebook, which was widely read and respected throughout the United States. He reported the district to be booming. Congress's population was estimated at 130, but he noted that its post office had been consolidated and moved to Chattanooga. The population of Ironton was placed at 125 (the 1885 Colorado census reported 181), and Red Mountain Town (including its nearby mines) had increased to 300 year-round inhabitants. Crofutt speculated that the Yankee Girl and National Belle might be among the most profitable mines in the world. Yankee Girl ore was optimistically reported to be running from four hundred to ten thousand dollars

This very early Yankee Girl photograph was taken in about 1883 and shows the day shift ready to proceed into the first-level tunnel. In the background, a pack train has been loaded with ore. This day's shift includes eight miners and six packers. Note the gun on the man in the center. *(Author's collection)*

per ton, but with an *average* of eight thousand dollars. "The National Belle is another mine that pays those that *wring* her, *big*."[13]

The exceedingly good reputation of the Red Mountain mines sometimes prompted the local owners to overestimate the true value of their property. They were also prone to fighting among themselves. The *Muldoon* mentioned "a strange fatality seems to attend many of the Red Mountain properties. Parties will start in on a splendid-looking property and after reaching their ore body, and with everything favorable to taking out pay, will immediately commence to quarreling and put a stop to further development. This reporter has had his attention called to a number of cases of this kind within the last few months and knows positively of some eight or ten claims that show pay mineral, but which lie idle as a result of quarreling between the owners."[14] In later issues, Day pointed out that the Red Mountain district seemed to be in a stalemate, since most of the prospectors were too poor to work their properties but were asking such high prices that an investor could not afford to buy a property and still produce a profit.

The lease system came into popularity in the mid-1880s as one answer to high production costs, low silver prices, and the high asking prices for local mines. Even the successful National Belle was worked, in part, under such an option.[15] A mine owner would lease his claim to an experienced miner or prospector, usually taking a royalty interest in the ore produced as his compensation. The mine owner profited by having his mine worked by a professional and by having no expenses while his mine was developed. The lessee profited because he did not have to pay the enormous prices that were being asked for the outright purchase of some of the better mines. "The lessors as a rule are men who live away from camp and who do not seem to care much whether their prospects are worked or not. The lessees, on the other hand, generally reside in the vicinity, and generally know what they are about when they take a lease . . . The leasing of mines will stimulate development and as a matter of course add largely to our annual output."[16]

As metal prices fell, some local mine owners hit upon another obvious way to reduce costs—lower the miners' wages. In Silverton, a meeting was quickly sponsored by the Knights of Labor. The miners present declared the minimum acceptable wage to be $2.50 per day plus room and board (which was worth about another dollar). The organizers wanted all of the miners present at the meeting in order to join the union, but organized labor was still a new phenomenon and only a small number of workers actually took the step. On the other side of the divide, Dave Day, loyal Democrat and champion of the common man, announced that "the *Muldoon* will oppose any and all attempts to reduce the wages of miners. A good miner earns every dollar he receives in this country." Day reported that miners made three to five dollars per day, common laborers two to three dollars per day, and servant girls twenty to thirty dollars per month. "There is no demand for preachers, lawyers, book agents, tramps or ornamental nuisances."

The decline in metal prices continued throughout 1885, with the price of silver eventually falling to less than one dollar per ounce in early 1886. The value of lead fell twenty percent to $.039 per pound, and copper dropped from $.185 a pound in 1882 to $.11 a pound in 1885—a forty percent decline in just three years. Many Colorado mines could not operate at these prices.

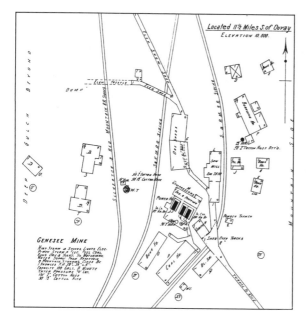

Many of the Genessee's buildings were dwellings or bunkhouses. A series of sheds covered most of the ore-car tracks, and two sidings came off the Silverton railroad. The grounds also included a sawmill, drying facilities, and a powder-thawing shack. (*Sanborn Map Company; author's collection*)

The richer ores of the Red Mountain district were still well worth mining, but some of the lower-grade ores that had been made economical by lower transportation costs were again made uneconomical by the falling metal prices. As the ores became richer and production costs were lowered, there should have been a great boom on Red Mountain, but because of the falling silver prices, most of the mines were only breaking even.

By July 17, 1885, the *Muldoon's* Red Mountain correspondent announced that "the weather is delightful and business is very up."[17] The wagon roads to the divide were open, and most mines immediately sent their winter's accumulation of ore to Silverton or Ouray. By the end of summer the Silver Bell was optimistically declared to be "a full sister" of the Yankee Girl, since assays of some select ore ran up to four thousand ounces of silver per ton. The Vanderbilt had mapped out great quantities of a lower-grade ore, and the Guston ore continued to get richer. Blasted, sacked, and shipped without sorting, it averaged forty-seven ounces of silver and thirty-seven percent lead. The *Rocky Mountain News* on November 25, 1885 reported "a rich strike in the Guston is being kept very quiet for reasons known only to the management. Assays have returned more than four thousand ounces of silver." The same article announced a rich strike at the Silver Link, where most of the ore had averaged only thirty dollars per ton, but assays of a small high-grade vein of three to seven inches ran 1,475 ounces of silver per ton! In the summer of 1885, Perry Terpenny developed an eleven-foot "hole" at the Vanderbilt, but his ore body was obviously extensive and valuable. Because the ore contained so much water, drying facilities became a major cost-cutter at the Genessee and Vanderbilt mines. As soon as the dryer was installed, ten percent of the ore's weight was eliminated, thereby considerably lowering freight costs.

In the hope of further cutting expenditures, eight of the bigger mines again brought in major new machinery in the fall of 1885. The major excitement was at the Yankee Girl, which had received a new 120-horsepower power plant. "It is the largest in the San Juan country and has but few equals in Colorado."[18] With the new machinery, the mine was expected to drive its shaft down to the one-thousand-foot level. As the year came to a close, the locals continued to be optimistic in spite of falling silver prices. Four times the amount of ore was now being shipped as at the same time the previous year. The *Solid Muldoon* estimated output for the Red Mountain district for 1885 at 14,111 tons of ore, worth $2,116,650. Red Mountain was the top district in the San Juans, and in Colorado only Leadville was doing better.

When summer finally came in 1886, Red Mountain Town was especially active. Three full stages ran daily, the local sawmill ran full-time, and a number of new buildings were under construction. Among other amenities, the town's citizens had installed a waterworks, constructed a one-room schoolhouse, and organized their own hook and ladder company to fight fires. At the mines, the Guston employed forty men, the Silver Bell thirty. "Last fall the *Muldoon* asserted that the Silver Bell was a full sister to the Yankee Girl . . . Now we take it all back. 'The Bell' is the Yankee Girl's mother, and today the most valuable property on Red Mountain."[19] Four weeks later, the same paper reported that "the largest shipment ever made by any mine in the Red Mountain area was sent out by Silver Bell teams on Friday. Twenty nine tons was the effort." Select Silver Bell ore assayed as high as one thousand to two thousand dollars per ton!

Day reported that only undeveloped or semideveloped properties could be purchased. "The Yankee Girl has now made two million dollars and is not for sale."[20] There were many capitalists looking to bond, lease, or buy mines, but "Red Mountain properties are being held at stiff figures and transfers are made only at royal figures."[21] The Yankee Girl continued its role as the leading mine on the divide. "The present ore body in the Yankee Girl is possibly unequaled for size and richness in the history of mining, being a fraction over thirty five feet and comparitably [sic] solid."[22] Soon the ore body had increased to fifty-six feet in width.

By summer 1886, the *Solid Muldoon* estimated that two thousand men were working on the divide. The first week that enough snow melted to allow good shipping, the Yankee Girl sent out "the first entire train load of ore from a Colorado mine . . . Twenty three car loads!"[23] The Saratoga was the major new discovery of 1886, with "assays running $200 to $2,400 in silver and also free gold!" However, overall production costs continued to rise at the very time that silver prices were plummeting. Even Dave Day was finally moved to suggest that "in times of adversity, when mine operators are conducting their exercises at a loss, miners should not be too exacting. Wages are entirely too high for the price of silver and it is better to submit to a slight reduction than close down properties that must remain idle all winter."[24]

The only cost factor that fell was shipping, which was now in the range of twenty to thirty dollars per ton from mine to smelter. But rather than being able to take advantage of the savings, mine after mine had to either shut down or stockpile its ore because the price of silver was so low and other costs were so high. The Guston, Silver Bell, Vanderbilt, and Genessee mines all either curtailed production or shut down completely. If matters weren't bad enough, there was a suspicion that the Pueblo and Denver smelters were not reporting the full value of the ore shipped to them. The Yankee Girl claimed it was cheated by six thousand dollars on three carloads of ore. The Silver Bell installed its own sampling works so that it would have a close estimate of the value of the ore it shipped to the smelters.

As silver prices fell, many of the big Red Mountain mines continued to ship ore, but Red Mountain was one of the few mining districts in the United States that had rich enough ore to still produce a profit. In the hope that metal prices would soon rebound, many of the mines concentrated on development work, such as the construction of roads or the installation of labor-saving machinery. Work forces were severely reduced at most of the mines. The Silver Bell cut back to fourteen men and the Guston to twenty, but the Yankee Girl continued with a work force of eighty miners plus several dozen laborers. The Yankee Girl shipped ten to fifteen tons of rich ore a day and continued to pay regular, if reduced, dividends to its stockholders. In fact, in terms of dividends, the Yankee Girl was second in Colorado only to the Small Hopes Mine of Leadville, having paid out over one million dollars in dividends in the year 1886 alone. The Silver Bell was second in production; it shipped more ore than the Yankee Girl, but of a lower grade. The Guston was third for 1886, shipping about 175 tons per month with an average assay of seventy-five ounces of silver per ton.

The year 1886 could be summed up as being one of uneasy prosperity. The mines had produced much greater quantities of an even richer ore, but with ore prices down and costs up, the profit margin was sometimes slim. The Red Mountain towns had grown, but their citizens constantly

Red Mountain Town was the premier settlement on the Red Mountain Divide in 1887. The Baxter Hotel is the large building to the left of Main Street. The ladders on the roof were for snow removal. Rough grading had been started on the railroad, but no track had been laid by this time. (*T. M. Moore photo; Colorado Historical Society*)

worried about being out of work. The management and ownership of most of the mines remained optimistic, often bringing in heavy machinery and even committing to small luxuries like the Guston manager's snug little bay-windowed cottage—said by many to be the finest manager's quarters in the San Juans.

Enough optimism existed that a new settlement called Liverpool was started "on the flats below Guston, near the Silver Bell mine." It obviously wasn't very substantial, because two weeks later the *Solid Muldoon* reported that "the big gale on Red Mountain played havoc with the new town of Liverpool, but it will be rebuilt as quickly as possible under the circumstances."[25] By May 1887, Day reported Liverpool to contain a general store, meat market, two saloons, and several boardinghouses. The town was even surveyed and platted, but within a year it was reported to be deserted.

Dave Day was the eternal optimist. He predicted that at "1,000 feet in depth, Red Mountain will disclose a body of ore that will be an eye opener. Remember the prediction."[26] Day felt that the ore in the Red Mountain volcanic pipes was pushed up from a huge body that lay at the bottom. It was a great idea, but not geologically valid. In his yearly wrap-up, Day boldly announced that "the Red Mountain mines are conceded to be the richest in the State, if not in the world, and the ore, on the average, is the most valuable ever produced by any mining camp."[27] Day estimated output for the Red Mountain Mining District for the year 1886 at 15,100 tons of ore worth $2,642,500.

The weather cleared so quickly in 1887 that the roads were open as early as March and prospecting was possible by early April. There was another reason for optimism – the price of silver had gone back up to a dollar. But additional problems seemed to blossom with the spring flowers. "Indications of lawsuits and bad blood generally are nearly ripe enough to cover a few mines at Red Mountain."[28] Even small suits seemed to flourish, such as the one that Red Mountain Town resident John Toy brought against his neighbor Andy Paubon for throwing garbage in Mr. Toy's backyard.

The biggest of the lawsuits involved control of the Guston Mine. D. C. Hartwell and Mrs. William Weston were two of the Guston's Class B shareholders, which meant the mine, if in financial trouble, could call on them for additional money. When a call was made, Weston and Hartwell failed to make their payments, and the Guston Mine was sold to an English syndicate. Mr. Weston had been the manager of the Guston, and there were allegations that his mismanagement had caused most of the mine's problems. Nevertheless, the two stockholders filed suit against the English company, claiming that the new English capital made it unnecessary for the stockholders to invest any more money. Mrs. Weston and Hartwell asked the court to appoint a receiver and declare the sale to the English null and void. Operations were suspended at the mine until the lawsuit could be tried.

Dave Day felt that Hartwell had done no purposeful misconduct but was furious at Mr. Weston and wrote: "The *Muldoon* has won a national reputation as an exposer of mining frauds. Since our entry into Colorado journalism we have exposed and driven to the wall, some of the worst 'wild-cat' schemes the history of mining has produced. We propose now to devote a slice of the future . . . to roasting William Weston of Ouray." Among other things, Day accused Weston of misusing company funds, mismanagement of the development of ore bodies, and purposely overstating the amount of ore in the mine. "The above is a record of a manager who seeks to pass only among strangers as a mining man."[29]

The English company easily won the lawsuit, and the Guston was reopened with T. E. Schwartz (also superintendent of the Yankee Girl) as manager. There were serious questions as to whether the Guston could ever produce at a profit again, but by August the mine was producing a medium-grade ore from its third level, and two weeks later a good grade of ore was found on its fourth level. "The finding of this ore in an abandoned mine speaks volumes of Mr. Schwartz as a mining engineer . . . Indications point to a boom for the Guston."[30] By July 1887, the same syndicate that ran the Yankee Girl and the Guston had also taken over the National Belle.

Schwartz continued to do well in his role as manager of the Yankee Girl. In 1887, its stock was selling for ten dollars a share, making its total capitalization $2,500,000. Standard Oil Company was reported to own the controlling interest. On its seventh level, "ore had been discovered by the acre." The Yankee Girl still kept eighty miners busy, with enough ore in sight to keep them going for five years. By the end of the year, the mine had built its own concentrating plant, which took forty tons of ore a day and concentrated it into ten tons for shipment. The Yankee Girl had produced three million dollars in ore during the five years the mine had been open.

The Silver Bell was one of the most productive Red Mountain mines in 1887. It shipped ten to twenty tons a day and worked fifty men. "The Bell" had been the first San Juan mine to put in a crushing plant and was estimated to have a five-year supply of ore in sight. But the mine had its problems. It pumped four thousand gallons of water an hour from its shaft and had not been able to keep up its cash flow. The Silver Bell was so much in debt that it often couldn't pay its miners, many of whom were forced to file liens against the property to ensure their payment. One day the mine was open, the next it was closed, the next it was being foreclosed on, and then it was operating again. Nevertheless, it was reported to have produced over $750,000 in five years.

The Genessee-Vanderbilt was purchased by a syndicate in October 1887 and worked twenty men. It was mining a very consistent low- to medium-grade ore. "Not a pound of mineral has been taken from it that does not have a marketable value and brought at least $30 per ton in silver and lead."[31] New machinery had been brought in and a new shaft house built. The mine was reported as ready to begin deeper mining, but it was waiting for the railroad to arrive before beginning any extensive shipment of ore. Most of the mines on Brown Mountain also had hit large quantities of low-grade ores. The Maud S., Belle of the West, and Saratoga were three of the best there.

During 1887, the population of Red Mountain Town continued to grow steadily. The 1887 Colorado State Business Directory listed its population at five hundred, and the number of businesses had grown proportionately. After an absence of any type of newspaper on the divide for a period of two years, the Red Mountain Journal started publication on October 1, 1887. The likes of a small town had also begun around the Guston Mine. "The town of Guston, near the mine from which it takes its name, has nine buildings erected and ten more underway. The business houses consist of two saloons,

This is a "backyard" photograph of the buildings on the west side of Main Street in Red Mountain Town when it was at or near its peak. As can be seen, there were a number of cabins, houses, and sheds packed in around Main Street. The National Belle Mine, to the left, dominates the town. (*Denver Public Library, Western History Department*)

one shoe shop, two restaurants and a miner's supply store . . . Three hundred miners do their business there and a petition has already gone in for a post office."[32] Ironton also was prospering, but the other settlements on the divide had begun to shrink in size.

On December 15, 1887, the D&RG railroad completed its extension from Montrose to Ouray, and ore could now be shipped much more inexpensively from the Ouray side of the divide than from Silverton. Day mentioned in his year-end summary for 1887 that total output for Ouray County was down one-fourth because the mines were waiting for the railroad to reach Ouray before they shipped huge stockpiles of low-grade ores. "Of course, they would be classified as high-grade ores in Leadville." Day detailed "low-grade" ore as averaging about twenty-one dollars per ton.[33] With the arrival of the railroad, Day predicted a gush of ore to come out through Ouray, but it was discouraging to Day that the mines closest to Ouray were all of the lowest grade. A reporter from the *Denver News* estimated Brown Mountain ores to average seven dollars in gold and thirteen to twenty dollars in silver and suggested the D&RG drop its rates to eight dollars per ton so that low-grade ore could be shipped economically.[34] Since it was also necessary to pay the cost of shipping to Ouray, the figures still wouldn't indicate that Brown Mountain ore could be shipped through Ouray at a profit. But the Saratoga Mine was building a mill in Ironton Park, and if a railroad could be constructed

In the late 1880s, a virtual maze of roads, mines, and railroad spurs existed on the lower slopes of Red Mountain No. 2. The Yankee Girl Mine is to the right, the Robinson-Guston is to the left. If you look closely, you can make out two different trains on the Silverton tracks, on the center right. (*S. G. White photo; Colorado Historical Society*)

Ironton in 1889 still had only one long street (named "Ouray"), which was lined with saloons, livery stables, hotels, and houses, in no particular order. The men on the left have come out of the saloon to greet a pack train from Ouray and have their picture taken. (*Colorado Historical Society*)

to the site, the ore could be concentrated and costs lowered enough to make the ore economical.

During most of 1887, rumors had been flying about that Otto Mears was up to something. Dave Day, tongue in cheek, suggested that Mears was going to float ore to Silverton by balloons. Mears himself wasn't taking any chances and did all he could to keep his project under wraps. When word finally leaked that Mears's project might be a railroad, the proposal was met with skepticism. Some felt that the slopes were too steep from Chattanooga up to the divide. Others pointed out that even the large D&RG railroad had given up on the plan. Dave Day (who had mentioned as early as July 1886 that "Mears is urging a railroad from Silverton to Chattanooga")[35] was concerned with the weather: "Mears will wake up some storming morning and find that his Silverton–Chattanooga summer route has bumped up against one of the Polar region's semi-daily slides and gone over to Ophir for vacation. Rail-roading around Silverton is about as profitable as engaging in some townsite schemes that we have heard of . . . If a branch [railroad] is to be built from Chattanooga it will be at the expense of a corporation other than the D&RG. This is official."[36] Later, Day conjectured that Guston would be the railroad's likely terminus, then later Ironton, and finally he predicted that the railroad would be in Ouray by August 1888.[37] It was as if Day didn't want to admit the possibility of the railroad, although he knew it was bound to happen. If he ignored it, maybe it would go away. If the railroad didn't build into Ouray, Silverton had won the battle to supply the Red Mountain towns and mines.

TEN

THE RAINBOW ROUTE

Otto Mears and other capitalists interested in the Red Mountain Mining District realized that although the wagon roads had lowered freight rates substantially, a railroad could drop rates even further. Each freight car carried a wagon or two in ore, and the railroad was more reliable, cheaper, and faster than the freight wagons. Mears made a careful survey of the Red Mountain mines, took stock of the value of their ores, and figured his construction costs. Unlike the D&RG, he was sure he could operate a railroad from Silverton to Red Mountain at a profit—perhaps as the most profitable railroad in Colorado. Mears predicted that ore with as little as twenty ounces of silver could be shipped economically on the railroad to the smelters.

On July 5, 1887, Otto Mears (President), Fred Walsen (Treasurer), John W. Wingate (Secretary), John Porter of the Durango Mining and Smelting Co., Sam Wood, George Crawford (Vice President), and O. P. Posey signed the incorporation papers for the Silverton Railroad Company. Its charter was issued by the state of Colorado three days later. Many of the local mines helped raise capital for the railroad by buying stock, the Yankee Girl alone subscribing for fifteen thousand dollars. The new railroad was started without a lot of money (invested capital was only seventy-six thousand dollars in 1888). It would eventually cost ten times that amount for its total construction and the purchase of all its equipment.[1] The intention was to follow the

162

The Silverton Railroad's survey crew has stopped in front of the house of the superintendent of the Yankee Girl Mine. The chief engineer, C. W. Gibbs, is the second person from the right. The railroad had already progressed to the top of Red Mountain Divide and was proceeding north. (*Denver Public Library, Western History Department*)

1883 survey made by Thomas Wigglesworth for the Denver and Rio Grande Railroad. Mears knew that the D&RG had abandoned the project not because the route to Red Mountain was impossible or unprofitable but because of the railroad's internal financial problems. The D&RG had concluded that it was impossible to extend the line the additional eight miles from Ironton to Ouray, but Mears felt the completion of a loop to be at least a possibility. The railroad would be narrow gauge (three feet between the tracks) and Mears planned to use thirty-pound rail, which was about the lightest possible. Narrow gauge allowed the rail to wind more easily along the mountainsides. The thirty-pound rail was cheap but, as time would show, did not hold up very well.

Because of heavy rains and the problem of raising sufficient capital, grading on the railroad did not get started until August 11, 1887, and track-laying did not commence until October 21, 1887. Once construction did get started, the laying of rail went quickly because the crews were, for the most part, following the route of Mears's wagon road. A hundred and fifty men were put to work, but an anxious Dave Day wrote, "at this rate the road will reach the Yankee Girl sometime in the year 1900."[2] The first train reached Chattanooga on October 20, 1887, where construction stopped for the winter. Otto Mears announced his hope that the Red Mountain mines would send out thirty carloads of ore per day on the Silverton Railroad the next year, and he suggested the mines store their winter production until they could ship on his line. Day realized that the railroad was certain to be successful. "Otto Mears has in his Silverton and Ouray Railroad a bonanza . . . Mears will be in a position to exact his own price, as he will certainly hold the key to the San Juan country."[3]

Even though it was still some distance away, the citizens of Red Mountain Town were excited at the prospect of the coming railroad. The *Red Mountain Mining Journal* suggested in its very first issue that "when the [railroad]

This photo was probably taken in September 1888 at the Chattanooga Loop. Silverton loco-motive number 100 is pulling a D&RG boxcar and a combination baggage-passenger car up the divide. In the lower part of the photo, a D&RG locomotive's tender and the handcart it is pulling are both filled with a work crew. Otto Mears stands beside the train. (*Denver Public Library, Western History Department*)

graders begin moving dirt through Red Mountain, a day be set apart by a number of our citizens and leisure hour people and that they make 500 feet of grade for the railroad. At the same time we should arrange to have a silver spike driven in the most central part of the track . . . We must certainly do something to show our appreciation for the coming event."[4]

Although work on the railroad had ceased with the first deep snows, the winter of 1887–1888 was spent planning the best ways to tackle the obstacles to come and buying equipment. On November 2, 1887, the Silver-ton Railroad bought its first locomotive (a class 60, 2-8-0 locomotive num-bered 42 and named "Anglo Saxon"). It was purchased from the D&RG for sixty-five hundred dollars and was immediately renumbered 100 and renamed "Ouray."

In the spring of 1888, Mears appointed Charles W. Gibbs, former assistant to Thomas Wigglesworth of the D&RG, to the position of chief engineer of the Silverton Railroad. Gibbs played a very important part in the railroad's construction, because Mears was often not physically on the site, having been previously appointed to oversee the building of the new Colorado capitol in Denver. It was at Mears's suggestion that the capitol dome be covered with its famous gold leaf, and a stained glass portrait of Mears was placed in the senate gallery to honor his many achievements. Gibbs more than capably

Even though it only had one coach (the "Yankee Girl"), there was a total of fifty passengers and crew on board the Silverton train this fine day in 1891. The location is Summit or Sheridan Junction at the top of the Red Mountain Divide—the hotel is to the right, the shed for the train is to the left. This was the highest point on the Rainbow Route. (*Denver Public Library, Western History Department*)

supervised the construction of the railroad, but he later described the Silverton Railroad as "the steepest [five-percent grade], the crookedest [thirty-degree curves] and the best paying road in Colorado."[5]

Although the winter snows were light, it was late May in 1888 before construction could start again. By June 1, the railroad's construction crews were making their way up the famous horseshoe curve at Chattanooga. Extensive use was made of inexpensive Mexican labor, with up to four hundred men working at any one time. At Chattanooga, Gibbs designed and built the first of several small bridges needed by the railroad. Usually bridges were a major part of the necessary engineering for a railroad, but on the Silverton Railroad, bridge construction was an easy task compared to other problems that needed to be conquered. Gibbs eventually designed and helped build three major engineering marvels on the Silverton Railroad.

The first was the layout of the track at the Chattanooga Loop, which made a two hundred–degree turn and then carried a five-percent grade for the next one and three-quarters miles. The Chattanooga Loop and some of the railroad's other curves on the divide were so tight that it was remarked "a burro needed hinges to get through them." By mid-July, regularly scheduled passenger and freight trains were running to Chattanooga. The Silverton Railroad reached Red Mountain Pass (which it dubbed the station of Summit) on July 22, 1888, and, at 11,075 feet in elevation at that station, it was immediately hailed as the highest railroad in the United States. At Summit, a large frame building was built to serve as an engine house, and a wye was constructed for turning the locomotive. In September, the railroad's first board of directors meeting was held in Silverton, and its stock and bonds were officially issued. Mears was continually looking for money, and he issued stocks and bonds on the Silverton Railroad well into the 1890s. He often took trips to the East to promote what he called "Rainbow Route money."

The Silverton Railroad reached Red Mountain Town on September 19, 1888, and Gibbs constructed his second marvel – the depot and the wye inside the incorporated limits of "The Town." Although wyes had been used before, they were seldom actually constructed in a business district, and never before had a depot been placed in the middle of a wye! This peculiar placement was necessary at Red Mountain Town because of the narrowness of the site, the geography of Red Mountain's two creeks, and the location of the National Belle at the Knob. Each leg of the wye was only 150 feet long, which was barely long enough for the locomotive and two or three cars – but the system worked!

By the end of 1888 the line had been extended a total of eleven miles to a point near Corkscrew Gulch, although officially only seven miles of track were open and operating. Spurs were being constructed for the Yankee Girl, Genessee-Vanderbilt, North Star, Silver Bell, and Guston mines. By December, Mears was shipping ore from the Yankee Girl, Genessee, and Guston. The earth-moving for the grade had been finished along the entire route, but the bridge over Red Mountain Creek wasn't finished, Corkscrew Gulch hadn't been conquered, and much of the track had not been laid. Nevertheless, the town of Ironton was booming in anticipation of the railroad. Wooden side-walks had been constructed on Main Street, a new schoolhouse had been built, and a water system was in the planning stages.

Since it had been another easy winter, track-laying resumed by early May 1889. The biggest challenge lay between Red Mountain Town and Ironton, where Corkscrew Gulch wound its way tortuously between Red Mountain No. 1 and No. 2. At first, Gibbs thought he could make it through Corkscrew by using a switchback, a wye, or a loop, but the details just didn't work out. There were important mines directly downhill from Corkscrew, and the little 2-8-0 engines didn't track well in reverse – especially in snow. Safety and efficiency also required the engine to be located downhill from the ore cars when on the spurs to the mines.

The day the first train arrived, on September 17, 1888, was an exciting one for the town of Red Mountain. The Silverton Railroad train consisted of only a locomotive, a D&RG freight car, and the combine called "Red Mountain." Several celebrities are in the process of transferring to stages and a coach for the ride to Ouray. There was no depot yet. Otto Mears stands at the rear platform; Ernest Ingersoll is in front of him. *(Thomas M. McKee photo; Denver Public Library, Western History Department)*

So the third engineering marvel was built. A fifty-foot turntable was placed on the main line of the railroad. At the Corkscrew turntable, the locomotive uncoupled, turned on the turntable, and went to the lower track. The cars then came down through the turntable by gravity, went to the lower track, and all was normal again—except the passengers were facing backward instead of forward. This led to the common saying in the Red Mountain district that the passengers never knew "whether the Silverton's engine was going or coming back."

By June 14, 1889, the turntable was in operation, although after only minimal winter operation it became obvious that it would have to be covered for protection from the heavy snows. Gibbs continued to lay track from Corkscrew along the additional mile and a half of grade toward Ironton. A twenty-five-hundred-dollar depot was built on the edge of town, and then laying of track continued to the small settlement of Albany (actually just the big Saratoga mill and a few cabins), where a final wye was built. In retrospect, the last part of the construction was unnecessary because the mines near Albany were never very successful, and further construction was stymied by the sheer walls and steep grades of the Uncompahgre canyon.

Mears didn't give up easily on this last challenge. He even went so far as to buy land in Ouray for a depot. But a six-percent grade was about maximum for the traditional locomotive, and that grade could only be maintained

By June of 1889 the newly constructed Corkscrew turntable had been covered, and the workers were busy building a shed over the track at the backside of the turntable building. A passenger train has passed through the turntable and is going uphill toward Guston. (*W. Carpenter photo; Denver Public Library, Western History Department*)

for very short distances. The normal grade could have been achieved by extensive rock-shelf construction and tunneling, but the feat would have been terribly expensive. A much cheaper idea was an electric railroad that was calculated to negotiate a seven-percent grade. A cog railroad could have negotiated ten-percent grades and would have allowed Mears to follow a route along the west side of the Uncompahgre canyon, leaving his wagon road open to pedestrians, horseback riders, and wagons. But Mears's concepts were only dreams, and in the meantime the stagecoach met the train at Ironton and transported baggage and passengers the last few miles to Ouray.

The total cost to build the Silverton Railroad and purchase the necessary equipment was $725,000. The railroad issued $425,000 in bonds, and the rest came from small purchases of stock, gifts, or Mears's own pocket. It was an unheard-of amount of money for one man to raise in those days. Mears set the passenger fare at twenty cents per mile. The smaller Silverton locomotives could only pull a maximum of four passenger or baggage cars, so a passenger train ran twice a day, every day. It left Silverton at 7:00 A.M.,

Ironton's little white church is visible on the hillside to the left in this 1889 photograph. The depot is slightly to the left of and above the church. The main line of the Silverton Railroad passes above the town. The tailings pond that exists today does not cover the town site itself but rather the flats to the east of town. (*W. H. Jackson photo; Colorado Historical Society*)

Ironton at 9:10 A.M., Silverton again at 1:10 P.M., and Ironton at 3:20 P.M. Additional trains were often run for special events like dances or emergencies, such as the one on February 8, 1890, when a special "mercy train" carrying Dr. J. W. Brown made it from Silverton to Red Mountain in twenty-three minutes to bring help to an injured miner.[6] The train caused at least one new problem – forest fires. The July 12, 1889 *Solid Muldoon* mentioned that "the forest fire occasioned by Mears' locomotives, aside from destroying considerable timber, came near to taking the Genessee-Vanderbilt ore house and other buildings on neighboring mines."

Passenger traffic was actually of secondary importance, because the coming of the railroad meant that low-grade Red Mountain ore could now be profitably shipped. In Dave Day's official announcement of the opening of the Silverton Railroad he wrote, "A heavy burden has been lifted from the shoulders of the mine owners and operators by the decrease in traffic rates and prices of fuel and supplies of every character."[7] Four regular freight trains were run each day, and extra freights were put on line when necessary. Since, during a good part of its existence, the Silverton Railroad only owned one locomotive, it was often necessary to borrow locomotives from other lines. The freights could pull three to five loaded cars up the divide, depending on the size of the locomotive used. It was normal to bring down ten loaded cars at a time.

Due in large part to the railroad, the Red Mountain Mining District entered another era of prosperity. In fact, after the coming of the railroad, the Red Mountain district was as lively as at any time since the initial boom of 1883. Thousands of tons of low-grade ore were now economically shipped out, and wealthy investors could easily be brought in to inspect prospective purchases. The old truism "it takes money to make money" is especially evident in the mining business, and eventually millions of dollars of English and American capital were invested in the local mines. It became a close race as to whether more money was made in the district by selling stock or by mining ore.

The coming of the railroad also coincided nicely with the development of new ore-reduction processes that allowed better recovery of the precious metals. An even lower-grade ore could be milled at a profit, again putting more emphasis on the inexpensive shipping costs brought about by the railroad. Shipping rates from the Red Mountain mines to the Pueblo smelters, which by mule had run as high as one hundred dollars per ton, now fell to less than forty dollars per ton. Even cheaper rates were available if closer smelters (such as those in Durango) could be used. From 1888 to 1890, the San Juan and New York Smelting Company in Durango continued to improve its processes until, eventually, none of the little Silverton smelters could compete. A large percentage of Red Mountain ore was then smelted in Durango, but the San Juan and New York smelter always operated very close to a loss because of continually falling silver prices.

With the advent of the railroad, the Red Mountain towns all looked successful. Real estate prices jumped twenty-five percent throughout the district. Silverton merchants were excited that the Red Mountain ore would now come out through San Juan County, and most of the needed supplies would be brought into the district on the return trip. Huge amounts of coal could now be shipped in from mines near Durango, which further lowered costs. All of the activity caused the February, 14, 1889 *San Juan Democrat* to remark that "Red Mountain is destined to become a great metropolis, as one of these days it will take into its corporate limits such suburban villages as Sheridan Junction, Ironton, Guston and the high line trail [the pack trail to Telluride]." Although the price of silver had already rebounded slightly in the late 1880s (silver was $.91 per ounce in May 1889 and up to $1.17 in August 1890), federal legislators bowed to pressure from western constituents and, through the Sherman Silver Purchase Act of 1890, raised the government's guarantee of silver purchases to a total of 4.5 million ounces. The purchase guarantee amounted to virtually all silver produced in the United States at the time. Silver prices continued to rise sharply, eventually hitting $1.50 for a short period of time.

By 1890, the railroad facilities had been well developed at Red Mountain. The depot was built on piles in the center of the wye. The extreme north end of Red Mountain Town's Main Street is to the left, and the small two-cell jail is the first building on the right. A freighter unloads a boxcar, and locomotive number 100, "Ouray," turns on the track. (*Charles Goodman photo; Colorado Historical Society*)

The price of silver had fluctuated so widely in the 1880s that the sale of "futures" had become popular. This, in turn, seemed to make the fluctuations even worse as the price came to be based mainly on speculation. No one knew what the price of silver would do next, but most of the men on the divide were certain it would go up. Some investors even predicted the price of silver would catch the price of gold.

In the fall of 1889, as the price of metals rebounded, many more men were hired at the Red Mountain mines. But, unfortunately, the weather didn't cooperate, and in 1890 winter storms often closed the Silverton Railroad. If a mine continued production, it wasn't long before its ore house was filled. Ore was sometimes stacked alongside the tracks, and it wasn't long before there was no more storage available. It was a nightmare for the mine owners – the price of silver was high, but they couldn't ship their ore. Most of the mines had to cease production until shipping could be resumed. By spring of 1890, the mines were working again at full capacity. The *Muldoon* reported that "Red Mountain is more active than for years, thousands are being spent in mills and machinery, and over a quarter of a million in shipments are made monthly."[8]

Unfortunately, the rise in the price of silver was short-lived. By the end of 1890 it was evident that the federal government was buying much more silver

Sometimes we forget just how small the narrow-gauge locomotives were and how deep the snow could get at Red Mountain. This photograph was taken in the neighborhood of the Guston or Yankee Boy mines near the end of a harsh winter. Locomotive number 100 leads another locomotive (visible behind it and to the right) into the snow-clearing operations. *(Frank Pecchio photo; Denver Public Library, Western History Department)*

than was needed, and the price of silver again slipped to below a dollar by January 1891. The roller coaster rise and fall of silver prices played havoc with the operation of the Red Mountain mines. By late 1890, only the Guston Mine might be called truly prosperous. The Guston might have been called the mine that the Silverton Railroad built. Its development had gone slowly until 1888, but when the railroad was under construction and the price of silver rebounded, the Guston had been purchased by an English syndicate that went public with its stock. By May 1889, the Guston had been pronounced the leading mine of the Red Mountain Mining District by both Dave Day and the Ouray County tax assessor.

Even the Yankee Girl seemed to be in trouble, although its shaft was down 960 feet and it was still producing more ore than any mine in the district. The trouble was that it required "a vast amount of currency to mine at that depth."[9] A sure sign of the Yankee Girl's future was the resignation of manager T. E. Schwartz in August 1889. He quoted two reasons for leaving: short-sighted owners who hampered development work, and ever-greater quantities of acidic water that had decreased output significantly. Schwartz shifted his efforts to upgrading the Genessee-Vanderbilt. In October 1888, the owners of the Genessee had bought the Vanderbilt for a reported half-million dollars,

The Guston-Robinson complex takes up most of this photo from about 1890. The Congregational church sits on the hill at the right; above and to the right of the church are the Yankee Girl stacks, and behind them is the Knob. The settlement of Guston is scattered among the hills to the right, and the buildings of the Guston Mill and Mine are on the left. (*Thomas M. McKee photo; Denver Public Library, Western History Department*)

and early the next year the workings were combined when the new owners discovered that the four pipes at the surface turned into one common ore body at depth. No extremely rich ore was ever found, but the Genessee-Vanderbilt had large amounts of low- and medium-grade ore to ship.

In late 1889 there was an attempt to sell the Yankee Girl Mine to British interests, but Day declared that there was "some kind of scheme afoot." He claimed the last of the rich ore in the mine had been shipped,[10] but the Yankee Girl, at least for the near future, continued to produce an enormous amount of valuable ore for a mine that was supposed to be played out. At the time of Day's pronouncement, it was shipping ore from a vein that ran three thousand dollars per ounce—the highest grade ever to come out of the mine. All during 1890 and 1891 the Yankee Girl shipped the highest dollar amount of ore in the district, but the mine was being gutted—all the previously known rich ore was being shipped, and the only new discoveries were low-grade ore. In 1890 and 1891, the Yankee Girl and the Guston combined to ship more than half of the ore that came out of the Red Mountain district—each showing a profit of twenty-five thousand to ninety thousand dollars per month.

At the Guston, Schwartz was setting up a systematic plan of deep development even before shipment of its ore began. The price of Guston stock skyrocketed from $.06 a share to almost $15.00. During 1889, many carloads of "first-class ore" that averaged 300 to 450 ounces of silver per ton were sent out. Most "second-class ore" averaged one hundred to three hundred ounces of silver. At a depth of two hundred feet, some handpicked ore contained fifteen thousand ounces of silver and three ounces of gold. It was the richest ore discovered in quantity at any time during the history of the Red Mountain Mining District. Schwartz resigned as manager of the Guston in March 1890, but the *Solid Muldoon* of March 14, 1890 reported that "Schwartz has left clear sailing for his successor and we'll look for great things to come of the Guston in the future."

With the high price of silver, the output of the Red Mountain district in 1890 increased to twenty thousand tons of ore worth over four million dollars. Almost forty percent of the dollar growth was due to the increase in the price being paid for silver. The United States Mint validated the 1890 output of silver alone for the Yankee Girl at $1,352,994 and for the Guston at $1,173,051. The former paid a dividend of forty-five percent of the par value of its stock and the latter an eighty-percent dividend. In July 1890, the rumors proved true, and the Yankee Girl was, in fact, sold to an English syndicate for $1,300,000. It wasn't until November 1891 that the Guston actually passed the Yankee Girl in terms of value of ore shipped; by December of the same year, the Yankee Girl's production had fallen to twenty-eight thousand dollars for the month as compared to over one hundred thousand dollars at the Guston. In 1891, the Guston produced ore totaling $824,000, but the amount of water coming into its shaft had increased from thirty-five to fifty gallons per minute, and the sulfuric acid content also was getting higher. Nevertheless, the mine was like a rock in the highly unpredictable times of the late 1880s and early 1890s. Not one in ten Colorado mines ever paid a cent of dividends to stockholders. Yet in the ten-year period between 1888 and 1897, the Guston was able to return over one million dollars to its investors.

By 1891, Guston had also become a "town"—a collection of houses scattered up and down the little hills and gullies near the mine. As Red Mountain Town had been the early bloomer at Red Mountain, the town of Guston was the late bloomer. By 1892, more than two hundred people lived near the mine, and a post office was established on January 26, 1892. The Robinson Mine was eventually incorporated into the Guston workings, and reference to the "town of Guston" was usually expanded to include the workings and houses at the Yankee Girl and Genessee-Vanderbilt.

Although Guston was growing quickly, the older settlement of Red Mountain Town also continued to prosper. By 1890, its population had risen to over six hundred. A schoolhouse had been built, and the town had a telephone office. In 1890, Frank Hall, in his *History of Colorado,* could write "the town

In 1890, Red Mountain Town's Main Street had been extended for another block to the south, and the sidewalk continued for another block to the residential section on the west. The schoolhouse is at the far left. The toll road to Ouray begins at the end of Main Street, and, although it is hard to see in this photograph, the train waits at the depot on the far northern end of town. *(W. H. Jackson photo; Colorado Historical Society)*

of Red Mountain, at first a collection of small tents, now bears the characteristics of a hurriedly built mining settlement."[11] That same year, Reverend Gibbons wrote that "Red Mountain camp was on the top of the range, 11,000 feet above sea level. Everyone had work, and if I remember aright the wages was three dollars and fifty cents a day. It was easier to get money than specimens of the peacock and ruby silver, which came from the famous Yankee Girl."[12] For better or worse, the town was at its peak.

On the other side of the divide, the settlement of Chattanooga was suffering. In the late 1880s the town had been hit by a major snowslide. Its population at the time of the disaster was fifty-two; after the slide its adult population was reduced to only two. "One of these inhabitants kept a saloon which was sort of a half-way house between Red Mountain and Silverton. The other, who was a widow with many children, appeared to be in the laundry business, for the clothes lines were always full."[13]

Ironton had, for all practical purposes, become the terminus of the Silverton Railroad, and as such the town boomed as a transportation and freighting center. The coach from Ouray stopped there several times a day, and the two trains that arrived daily sometimes carried as many as two hundred passengers. In the summer, many of the stage and train passengers were tourists who were making "The Circle Route"—the scenic loop from Denver through Colorado's spectacular mountains. The very first advertisements for the Rainbow Route, which were (à la Mears) very ornate and beautiful, touted the Silverton Railroad as "the gold and silver clasp to the girdle of attractions on the trip 'Around the Circle.'" Tickets cost $18.50, and the trip took five days. Layovers could be taken at any of the towns along the route as long as the round trip was completed within thirty days. It was estimated that ten thousand tourists decided to take "The Circle Route" in the summer of 1889.

The town of Ironton completed its water works and built an electric plant in 1889. The completion of its water system prompted Dave Day to write that "Ironton's citizens are quite proud of their new water works, and most of them are learning to wash before breakfast and bathe once a month. As a beverage, they have no use for water."[14] By 1890, the census listed the town's population as 323. Ironton had its promoters, some of whom got a little carried away: "A number of God's own people inhabit this beautiful dell, sorrow and strife do not exist there, while peace and plenty reign supreme."[15] Dave Day predicted that "Ironton will be the new metropolis of the Red Mountain country and the fellows on the Divide should reconcile themselves to this fact."[16]

After the arrival of the railroad, most of the Red Mountain mines continued to struggle to make a profit because of the wildly fluctuating price of silver. The Silver Bell was sold to capitalists in June 1890 for $150,000. Some of its production was a very rich silver ore that contained up to one thousand ounces of silver per ton, but "The Bell" continued to have major cash-flow problems. Several times in the early 1890s the papers reported that "the Deputy U.S. Marshall went up to Ironton this morning to sell the Silver Bell again."[17] Unfortunately, as the mine got deeper, the ore changed to a much lower grade, which consisted chiefly of pyrites and carried less than twenty ounces of silver. The Silver Bell, the National Belle, and several other Red Mountain mines were bought by American Belle Mines of London in 1890, capitalized for two million dollars, and worked until 1894.

In the first few years after the arrival of the Silverton Railroad, the district was continually worked at close to full capacity. Each year the Red Mountain mines had shipped an average of twenty-five hundred carloads of ore and, correspondingly, imported fifteen hundred carloads of coal. Dave Day reported that "Otto Mear's Rainbow Route is taxed to its utmost capacity to carry coal and supplies to the upper Red Mountain country,"[18] and "the Rainbow Route is doing a splendid business. The receipts are in excess of $500 per day."[19]

It was David Day who named the little Silverton Railroad "The Rainbow Route." The nickname was so popular that it was immediately taken up by the railroad and used in some of its earliest advertising. The *Silverton Weekly Miner* explained why the name was appropriate: "Originating in Silverton, where it connects with the D&RG system, it runs north twenty miles and ends. Half the distance it ascends the mountain at an average grade of 212 feet to the mile, crossing the pass at an altitude of 11,650 feet. From this point, surrounded by the snows of centuries, it descends to Ironton, at about the same grade, making a bow over the mountains, hence the name "The Rainbow Route."[20] The wealth of scenery along the way and the pots of gold (unfortunately mainly silver) at the mines in the Red Mountain Mining District were also certainly good reasons for the name.

The Silverton Railroad surely seemed to be a pot of gold. It made twice the normal rate of return for a railroad – enough profit to allow Mears to finance a great part of the construction of the Rio Grande Southern Railroad from Durango to Ridgway. One reason Mears made such good profits was the railroad's evidently misstated mileage. Passenger rates were a hefty twenty cents per mile. Mears made an extra profit by showing the Silverton Railroad as twenty percent longer than it actually was, thereby making his effective rates twenty-four cents per mile. Another initial reason for the railroad's good economic showing was Mears's incredible timing, matching the building of the Silverton Railroad with the high prices of the Sherman Silver Purchase Act of 1890.

Since the Silverton Railroad was taking the vast majority of the ore from the Red Mountain district, the D&RG decided to drop freight rates in Ouray. Although the Silverton could pick up the ore at a mine's doorstep, the railroad route from Ouray to Denver was still quite a bit shorter than through Durango. When rates were cut to eight dollars per ton for low-grade, nine dollars per ton for middle-grade, and ten dollars per ton for high-grade ore, some of the Red Mountain mines shipped through Ouray. Day had pushed for the lower rates for years and now notified his readers that "miners can now commence on their low grade mines or else indulge in a roasting from the *Muldoon*. We have secured a reduction in the rates and want a positive and pronounced response."[21]

The building of the Silverton Railroad had actually helped to strengthen the economy of both Silverton and Ouray. "The effect has been witnessed in the increasing number of mines developed, and in the heavy increase of receipts at the smelters, in the multiplication of people, and the steady growing of wealth acquired."[22] Although some ore had been refined in Silverton, in 1889 Otto Mears helped organize a group to build a Durango smelter that could properly treat the high copper content of most Red Mountain ores. The smelter became known as the Standard Smelter and sat on the banks of the

Animas River to the south of town. With an adequate smelter in Durango there was no reason for any of the mines to ship via Ouray. Durango merchants benefited from the smelter and, on the return trip, the Silverton Railroad brought thousands of tons of Durango coal to the Red Mountain Mining District.

By the early 1890s, the Silverton Railroad owned three locomotives, two passenger cars (named "The Red Mountain" and "The Yankee Girl"), a baggage-express car, and fifty freight cars. Mears's pride and joy was a Pullman car he named "Animas Forks" because it also ran on the line from Silverton to that town. It was rebuilt into a combination restaurant and sleeping car that carried an elaborate variety of wines and liquors as well as a wonderful menu that included such exotic items as oxtail soup, caviar, fresh asparagus tips, and plum pudding. Certainly such a car was not needed on the short little railroad, but it helped to impress the capitalists being brought into the Red Mountain district and gained the Silverton Railroad notoriety – exactly the type of free publicity Otto Mears was hoping for.

Another of Mears's advertising gimmicks was his unique railroad passes. All railroads gave free paper passes to dignitaries, clergymen, and the owners of other railroads, but Mears didn't give out the usual cheap cardboard pass. The Silverton's were made out of lambskin, white buckskin, silver, and even gold! They were not just in the normal card shape but were made into watch fobs, lockets, medallions, and even spoons. Pass number one of both the 1888 lambskin and the 1889 silver version went to his good friend and supporter David Day.

The Silverton Railroad's profits increased from $21,000 in 1889 to $29,000 in 1890 to $38,500 in 1891. The railroad so completely dominated the transportation of ore from Red Mountain that Frank Hall in his *History of Colorado* reported all the mines of the Red Mountain district to be in Ouray County, "but the products of these mines are conveyed to Silverton as the *only* outlet to market . . . From the fact that both Ouray and San Juan counties claim credit for the products of Red Mountain, which is the largest producer of Southwestern Colorado, it is almost impossible to discover the true output of each county."[23]

The Red Mountain mines, although producing vast amounts of ore, were now faced with ever-greater amounts of sulfuric acid in the mine water. The problem was brought about by water and air reacting with the pyrites and copper sulphides. The acids ate holes in anything made of iron or steel. Almost every day a tube had to be replaced in the boilers, and hoisting cables had to be coated constantly with heavy, sticky grease. Every month the shaft cages had to be taken apart, repaired, painted, and put back together. Even the nails in planks were eaten away, sometimes dropping heavy timbers on

The Yankee Girl Mine was at its peak in 1890. In addition to the switchback that entered the property at the center of the photograph, the Yankee Girl owned the central spur that the boxcar to the lower left is on, to bring in fuel, as well as a still lower spur used to pick up ore. (*W. H. Jackson photo; Colorado Historical Society*

miners or making ladders unsafe. The acids were so strong that on one occasion they were reported to have eaten through a three-inch pipe in just nine hours.[24] The *Muldoon* reported that at the Yankee Girl, "the iron pipes from the pumps have been taken out regularly, the threads joining the pipes having been eaten away, thereby rendering them useless, and two weeks to a month seems to be the limit of life of iron piping."[25] Day suggested that threadless pipe be used—bolted together through overlapping flanges "like is done in acid factories." The mine actually opted for iron pipe lined with a wooden casing. Water was a major problem simply because there was so much of it. Most Red Mountain mines eventually came to a point where the pumps could no longer pull the water out. Then there were only two possible choices: an adit (a horizontal tunnel) could be driven to drain the mine, or the mine could choose to close.

Despite the district's problems, the *Muldoon* remained optimistic and boasted that "Red Mountain is the banner district of the world . . . We challenge the State of Colorado, the United States, the Earth to duplicate the Red Mountain country."[26] Day also took the time to congratulate Posey and Crawford for getting so much English capital into the district. In March 1891 they had sold the American Belle group to an English syndicate for $1,750,000. The English were anxious to invest in the Red Mountain Mining District because they usually made a good return on their money. Dave Day pointed out that

This photograph of the east side of Main Street was taken in the winter of 1891–1892, before the fire that burned Red Mountain Town to the ground. The City Laundry building is second from right, the Rainbow Restaurant is the white building near the center, and the two-and-a-half-story building at the left with men standing on the upper porch is the Red Mountain Hotel, where the fire started. *(Thomas M. McKee photo; Denver Public Library, Western History Department)*

"for every dollar of English capital placed in Red Mountain, the investors have taken out $50."[27] It was a gross exaggeration. Some investors in the Yankee Girl and Guston were getting close to a one-hundred-percent-a-year return on their original investment; however, many other Red Mountain mines never returned a dollar in dividends. By the spring of 1891, Posey and Crawford had tied up so many Red Mountain mines that they began to negotiate to buy the Silverton Railroad. Otto Mears admitted the negotiations were taking place but mentioned that the principals were still two hundred thousand dollars apart on the price.

With high silver prices, the spring of 1891 was a good time for production. Most mines were clamoring to get their ore out by May of that year. Day announced that "the yell for cars that emanates from Red Mountain can be heard in Utah."[28] The shipments were slow to start because melting snows had washed out or made the track unstable in many places, but by June activity on the divide was downright hectic. Since the price of silver remained high for most of the year, the mines were being worked for all they were worth. More ore was shipped than at any other time in the history of the Red Mountain district. The Yankee Girl's annual report ending June 30, 1891 showed that it produced $805,255 in ore and paid dividends of $520,000. The Guston paid only forty-four thousand dollars in dividends in 1891, but its reputation remained strong. Its total paid dividends had passed the one-million mark, and the market value of its stock was $1,925,000. By December 1891, the price of silver was again taking a nosedive. "Snowstorms have interfered with ore shipments this week, but the low price of silver and lead justifies a reduced output."[29] By February 1892, silver had fallen to $.90 per ounce.

Meanwhile, Dave Day's desire to get the D&RG railroad to Ouray, matched with his often self-righteous attitude, got him into serious trouble. In 1886, when the Ouray branch of the D&RG was under construction, Day decided the railroad could not possibly come to Ouray because of steep grades. He felt the tracks had to stop at the small settlement known as Portland, a few miles north of Ouray. He began buying land and promoting Portland as "the metropolis of the San Juans." Ouray citizens were irate that he had abandoned their town so quickly. Soon they were boycotting Day, although he claimed the boycott did him little harm. The final irony was that the D&RG switched its planned route to the west side of the Uncompahgre River and brought the railroad to Ouray successfully. Although Day returned every dollar that had been invested in his venture, the merchants of Ouray never forgave him and cut back severely on their advertising. At Mears's request, Day finally agreed to move to Durango. The last issue of the *Solid Muldoon* was published February 12, 1892, and Day announced that "our regrets for leaving Ouray are of a purely social character, as the move viewed from a financial and business standpoint is superb."

ELEVEN

<hr>

THE BUST

By January 1892, all of the Red Mountain mines had major production problems, from which most would never recover. In late 1891, the shaft house of the Silver Ledge Mine burned, igniting forty pounds of dynamite in the powder house and blowing most of the mine's surface buildings into small pieces. By 1892, the Genessee-Vanderbilt's shaft carried so much water that it was necessary to blast an 820-foot tunnel through absolutely barren rock for drainage. Then, on August 13, 1892, despite the courageous efforts of the extremely efficient fire department, a fire destroyed the entire business section of Red Mountain Town. About fifteen large commercial buildings at the northern end of Main Street, as well as many smaller structures, were decimated. The fire started in the Red Mountain Hotel, and the town's dried frame buildings were packed so close together that the northern part of town was instantly ablaze. "The Town of Red Mountain is ashes. The fire broke out about 3 o'clock this morning and by day-break not a single important building in the place was left standing. The loss was estimated at $75,000. There was insurance of only $15,000."[1]

The immediate suspicion was that the fire was purposely started; it definitely was well on its way before the fire department responded. A child swore that she saw men pouring coal oil on the floor of the vacant hotel the day before the fire. She recalled the pandemonium of the night: "Women threw

Smoke still rises from the ruins of Red Mountain Town in this photograph, taken after the devastating August 12, 1892, fire. Women and children are included among those who arrived to witness the disaster; the fire hoses, to the right, still hadn't been reeled in. The destruction was obviously complete. (*Colorado Historical Society*)

china from second floor windows in an effort to save their precious possessions; couples quarreled over what to save until the whole house burned down with everything in it destroyed."[2] Only the jailhouse and the depot on the northern end of town were saved.

One miner reminisced that "everybody began piling furniture and bedding in the middle of the street. I can see them yet—men staggering out of the pool halls with billiard tables and roulette wheels, and women carrying silly things like lamps and quilts. Before they got them all piled up the wind changed, and the flames licked everything up."[3] Some felt that the fire was overdue. "The town has never been provided with serviceable water works and the calamity which befell Red Mountain has often been predicted . . . In one hour from the starting of the fire, the people of Red Mountain found themselves homeless, and practically without food. Tents, clothing and provisions were at once ordered from Silverton, and Moses Livermann, general manager of the Silverton Railroad, tendered the citizens a special train."[4]

Red Mountain Town never really fully recovered, although some tents were in use and a few buildings were being rebuilt the same day as the fire. Guston's preacher moralized that God had sent judgment to Red Mountain Town for His treatment while trying to start His new church. In fact, he had predicted that "God would perhaps send judgment to Red Mountain Town, as he once did some thousands of years before to wicked Sodom and Gomorrah . . . You can't fight God and prosper."[5]

Perhaps the most important factor that sealed the fate of the Red Mountain Mining District happened several hundred miles away when, in 1891, Cripple Creek roared into prominence as a gold-producer. It quickly became the new "glamour girl" of the mining world and completely overshadowed the Red Mountain district. On a more local level, "The Gold Belt" was discovered at the same time a mile north of Ouray. Colorado's glorious silver days were over. The state owed its beginnings to gold and now returned to gold. "The Silver State" was a slogan that had only applied to Colorado in the 1870s and 1880s. Although the district was not totally dead, the boom times of the Red Mountain Mining District had lasted less than ten years.

Those in the Red Mountain district kept up their hopes. Looking back is so much easier than trying to understand events at the time they are happening. On January 22, 1892, David Day announced that Mears's Ouray–Ironton Electric Railway, Power and Light had been granted all necessary franchises to begin construction. Mears said he "had never given up the idea of finishing the connecting link," and he predicted that the electric railroad would substantially lower transportation costs. He went so far as to have a survey completed in the summer of 1892, and charted the entire eight-mile route in detail. Even with thirty-five-degree curves and a seven-percent grade, the electric railroad would require considerable tunneling, and its cost was estimated at a staggering eight hundred thousand dollars. Perhaps Mears believed the Silverton Railroad could bear the cost. Treasurer John McNeil wrote in March 1892 that "there is every reason to expect that the earnings for the year 1892 will increase in the same proportion as the past, and will continue for a great many years."[6]

In the meantime, the price of silver continued to slide. This time the decline seemed never to stop. Silver was at $.87 an ounce at the beginning of 1893, $.78 a couple of months later, and down to $.63 by June, when the British decided to stop mining silver rupees in India. The United States was in a recession and could not afford to keep up its purchases. Rumors of the repeal of the Silver Purchase Act started spreading, and when President Cleveland actually asked for such, the House of Representatives was quick to give its approval. But western senators began a filibuster, holding off passage of the act. Based on fears of the repeal, the economy of the San Juans went into a recession. The *Silverton Standard* reported: "So far there has been no suffering among the poor people in town. The town trustees at their last meeting instructed the marshall to give employment to the men with families only, and let the single men rustle somewhere else."[7]

Because of the long Senate filibuster, it wasn't until October 30, 1893 that the Silver Purchase Act was repealed by a vote of forty-eight to thirty-seven. The price of silver fell to fifty cents an ounce within minutes of the repeal. The crash of 1893 hit the San Juans hard. Banks closed, businesses failed, large bands of men roamed the country looking for jobs. Total panic had struck. Boomtowns became ghost towns in a matter of weeks. Thousands of miners were soon out of work, which further strengthened the working man's desire for better conditions and more stability in the working place. Many miners began to turn to unions as the answer to their fears.

At the Red Mountain district, some of the mines were so profitable that they continued to operate even as hundreds of mines closed across the United States. However, operating expenses continued to climb. In most mines, larger and more expensive pumps were continually needed to contend with ever-larger quantities of water that contained ever-higher levels of acids. As the price of silver fell, most Red Mountain mines cut back sharply on their ore shipments. The grade of most ore was falling, and some of the English-owned companies waited for an improved smelter to open in Silverton before shipping their ore. As the number of miners employed at the Red Mountain mines dropped, the volume of railroad passengers fell. The passenger and freight traffic dropped so rapidly that Otto Mears's Rio Grande Southern Railroad was forced into receivership on August 1, 1893; for the present, the Silverton Railroad continued to be profitable enough to operate.

One ray of hope occurred in 1893, when a very rich strike of gold was made at the Hoosier Boy Mine near Chattanooga. The gold lay in the quartz in both wires and cubes. Prospectors rushed to the Red Mountain district and eventually filed fifty-two new mining claims, but the hope that the Red Mountain district might contain large amounts of gold was short-lived, and most of the prospectors soon left.[8] Even with all the disappointments and hardships, at the end of 1893 there were 400 people living in or near Red Mountain Town, and almost 250 hardy souls still occupied Ironton.

In an effort to keep up with the falling price of silver, the Red Mountain mines dramatically cut the cost per ton of ore produced. Development work was minimized, transportation costs were cut by the railroad, and the mines concentrated on the production of ore that was easy to reach. For example, by taking such steps, the cost of production at the Guston fell from $53.50 per ton in 1888 to $18.90 per ton in 1892. But the severely depressed price of silver, together with the decreasing quality of the ore, slowly strangled the Red Mountain mines. In 1894, the Silver Bell became the first of the prominent Red Mountain mines to close, although it was to reopen and reclose sporadically over the years. In 1894, the value of its ore averaged only twenty dollars per ton, but it had reached a depth of 706 feet and produced ore totaling over one million dollars. The quality of the Guston ore had also fallen sharply in 1894, and water was now coming into its shaft at the rate of sixty gallons a minute;

it was saved from closure by a last-minute strike of very rich ore. Otto Mears was himself in serious personal trouble, putting even the Silverton Railroad into jeopardy. He wrote: "There is no way for me to raise any money here on any other property I have. I am very sorry the circumstances are such that it is impossible for me to do anything at present. It is very hard for me today to raise even sufficient money for my household expenses."[9]

On February 16, 1895, Red Mountain Town was struck by an avalanche. The town's location had seemed to be completely safe, but the slide started on Red Mountain No. 3 and hit with such force that it went over the flats to the east of town, cleared a small divide, and ran into Main Street. Luckily, most of the slide's path was through an area of town that was not heavily developed, and only two houses were damaged. On June 13, 1895, Red Mountain Town burned for the second time, and a great part of what didn't burn in 1893, as well as many structures that had been rebuilt, were devastated on this occasion. "Fire was discovered in the rear of the upper apartments of Statting's saloon at Red Mountain at 1:00 A.M. this morning, and despite the efforts of all the citizens, the entire block, composing the entire town, was soon in ashes. Only one commercial building was saved." The *Ouray Herald* predicted that "this time the town is not likely to be rebuilt."[10] For all practical purposes Red Mountain Town was a ghost town.

In 1896, William Jennings Bryan ran for president on a platform that included the restoration of the silver standard. Silver was pushed as the metal of the people; gold was the metal of the rich. The entire San Juan region campaigned tirelessly for Bryan, and he won by a ten-to-one margin in Colorado but was defeated nationwide. The last hope for the Red Mountain Mining District seemed to disappear. Gradually it became obvious to the mine owners that the price of silver would never recover. One by one, the mines began to close–those with low-grade ore first, then, gradually, the richer mines. Businesses shut down, miners lost their jobs, and the remaining towns began to lose their populations.

Otto Mears seemed to give up on the San Juans, and he left Colorado to build railroads on the East Coast. In 1896, the Silverton Railroad was forced into receivership and shut down temporarily. In the summer of 1897, after Mears's friend Alex Anderson was appointed receiver, the Silverton reopened operations. Shortly thereafter, the National Belle Mine was compelled to shut down, and the Yankee Girl operated with a minimal work force. The Guston found it necessary to close in 1897, and the New Guston, Ltd., was liquidated. By February 1898 the Yankee Girl was forced to close due to high water and low ore prices.

Today there are widely fluctuating estimates as to how well the major Red

Mountain mines did before they were forced to close in the mid-1890s. The Yankee Girl undoubtedly produced in excess of four million dollars in ore, but some sources quote a figure as high as twelve million dollars. Five different chimneys (named the Yankee Girl, Orphan Boy, North, West, and South) had been mined to a depth of 1,050 feet. The first seventy-five feet had averaged 67 ounces of silver, and the next eighty feet averaged 242 ounces of silver. At the three-hundred- to four-hundred-foot levels the ore had been very rich – much of it as high as one thousand ounces of silver per ton. But as the shafts went deeper, the chimneys narrowed from twenty to thirty feet across to ten feet or less across, and the ore values decreased significantly.

The production of the Guston-Robinson exceeded 2.5 million dollars, although some quotes are as high as 7 million dollars. Five chimneys had been mined, but most production had been of an average-grade ore from a single pipe. The Robinson bottomed out at seven hundred feet and the Guston at thirteen hundred feet. Small amounts of the latter's ore had been as rich as fifteen thousand ounces of silver per ton – the richest on Red Mountain. When it finally closed in 1897, the Guston had returned half its gross income as dividends to investors.

The Genessee-Vanderbilt did most of its production between 1891 and 1896. Both mines followed the same chimney, thus the decision to merge. It bottomed out at seven hundred feet, with a little more than one million dollars in production. Its ore was middle-grade, and the cost of development and production came very close to the total of its net income.

The National Belle produced close to two million dollars in ore before closing in 1897. The mining in the "Belle" was mainly in irregular and unpredictable caves, and very little ore found below the three-hundred-foot level was worth mining. The National Belle never did have any sizeable amount of rich ore. Its ore usually ran from ten to twenty-five ounces of silver and less than one-tenth of an ounce of gold, but its low cost of production allowed the ore to be shipped at a profit.

All told, the Red Mountain Mining District from 1871 to 1900 produced at least fifteen million dollars in ore – some authorities would claim a figure as high as thirty-five million dollars. Later operations (mainly during and after World War II) added many more millions to that total. At today's metal prices the total output of the district would come close to a quarter of a billion dollars.

Many of the Red Mountain mine owners couldn't believe the end had come. They attempted to keep producing – even at a loss if necessary. Other mines hit rich pockets of silver ore that allowed production to continue for short periods of time. Some operations were kept alive by mining small

In this photograph, taken in the early 1900s, the Silver Ledge Mine dominates the center fore-ground, and its mill is in the valley near what is left of the town of Chattanooga. The railroad grade is at the center on the far right, and the trail comes up the divide at the lower right. *(Denver Public Library, Western History Department)*

amounts of gold that had always been in the ore but that had been ignored until this time (at one time a find of less than one ounce of gold was not even paid for by the mills). Gold actually began to appear in greater amounts in the deeper Red Mountain ores, although it certainly was not plentiful. Some Red Mountain mines struck other minerals, such as fluorspar, that allowed profitable short-term production. Base metals such as copper, zinc, and lead experienced an increase in price due to an expanding American industrial economy. Whole new markets opened up a demand for metals such as copper for use in electric wire and lead for automobile batteries. All metals were recovered more efficiently in the twentieth century, when better milling and smelting procedures were developed.

Even though the year 1898 brought a rise in metal prices (and by July 1898 the Congress and the Silver Bell regularly shipped a wagon full of ore to Red Mountain Town each day to be loaded on the train), the glory days were over for the Red Mountain Mining District. A strike at the Durango smelter in late 1898 completely shut down the few mines that had remained open. On November 16, 1898, the Guston post office was closed. The winter of 1898–1899 was especially harsh; the January 6, 1899 *Silverton Plaindealer* reported five feet of snow on the ground at Red Mountain Town. Only ten men and two women lived in "The Town" that winter, and only nine families were at Ironton. At the turn of the century only the Silver Ledge, Congress, and Silver Bell were being worked, and they would not have been in operation if it hadn't been for the recent discovery of small pockets of rich ores in them. The 1900 census gave Ironton a population of seventy-one in the summer, but it was just too much hassle for most families to try to spend all winter on the Red Mountain Divide.

At the turn of the century, labor strikes became prevalent throughout the San Juans. One portion of the labor problem was brought about by the economy and another portion by immigrant laborers. As early as 1891, the workers at the Guston had complained of immigrants (who were willing to work for less money) replacing the local miners. As the price for silver fell, owners insisted they had to cut wages. Some men simply couldn't afford to be out of a job and therefore agreed to lower pay. In the period of 1901 to 1904, violent strikes hit the San Juans – especially in nearby Telluride. Lives were lost and men were injured, but worst of all, the reputation of the San Juans was tarnished. It became almost impossible to attract outside capital to the district.

One small ray of hope for the Red Mountain district was the Treasury Tunnel (also called the Hammond Tunnel) that had opened across the valley from the Yankee Girl in 1896. It was started in the hope of tapping gold that was known to exist between Ouray and Telluride. The plan was to work the old mines at lower levels with hope of hitting new discoveries along the way. The Treasury Tunnel had been started at the very time that many of the other Red Mountain mines were shutting down, but it really wasn't working in the Red Mountain district proper. A two-thousand-foot railroad spur was run across the valley to tie into the Yankee Girl track, and the Treasury Tunnel operated for about ten years before shutting down.

In 1898, work had started on the Meldrum Tunnel, which was another major hope for the recovery of the Red Mountain Mining District. Andrew S. Meldrum originally had been a blacksmith at the Sheridan Mine near Telluride, and he made a fortune by grubstaking others. His "investments" included John Robinson, and Meldrum thereby became one of the original owners of the Yankee Girl and Guston mines. Meldrum originated the idea of blasting a tunnel large enough for a normal narrow-gauge freight train to go from the Red Mountain district almost directly west to tie in with the Rio Grande Southern Railroad near Telluride.

The Meldrum Tunnel was projected to cost three million dollars; it would be financed by the sale of stock and the proceeds of ore expected to be found along the way. The plan also included the blasting of ore chutes into several of the larger existing mines. The project was pushed as having "the stability of ordinary railroad investments" with the added bonus of being "vastly superior to any one mining proposition." Meldrum announced that "between terminals of this tunnel is included the most extensive, remarkable and rich system of mineral bearing veins known in the State of Colorado."[11]

In 1895, in an effort to raise capital, Meldrum prepared a detailed prospectus for use overseas, in which he discussed many of the mining problems that the Meldrum Tunnel was meant to solve – all problems that had plagued the Red Mountain mines for years. Drainage of the mines would be solved by placing deep trenches alongside the track, with the drainage water being used to power an electric generating station. It was noted that, above ground, the streams froze in the winter, but the underground water would be reliable year-round. Ventilation in the mines would be greatly improved, because air could come in one end of the tunnel and go out the other. Hoisting expenses would be minimized and freighting expenses lessened because the ore would be dumped by gravity directly into the railroad cars that could carry it all the way to the mill. The ore would make its own traffic for the railroad, and the mines would be their own consumers for the electricity. Supplies and miners could be brought directly to the inside of the mines by the railroad, again cutting freighting costs. It was also suggested that a reduction or concentration mill be built directly outside the tunnel, thereby allowing the low-grade ores to be shipped from the dumps of Red Mountain mines. The concentrates then could be shipped by one of two different routes to the smelters in Pueblo, Denver, or Durango – whichever was cheaper at the time. The tunnel would even complete "The Loop" for the thousands of tourists who would be expected in the summer.

Meldrum estimated that it would take a little over two years to complete the project, but revenue was expected to start coming in as soon as either end of the tunnel had been driven in two thousand feet – the point at which rich veins were projected to be encountered and ore shipped. The project "combines the production of precious metals, the furnishing of power, cheaper transportation, cheaper mining, with the possibilities of discoveries of new and heretofore unknown bodies of ore so that it has every element of success upon a most conservative basis with all the possibilities of greatest wealth from mining undertakings."[12] Meldrum estimated a net profit of $650,000 per year from the railroad and power company alone. But in 1900, with only 2.2 miles of a 6-mile project completed, he had to quit. The project had cost only $250,000, but financial help from Scotland was being funneled off by the Boer War. It is ironic that Andrew Meldrum, who had grubstaked John Robinson to his fabulous discovery at the Yankee Girl, was involved in this failed venture near the end of his life. Meldrum died a pauper and is buried in an unmarked grave at Ouray's Cedar Hill Cemetery.

Ironton at the turn of the century was well past its prime. But on the Fourth of July, when this picture was taken, flags were flying all over town. Not many people seem to be on hand to enjoy the event, though. (*Frank Pecchio photo; Denver Public Library, Western History Department*)

In 1898, another short-lived gold strike hit the Red Mountain Mining District – this time near Ironton. The *Silverton Plaindealer* reported that about 150 people had gone to the Red Mountain district, including several families who were already living in Ironton. "Ironton used to have 2,000 and the 2,000 made it a howling wilderness . . . That was in the palmy days of silver, before the country went into mourning for a dead industry. The pick and drill are again clicking . . . Whatever they lost in silver they are trying to recover in gold, copper and lead."[13] But, again, it was a short-lived boom. In 1899, the *Denver Times* reported Ironton to be in "the most dull portion of the district." Although it was the biggest settlement on the divide, the 1900 census gave Ironton a population of only seventy-one residents.

Nevertheless, the managers of the Silverton Railroad remained optimistic. Believing that 1899 would be a really good year for the Red Mountain mines, they had replaced a considerable amount of defective ties and track. But, once again, high costs, low prices, and large amounts of acidic water combined to keep almost all of the Red Mountain mines closed. The year 1900 was the last year the Silverton Railroad made any profit, and it was only $427.67. In 1902, the big excitement concerned an engine that rolled at Sheridan Junction, tearing off Engineer G. W. "Baldy" Thompson's head and burning his body "like a scalded turkey." Times were tough and, although the Silverton Railroad continued to operate, it did so only sporadically. Many of its spurs and parts of its main line were often inoperable.

In the very first years of the twentieth century, there were several attempts

The Barstow Mine was a late bloomer in the history of the Red Mountain district. Its ore was like that found in Telluride, but it produced nearly a million dollars worth of ore at the beginning of the twentieth century. *(Denver Public Library, Western History Department)*

to restore the Red Mountain Mining District to its former glory. Almost every week, articles appeared in the Denver papers announcing "Red Mountain Mines Show Bonanza Ore" or "Large Deals Pending in Ouray Mines." The articles were full of statements that "the new owners expect to ship"; an important deal is "expected to be consummated"; or, more realistically, "none of the ore bodies have been explored so nothing is known regarding their extent."[14] There was even an announcement that "the money necessary for the completion of the Meldrum Tunnel has been secured and work will be resumed," but nothing ever came of the project.

Because of new gold and fluorspar discoveries made in 1899 and 1900, the Barstow Mine (at first called the Bobtail, located to the west of the Treasury Tunnel) was the only mine worked on any scale on the north side of the Red Mountain Divide. The Barstow was following a fissure vein much more typical of the Telluride district than of the Red Mountain district. The ore in the vein was called "grey copper," but it contained almost no copper. It did contain an extremely rich lead ore that sometimes assayed up to two thousand ounces of silver and twenty-five ounces of gold. Average ore values were much lower—sometimes as little as ten ounces of silver and less than an ounce of gold. The Barstow had a short aerial tramway from the mine's upper portal to its forty-stamp mill. Snowslides were a major problem for the mine. Avalanches took out the mine buildings or buried workers several times, and wintertime work was always dangerous there. Serious operations stopped about 1917, but the mine had produced almost seven hundred thousand dollars by that time. After 1930, the Treasury Tunnel worked the Barstow from underground; parts of the mine were worked into the 1970s.

In December 1901, George Crawford, former director of the Silverton Railroad and part owner of the Yankee Girl Mine, announced plans to reopen the Guston, Hudson, and National Belle mines. Crawford knew that the Silverton Railroad and the Red Mountain mines were heavily dependent on each other. He had many times before put together syndicates to purchase Red Mountain mines, and the *Ouray Times* predicted that "Red Mountain will now bloom as she did when we had silver at the old-time prices." In fact, the Red Mountain district was so dead during 1902 that, when T. A. Rickard, Colorado State geologist, did an extensive survey of the mines in the Ouray–Telluride–Silverton area, he allocated only half a paragraph to the entire Red Mountain district. He stated that "at the foot of these iron stained ridges are situated the famous Yankee Girl and Guston mines, which were so productive fifteen years ago."[15]

Crawford incorporated the Red Mountain Railroad, Mining and Smelting Company on October 6, 1902.[16] Its purpose was to strike the ore bodies of the Guston, Yankee Girl, Robinson, and Genessee-Vanderbilt at lower levels, through what was to be called the Joker Tunnel, thereby giving easy access to their ore at depth and draining water by gravity from the mines. The portal was located next to the railroad tracks, just below the Silver Bell. Would-be investors were brought into the Red Mountain district from as far away as New York. The Red Mountain Railroad, Mining and Smelting Company bought the Silverton Railroad at a foreclosure sale in 1904 for only forty-three thousand dollars. The new company replaced the railroad's old thirty-pound rail with new forty-five-pound track. The old rail was used in the Joker Tunnel. By the summer of 1904, one passenger train and several freights again ran each day to the Joker Tunnel. Construction actually commenced on the Joker Tunnel itself on July 9, 1904.

Over on the Silverton side of the divide there was also increased activity. In 1904, the Silver Ledge Mill successfully separated zinc from the Red Mountain ore. It was a solution to an age-old problem, but it came too late for most of the Red Mountain mines.[17] The Silver Ledge continued to operate off and on for several more decades and even had a post office from September 6, 1904 to March 30, 1905.

In 1905, Otto Mears returned to the San Juans and revived his dream to traverse the distance from Ouray to Ironton. He found no interest in the idea of a cog railroad, but, never daunted, he immediately came up with another plan. The Mack truck factory had developed an experimental railroad truck that supposedly could run on steeper grades than a regular locomotive. It carried twenty-eight passengers and could also pull a freight car. An electric railroad was mentioned as a possible alternative. Mears himself could not finance the project, but he agreed to undertake it "provided it is the earnest desire of the community." As a show of faith, the local citizens were asked to subscribe to the majority of the stock in the company with the balance to be raised by Mears in the East. He was reported as "ready to go as long as compensating inducements were offered." Mears widened the toll road in 1905 and scattered railroad ties along the route, but he could not get the support of the people of Ouray. The Mack truck also did not perform as advertised, and the idea was abandoned.

In the meantime, the Joker Tunnel had been extended forty-eight hundred feet into the divide by 1907. About thirty-five men had been put to work, and they progressed directly to the main shaft of the Genessee-Vanderbilt; laterals branched off to some of the other mines. The Joker Tunnel was ten to eleven feet wide with a grade of three inches per one hundred feet. The tunnel floor had a two-by-four-foot excavation under the track, which allowed drainage of up to twelve hundred gallons of water per minute from the mines. The Guston was struck at a depth of about four hundred feet, the Yankee Girl at five hundred feet, and the Genessee at six hundred feet. Water levels in these mines were lowered immediately, and ore deposits were made accessible that hadn't been worked in years. The ore could also be trammed out of the tunnel instead of being raised hundreds of feet up shafts.

Crawford had leased or gained ownership of most of the mines on the divide and put men to work on the surface as well as on the lower levels. All together he now controlled two thousand acres of claims that included the National Belle, Hudson, Yankee Girl, Guston, Genessee, and many others. In the summer of 1906, as many as eighty men worked for the Red Mountain Mining and Smelting Company mining in the Genessee, Yankee Girl, and Guston mines or on the Joker Tunnel and the railway. By the end of the summer it was reported that more work had been done in the Red Mountain Mining District than in the last fourteen years together. "It looks more like the old days than ever before."[18] There was enough new mining on the divide in 1906 that a restaurant, rooming house, and hotel were opened at Red Mountain Town. Ore values were running about fifty dollars per ton, and two new veins had been uncovered at the Yankee Girl Mine. For ten years, work continued

The Joker Tunnel and a few of the cabins that were sometimes referred to as the settlement of Liverpool are shown in this photograph, taken around 1910 to 1915. The town of Guston is just beyond the ridge in the center of the photograph. The Joker was a last-ditch effort to revive the Red Mountain district. *(Colorado Historical Society)*

on the Joker Tunnel at a constant but slow pace; the ore shrunk in both quality and quantity at the bottoms of the old mines. Originally, the tunnel was to run all the way to the workings of the National Belle, Hudson, and Congress, but it never got past the Genessee. The tunnel eventually saw periods of disuse and occasional activity into the 1940s.

Even though it was near the Joker Tunnel, Ironton's population fell to forty-eight in 1910. Red Mountain Town dwindled to twenty-six inhabitants, and on February 28, 1913 its post office closed. After the Joker Tunnel closed in 1914, the Silver Ledge and Congress were the only major Red Mountain mines that continued to operate. The Congress shipped about one hundred carloads of low-grade ore each year from 1912 to 1918. Zinc, copper, lead, and other base metals were in great demand during World War I, and a few of the Red Mountain mines made small shipments during that period. The Silverton Railroad continued to operate at a loss. Its deficit in 1917 alone was over twenty-five thousand dollars.

In 1919, the Silver Ledge Mine shut down when its mill burned, eliminating the only local milling facilities designed to process the Red Mountain district's ore. Ironton was the last active town in the district. Its post office closed on August 7, 1920, but Ironton continued to have a saloon even after that time. The old way of life had changed forever. It was too easy for miners to live in Ouray or Silverton and commute to Red Mountain. New roads,

Red Mountain Town is well on its way to being a ghost town in this photograph, taken in the early 1900s. There are no people visible, and the National Belle is not being worked. The building in the left foreground is a general store and post office. To the north of it is a restaurant, saloon, and stable. On the right is a vacant house and another saloon. (*Colorado Historical Society*)

electricity, and telephones had all helped bring the transformation. In 1921, regular operations ceased on the Silverton Railroad, and on June 17, 1922, a hearing was held before the Interstate Commerce Commission to determine if the Silverton Railroad could be abandoned. Although attorneys for the mines and the town of Silverton all protested vehemently, the ICC allowed the request.

As historian David Lavender wrote: "The period between the First and Second World Wars was, for the Rockies, a time of cruel suspension and uncertain change. Not even children could pull the covers over their heads and pretend that the boogies were not there, for we were surrounded with the wreckage of hopes that once had blossomed as brightly as our own and then had withered, in spite of those who kept insisting that the old values were still sound. The most graphic of the ruins lay in the Red Mountain District . . . Depressed by each winter's heavy snowfall, the mill and mine buildings, the stores, the little bell-towered church—everything leaned a little more perilously each year . . . Rusted pipes and cables, overturned ore cars and detached chunks of machinery sprawled everywhere."[19]

In the late 1930s, the Saratoga smelter at the north end of Ironton Park was torn down and the bricks and lumber used to build a good-sized lodge. A trout pond was constructed and a ski-tow installed. The governor of Colorado attended the opening ceremonies, but the venture was not a success.

The St. Germain Foundation eventually took over the lodge, and soon thereafter a caretaker, melting ice off the roof with a blowtorch, burned the building to the ground. The basement garage is all that now remains.

The Beaver and Belfast Mine, located directly alongside the west side of U.S. 550 near Ironton, was owned by Harry and Milton Larson. They worked a low-grade ore off and on during the mid-1900s, but problems with smelting the zinc ore prevented them from making a very big return. Harry died in the 1940s, leaving Milton behind as the sole resident of the town of Ironton. Acquaintances dubbed Milton the mayor of Ironton, which eventually led to his being given an all-expense-paid trip to New York, where he was interviewed about his "mayorship." Milton died in the mid-1960s, making Ironton the last of the ghost towns on the divide.

When the Million Dollar Highway was upgraded for automobile traffic between 1921 and 1924, the road was moved from the east to the west side of the Ironton Park valley. This put the Treasury Tunnel on the main highway for the first time ever. At the time, only a small operation was carried on there – mainly the salvaging of equipment and materials for use elsewhere. It was the Great Depression and, if a man dug through the dumps himself, picking and sorting, a meager living could be made. In the 1930s, the San Juan Metals Company took over and actively mined in the Treasury Tunnel. A new mill, boardinghouse, and offices were built in 1937. Several companies that eventually became the Idarado Mine (Idarado is a combination of "Idaho" and "Colorado") took over the Treasury Tunnel in 1939. They also purchased and consolidated many of the mines on the west side of the Red Mountain valley. Production continued sporadically – twelve hundred dollars total production one year, sixty-six thousand dollars a year or two later. During World War II, with its huge demands for lead and zinc, the Idarado Mine operated very profitably. Eventually it took control of over eighty miles of interconnected tunnels that included the Ajax-Smuggler, Tomboy, Liberty Bell, Virginius, Barstow, Black Bear, and other veins. The old Treasury mill and the Pandora mill near Telluride were also rehabilitated. In 1956, all of the Idarado's milling operations were diverted to a new mill at Pandora. The mine produced ores of copper, lead, zinc, gold, and silver and, for many years, was first or second in Colorado in terms of production of these metals. A few employees of the Idarado have lived at the mine or the mill right up to the present.

The Idarado's tailings eventually filled in all the available areas near the mine and were then pumped more than a mile to a spot where they covered the area to the west of the original town site of Ironton. Now only a few houses still stand at the south end of that town. On June 13, 1939, a fire destroyed almost everything that was left of Red Mountain Town, Guston, and the points

The Idarado Mine was in the midst of its great expansion at the time this photograph was taken in the early 1940s. The Silverton Railroad was long gone; its grade is still visible in the background. The highway had been relocated to the west side of Red Mountain Creek, but it would be two more decades before it was paved. *(Denver Public Library, Western History Department)*

in between. In Red Mountain Town, only the jail, a residence, and the shaft house of the National Belle remain. The Genessee-Vanderbilt has been worked on and off right up to present times, and a few newer buildings stand in its vicinity. A few sheds or cabins still exist at Congress, Guston, and Red Mountain City.

The only remains of the Silverton Railroad are a few ties, an occasional spike, and the Corkscrew turntable (although its covering shed and most of the movable parts are gone). The snows have flattened many of the Red Mountain buildings. World War II saw all of the available scrap metals salvaged from the once-proud district. Treasure seekers carry off anything remotely usable or collectible. Even the dumps slowly flatten out as mineral collectors dig for specimens, and the rains wash the yellow- and red-colored minerals into Red Mountain Creek and the Uncompahgre River, and they eventually flow on to the Pacific Ocean.

For now, a quiet has come to Red Mountain. Only cross-country skiers and an occasional jeeping fanatic enjoy the district. But the story of Red

Mountain may not be finished. Many geologists believe there are still rich chimneys waiting to be discovered. Huge amounts of low-grade ore exist that may some day be considered high-grade as prices rise. When that day comes there will undoubtedly be a fight from environmentalists to save what many believe to be one of the most beautiful spots on this earth. If production does start again, where will the ore be milled? Where will the tailings be placed? How will the ore be shipped? There may well be many more chapters to write about Red Mountain.

Notes

Chapter One: The Land

1. Baggs, *Colorado,* 238.
2. Griffiths, *San Juan Country.* This is a wonderful in-depth study for the layman of the geology of the San Juan mountains.
3. New Mexico Geological Society's *Guidebook of the Southwestern San Juan Mountains, Colorado,* and Cross, *A Brief Review of the Geology of the San Juan Region of Southwestern Colorado* are excellent technical geologic studies.
4. Ransome, *Report of the Economic Geology of the Silverton Quadrangle* is the accepted technical review of the Red Mountain district.
5. Ingersoll, *Crest of the Continent,* 284.
6. Ibid., 284.
7. Hall, *History of Colorado,* 255.
8. Jocknick, *Early Days on the Western Slope,* 162.
9. Ingersoll, *Crest of the Continent,* 284.
10. Hayden, *U.S. Geological and Geographical Survey, 1876.*
11. The weather and climate of the San Juans is also well covered in Griffiths, *San Juan Country.*
12. Wheeler, *U.S. Survey Territories West of 100th Meridian,* 92.

Chapter Two: The Explorers

1. Hall, *History of Colorado,* 194.
2. *Rocky Mountain News,* January 23, 1861.
3. Smith, *Song of Hammer and Drill,* 6.
4. See Borland, "The Sale of the San Juans."
5. Hall, *History of Colorado,* 191.
6. Hayden, *Survey 1874,* 229.
7. This report is not technically correct, because Red Mountain Creek starts at the divide. The Uncompahgre follows what is now the Engineer Pass Road.
8. Rhoda, *Survey Report 1874,* 465. The area that Rhoda is describing is near the Riverside Slide, which leaves tremendous debris.
9. Wheeler *Survey,* 92.
10. Wheeler *Survey,* 108–109.
11. Hayden *Survey 1874,* 10.
12. To confuse matters further, even though this is called the Uncompahgre canyon, Red Mountain Creek flows through this area.

13. Williams, *Tourist Guide and Map of San Juan Mines.*
14. Fossett, *Colorado,* 511.
15. Williams, *Tourist Guide and Map of San Juan Mines.*
16. Smith, *Song of the Hammer and Drill,* 19.
17. *Ouray Times,* August 23, 1879.
18. Hall, *History of Colorado,* 254.

Chapter Three: The Mines

1. At 10,000 feet there is only half the oxygen in the air as there is at sea level.
2. This same discovery story has been reported many times, but in some versions Andrew Meldrum is the locator, sometimes two out of the four are present, and sometimes all four make the discovery.
3. *La Plata Miner,* September 23, 1882.
4. Ingersoll, *Crest of the Continent,* 284.
5. *La Plata Miner,* November 25, 1882.
6. Ibid., December 23, 1882.
7. *Denver Tribune,* January 9, 1883.
8. *Red Mountain Review,* March 17, 1883.
9. *La Plata Miner,* March 10, 1883.
10. Red Mountain Review, April 14, 1883.
11. Red Mountain Pilot, April 28, 1883.
12. Ibid., May 5, 1883.
13. *Red Mountain Review,* May 5, 1883.
14. Rickard, *The Economics of Mining,* 106.
15. *Rocky Mountain News,* July 3, 1883.
16. *Red Mountain Pilot,* July 19, 1883. See Ingersoll, *Crest of the Continent,* 284–285, for a slightly different account.
17. *Red Mountain Pilot,* July 21, 1883.
18. *La Plata Miner,* August 25, 1883.
19. See Smith and Rosemeyer, "Great Pockets, The National Belle Mine," for a good detailed account of the National Belle, its treasure cave, and chimney deposits.
20. *Red Mountain Review,* September 15, 1883.
21. Ibid., September 1, 1883.
22. *Denver Republican,* January 9, 1884.
23. *Red Mountain Review,* November 3, 1883.

Chapter Four: The Towns

1. *La Plata Miner,* December 30, 1882.
2. Ibid., January 13, 1883.
3. *Omaha Commercial Record* quoted in *Red Mountain Review,* September 22, 1883.
4. This doesn't match with earlier reports in the *La Plata Miner* that dozens of buildings were underway in January. In fact, even in March most of Red Mountain City's structures were probably tents.
5. *Red Mountain Review,* March 17, 1883.
6. Ibid., April 4, 1883.
7. Ibid., March 17, 1883.
8. *Solid Muldoon,* March 9, 1883.

9. Ibid., March 23, 1883.
10. *Red Mountain Review,* March 3, 1883.
11. *La Plata Miner,* April 4, 1883.
12. Ibid., April 4, 1883.
13. *Red Mountain Pilot,* May 19, 1883.
14. Quoted without reference to source in Wolle, *Stampede to Timberline,* 438.
15. Letter in author's possession.
16. *Red Mountain Review,* May 5, 1883.
17. Ibid., May 17, 1883.
18. Ibid., June 9, 1883.
19. Ibid., June 30, 1883.
20. Ibid., June 9, 1883.
21. Ibid., August 25, 1883.
22. Ibid., September 15, 1883.
23. Quoted in *Red Mountain Review,* September 22, 1883.
24. *Rocky Mountain News,* May 5, 1883.

Chapter Five: The Newspapers

1. See Smith, *Rocky Mountain Mining Camps,* for an excellent review of mining town newspapers.
2. *Solid Muldoon,* July 24, 1891.
3. Day, "Momentos of the Dave Day Family," 148.
4. Ripley, *Handclasp of the East and West,* 98.
5. *Solid Muldoon,* January 19, 1883.
6. *Denver Times,* July 5, 1883.
7. *La Plata Miner,* January 27, 1883.
8. Ibid., February 17, 1883.
9. *Red Mountain Review,* March 3, 1883.
10. *Solid Muldoon,* March 9, 1883.
11. *La Plata Miner,* March 17, 1883.
12. Ibid., April 28, 1883.
13. *Red Mountain Review,* April 28, 1883.
14. *Lake City Silver World,* April 1883.
15. *Red Mountain Pilot,* June 19, 1883.
16. *Red Mountain Review,* May 5, 1883.
17. *Red Mountain Pilot,* July 7, 1883.
18. *Denver Times,* October 14, 1899.
19. *Red Mountain Review,* August 18, 1883.
20. *Solid Muldoon,* August 17, 1883.
21. Ibid., September 9, 1884.
22. *La Plata Miner,* November 22, 1884.
23. Ibid., December 27, 1884.
24. *Solid Muldoon,* January 23, 1885.
25. Ibid., October 16, 1885.
26. Ibid., September 14, 1888.
27. *Rico News,* October 1888.

Chapter Six: The Road

1. Williamson, *Otto Mears,* 74.
2. *La Plata Miner,* September 23, 1882.

3. Ibid., December 30, 1882.

4. Ibid., January 13, 1883.

5. See *Solid Muldoon*, October 28, 1882; April 27, 1883; August 17, 1883; and November 28, 1884, for articles concerning the building of the road.

6. *Solid Muldoon*, May 11, 1883, and June 5, 1883.

7. *Red Mountain Pilot*, February 2, 1883.

8. Quoted in *Red Mountain Pilot*, March 31, 1883.

9. *Solid Muldoon*, April 13, 1883.

10. *La Plata Miner*, May 26, 1883.

11. *Red Mountain Pilot*, June 2, 1883.

12. *Red Mountain Review*, June 30, 1883.

13. *Red Mountain Pilot*, July 14, 1883.

14. *Solid Muldoon*, quoted in *Red Mountain Review*, July 7, 1883.

15. Quoted in *Red Mountain Review*, September 8, 1883. This same scheme was reported in the *La Plata Miner*, July 21, 1883.

16. *Red Mountain Review*, October 20, 1883.

17. As reported in *Red Mountain Review*, September 22, 1883.

18. *Solid Muldoon*, September 28, 1883.

19. *Omaha Commercial Record*, September 23, 1883.

20. *Red Mountain Review*, October 27, 1883.

21. *La Plata Miner*, June 21, 1884.

22. *Solid Muldoon*, October 3, 1884.

23. Ibid., September 1, 1885.

24. *Red Mountain Pilot*, December 6, 1884.

25. Gibbons, *In the San Juans*, 15–16.

26. *Red Mountain Pilot*, December 6, 1884.

27. *Solid Muldoon*, November 28, 1884.

Chapter Seven: Life on Red Mountain

1. *Solid Muldoon*, June 29, 1888.

2. *Red Mountain Pilot*, October 1883.

3. Gibbons, *In the San Juans*, 104.

4. *Solid Muldoon*, July 17, 1885.

5. Ibid., August 14, 1885.

6. Gibbons, *In the San Juans*, 27.

7. *Red Mountain Review*, April 14, 1883.

8. Gibbons, *In the San Juans*, 26–27.

9. *Solid Muldoon*, September 11, 1891.

10. Ibid., June 3, 1887.

11. *Denver Times*, June 27, 1891.

12. *Around the Circle*, 1887.

13. *Red Mountain Pilot*, December 6, 1884.

14. *La Plata Miner*, February 14, 1884.

15. *Solid Muldoon*, August 31, 1888.

16. *Red Mountain Review*, September 22, 1883.

17. Ibid., November 17, 1883.

18. *Solid Muldoon*, July 31, 1885.

19. *Telluride Republican*, October 1, 1887.

20. Gibbons, *In the San Juans*, 191.

21. *Solid Muldoon*, October 2, 1891.

22. Ibid., November 3, 1891.
23. Gibbons, *In the San Juans,* 32.
24. *Solid Muldoon,* July 10, 1885.
25. Gibbons, *In the San Juans,* 170.
26. See *Silverton Standard,* November 14, 1891.
27. Annie Davis, Reverend Davis's daughter, tells this story in Wolle, *Timberline Tailings,* 276.

Chapter Eight: The Snow

1. DAR, *Pioneers of the San Juan Country,* 182.
2. *Solid Muldoon,* January 29, 1886.
3. Ibid., April 2, 1886.
4. Ibid., January 12, 1886.
5. Ibid., February 25, 1887.
6. Ibid., April 23, 1886.
7. Ibid., April 16, 1883.
8. Ibid., January 21, 1887.
9. Gibbons, *In the San Juans,* 15.
10. Ibid., 19.
11. Ibid., 17–18.
12. Ingersoll, *The Silver San Juan,* 10.
13. *La Plata Miner,* September 27, 1884.
14. *Solid Muldoon,* December 24, 1886.
15. *Red Mountain Mining Journal,* November 26, 1887.
16. *Solid Muldoon,* May 30, 1890.
17. Ibid., August 10, 1888.
18. Gibbons, *In the San Juans,* 120.
19. Leonard, "In the Red Mountain Mining District."
20. *Solid Muldoon,* January 27, 1891.
21. Ibid., December 19, 1890.
22. Ibid., March 6, 1891.
23. Ibid., February 22, 1891.
24. Ibid., March 20, 1891.
25. Gibbons, *In the San Juans,* 76.
26. *Silverton Standard,* March 21, 1891.
27. Gibbons, *In the San Juans,* 33.
28. *Solid Muldoon,* January 18, 1889.
29. *Ouray Herald,* March 15, 1889.

Chapter Nine: The Silver Slide

1. *Solid Muldoon,* November 20, 1885.
2. *La Plata Miner,* October 11, 1884.
3. Ibid., November 22, 1884.
4. Hall, *History of Colorado,* 257.
5. *Rocky Mountain News,* November 21, 1884.
6. *La Plata Miner,* December 27, 1884.
7. Ibid., September 27, 1884.
8. *Ouray Times,* October 6, 1885.

9. *Solid Muldoon*, November 20, 1885.
10. *La Plata Miner*, January 13, 1885.
11. *Solid Muldoon*, January 1, 1886.
12. Ibid., August 14, 1885.
13. Crofutt, *Grip-Sack Guide to Colorado*, 134.
14. *Solid Muldoon*, October 3, 1884.
15. Ibid., February 7, 1885.
16. Ibid., March 20, 1885.
17. Ibid., July 17, 1885.
18. Ibid., September 4, 1885.
19. Ibid., May 28, 1885.
20. Ibid., March 5, 1886.
21. Ibid., July 30, 1886.
22. Ibid., May 28, 1886.
23. Ibid., July 2, 1886.
24. Ibid., August 6, 1886.
25. Ibid., December 24, 1886.
26. Ibid., December 24, 1886.
27. Ibid., December 3, 1886.
28. Ibid., May 13, 1887.
29. Ibid., November 25, 1887.
30. Ibid., August 17, 1888.
31. Ibid., July 29, 1887.
32. Ibid., December 2, 1887.
33. Ibid., January 11, 1889.
34. *Denver News*, February 25, 1889.
35. *Solid Muldoon*, July 9, 1886.
36. Ibid., May 13, 1887.
37. Ibid., July 29, 1887.

Chapter Ten: The Rainbow Route

1. *First Annual Report on Statistics of Railroads in the United States for the Year Ending 1888.*
2. *Solid Muldoon*, September 30, 1887.
3. Ibid., November 11, 1887.
4. *Red Mountain Mining Journal*, October 1, 1887.
5. *Transactions of the American Society of Civil Engineers*, Vol. 23, No. 450, September 1889.
6. *Silverton Weekly Miner*, February 9, 1890.
7. *Solid Muldoon*, June 21, 1889.
8. Ibid., August 15, 1890.
9. Ibid., May 10, 1889.
10. Ibid., December 20, 1889, and February 7, 1890.
11. Hall, *History of Colorado*, 310.
12. Gibbons, *In the San Juans*, 26.
13. Ibid., 33.
14. *Solid Muldoon*, November 6, 1891.
15. *Red Mountain Mining Journal*, December 31, 1887.
16. *Solid Muldoon*, June 14, 1889.
17. Ibid., June 14, 1889.
18. Ibid., December 5, 1889.

19. *Solid Muldoon,* July 25, 1890.
20. *Silverton Weekly Miner,* January 1, 1897.
21. *Solid Muldoon,* August 14, 1889.
22. Ibid., June 14, 1889.
23. Ibid., August 22, 1887.
24. Leonard, "In the Red Mountain District," 147.
25. *Solid Muldoon,* July 13, 1888.
26. Ibid., January 2, 1891.
27. Ibid., May 15, 1891.
28. Ibid., May 22, 1891.
29. Ibid., December 4, 1891.

Chapter Eleven: The Bust

1. *Ridgway Herald,* August 18, 1892.
2. Julian Benton in Wolle, *Timberline Tailings,* 274.
3. Wolle, *Stampede to Timberline,* 437.
4. *Ridgway Herald,* August 18, 1892.
5. Letter of Annie Rogers in Wolle, *Timberline Tailings,* 278.
6. *Annual Report of The Silverton Railroad,* 1892.
7. *Silverton Standard,* July 22, 1893.
8. Wolle, *Stampede to Timberline,* 436.
9. Sloan and Skawronski, *The Rainbow Route,* 120.
10. *Ouray Herald,* June 13, 1895.
11. Meldrum Tunnel prospectus in author's possession.
12. Ibid.
13. *Silverton Plaindealer,* July 29, 1898.
14. See *Denver Times* of 1900–1902.
15. Richard, *In the San Juans,* 59.
16. Joker Tunnel prospectus in author's possession.
17. Henderson, *Mining in Colorado,* 50.
18. *Ouray Herald,* August 24, 1906.
19. Lavender, *The Rockies,* 348.

Bibliography

Armstrong, Betsy R. *Century of Struggle Against Snow: A History of Avalanche Hazard in San Juan County, Colorado.* Boulder: The Regents of the University of Colorado, 1976.

————. *Avalanche Hazard in Ouray County, Colorado, 1877 to 1975.* Boulder: University of Colorado, 1977.

Armstrong, Betsy R., and Richard L. Armstrong. *Avalanche Atlas–Ouray County, Colorado.* Silverton: Institute of Arctic and Alpine Research, University of Colorado, 1977.

Ayers, Mary C. "Howardsville in the San Juan." *Colorado Magazine,* October 1951.

Baggs, Mae Lacy. *Colorado–The Queen Jewel of the Rockies.* Boston: The Page Company, 1918.

Baker, James H., and Leroy R. Hafen, eds. *History of Colorado.* Denver: Linderman Co., 1927.

Bancroft, Caroline. *Unique Ghost Towns.* Boulder, Colo.: Johnson Publishing Co., 1967.

Bancroft, Hubert Howe. *TheWorks of Hubert Howe Bancroft,* vol. 25 of *History of Nevada, Colorado and Wyoming.* San Francisco: History Company, 1890.

Bauer, W. H., J. L. Ozment, and J. H. Willard. *Colorado Postal History: The Post Offices.* Crete, Neb.: J. B. Publishing Co., 1971.

Beebe, Lucius, and Charles Clegg. *Narrow Gauge in the Rockies.* Berkeley, Calif.: Howell-North, 1958.

Boars, Donald L. *The Colorado Plateau, A Geologic History.* Albuquerque: University of New Mexico Press, 1983.

Bolton, H. E. *Pageant in the Wilderness–The Story of the Escalante Expedition to the Interior Basin, 1776.* Salt Lake City: Utah State Historical Society, 1972.

Borland, Lois. "The Sale of the San Juan." *Colorado Magazine* 28, no. 2 (April 1951).

Brown, Robert L. *Jeep Trails to Colorado Ghost Towns*. Caldwell, Idaho: The Caxton Printers, 1966.

————. *An Empire of Silver*. Caldwell, Idaho: The Caxton Printers, 1968.

————. *An Empire of Silver: An Illustrated History*. Denver: Sundance Publications, 1984.

Chronic, Halka. *Roadside Geology of Colorado*. Missoula, Mont.: Mountain Press Publishing Co., 1980.

Colorado Bureau of Mines. *Thirteenth Biennial Report of Mines in the State of Colorado*. Denver: Smith-Brooks Printing Company, State Printers, 1914.

Colorado State Business Directories. 1882–1894.

Cooper, Ray H. "Early History of San Juan County." *Colorado Magazine* 22, no. 5 (September 1945).

Crofutt, George A. *Crofutt's Grip-Sack Guide to Colorado*. Omaha: The Overland Publishing Co., 1885.

Cross, Whitman, and Esper Larsen. *A Brief Review of the Geology of the San Juan Region of Southwestern Colorado, 1935*. USGS Survey Bulletin 843. Washington, D.C., 1935.

Crum, Josie Moore. "Three Little Lines." *Durango Herald News*. N.d., 1960.

————. *Ouray County, Colorado*. Durango, Colo.: San Juan History, Inc., 1962.

Cummins, D. H. "Toll Roads in Southwestern Colorado." *Colorado Magazine* 29, no. 2 (April 1952).

Daughters of the American Revolution. "Sarah Platt Decker," in *Pioneers of the San Juan Country*. Colorado Springs: Outwest Printing Co., 1942.

Day, George Vest. "Momentos of the Dave Day Family," in *The 1961 Brand Book*, vol. 17. Denver: The Denver Westerners, 1962.

Delaney, Robert W. *The Southern Ute People*. Phoenix: N.p., 1974.

Denver & Rio Grande Railroad. *Around the Circle*. Denver: Denver & Rio Grande Railroad, 1892.

Dorset, Phyllis F. *The New Eldorado—The Story of Colorado's Gold and Silver Rushes*. London: The Macmillan Co., 1970.

Eberhart, Perry. *Guide to the Colorado Ghost Towns and Mining Camps*. Denver: Sage Books, 1959.

Fell, James E., Jr. *Ores to Metals*. Lincoln: University of Nebraska Press, 1979.

Ferrell, Mallory Hope. *Silver San Juan*. Boulder, Colo.: Pruett Publishing Co., 1973.

Fossett, Frank. *Colorado, Its Gold and Silver Mines*. New York: C. G. Crawford, 1880.

Foster, Mike. *Summits to Reach*. Boulder, Colo.: Pruett Publishing Co., 1984.

Fritz, Percy S. *Colorado, The Centennial State*. New York: Prentice-Hall, 1941.

Gibbons, Rev. J. J. *In the San Juan Colorado*. Chicago: Calumet Book & Engraving Co., 1898.

Gibbs, C. W. *Transactions of the American Society of Civil Engineers*, vol. 23, no. 450. N.p.: 1889.

Griffiths, Thomas M. *San Juan Country*. Boulder, Colo.: Pruett Publishing Company, 1984.

Gregory, Marvin, and P. David Smith. *Mountain Mysteries*. Ouray, Colo.: Wayfinder Press, 1984.

————. *The Million Dollar Highway*. Ouray, Colo.: Wayfinder Press, 1986.

Griswold, Don, and Jean Griswold. *Colorado's Century of "Cities."* Denver, Colo.: Smith-Brooks Printing Co., 1958.

Hafen, LeRoy R. "Otto Mears. 'Pathfinder of the San Juans.'" *Colorado Magazine* 9 (March 1932): 71–74.

————. "Ute Indians and the San Juan Mining Region," in *Ute Indians*, vol. 2. N.p.: Clearwater Publishing Co., 1974.

Hafen, LeRoy R., ed. *Colorado and Its People*. New York: Lewis Historical Publishing Co., 1948.

Hall, C. L. *Resources, Industries and Advantages of Ouray County Colorado*. N.p.: N.d.

Hall, Frank. *History of the State of Colorado*, vol. 2. Chicago: The Blakely Printing Co., 1890.

Hayden, F. A. *U.S. Geological and Geographical Survey of Colorado*. Washington, D.C.: 1874, 1875, 1876.

Hazen, Scott W., Jr. *Lead-Zinc-Silver in the Poughkeepsie District and Part of the Upper Uncompahgre and Mineral Point Districts, Ouray and San Juan Counties, Colorado*. N.p.: 1949.

Henderson, Charles W. *Mining in Colorado*. USGS Professional Paper 138. Washington, D.C.: 1926.

Holmes, Richard, and Marrianna Kennedy. *Mines and Minerals of the Great American Rift – Colorado and New Mexico*. New York: Van Nostrand, Reinhold Co., 1972.

Ingham, G. Thomas. *Digging Gold Among the Rockies*. N.p.: Edgewood Publishing Co., 1882.

Ingersoll, Ernest. *The Silver San Juans*. Reprint, Olympic Valley, Calif.: Outbooks, 1977.

————. *The Crest of the Continent*. Reprint, Glorieta, N.M.: The Rio Grande Press, 1883.

————. "The Heart of Colorado." *Cosmopolitan Magazine*. September to October 1888.

Jocknick, Sidney. *Early Days on the Western Slope of Colorado*. Glorieta, N.M.: The Rio Grande Press, 1913.

Jones, William C., and Elizabeth B. Jones. *William Henry Jackson's Colorado*. Boulder, Colo.: Pruett Publishing Co., 1975.

Kaplan, Michael. "Colorado's Big Little Man." *Western States Jewish Historical Quarterly* 4 (April 1972).

———. "The Toll Road Building Career of Otto Mears." 1881–1887. *Colorado Magazine* 52, no. 2 (Spring 1975).

———. *Otto Mears, The Paradoxical Pathfinder*. Silverton, Colo.: San Juan County Book Company, 1982.

King, Joseph E. *A Mind to Make a Mine*. College Station: Texas A & M University Press, 1977.

Kushner, Ervan F. *A Guide to Mineral Collecting at Ouray, Colorado*. Paterson, N.J.: Ervan Kushner Books, 1972.

———. *Otto Mears: His Life & Times*. Frederick, Colo.: Jende-Hagan Bookcorp., 1979.

Lavender, David. *The Big Divide*. Garden City, N.Y.: Doubleday & Co., 1949.

———. *The Rockies*. New York: Harper & Row, 1968.

Leonard, Charles McClung. "In the Red Mountain District." *Colorado Magazine* 33, no. 2 (April 1956).

———. "Forty Years in Colorado Mining Camps." *Colorado Magazine* 37, no. 3 (July 1960).

Lingenfelter, Richard E. *The Hardrock Miners*. Berkeley: University of California Press, 1974.

Marshall, John B. "Andy Meldrum and the Treasure of the Red Mountains," in *The 1967 Westerners Brand Book*, vol. 23. Denver: The Denver Westerners, 1968.

McConnell, Virginia. "Captain Baker and the San Juan Humbug." *Colorado Magazine* 48, no. 1 (Winter 1971).

Miller, David E., ed. *The Route of the Dominguez-Escalante Expedition, 1776–1777*. A Report of Trail Research Conducted Under the Auspices of the Dominguez–Escalante State/Federal Bicentennial Committee and the Four Corners Regional Commission, 1976.

Monroe, Arthur W. *San Juan Silver*. Montrose, Colo.: Self-published, 1940.

New Mexico Geological Society. *Guidebook of Southwestern San Juan Mountains, Colorado*. N.p.: 1957.

Ormes, Robert M. *Tracking Ghost Railroads in Colorado*. Colorado Springs, Colo.: Century One Press, 1976.

Ouray County Plaindealer. "Ouray Centennial-Historic Souvenir Issue." 1976.

Pearl, Richard M. *Colorado Gem Trails and Mineral Guide*. Denver, Colo.: Sage Books, 1965.

Ransome. *Report on Economic Geology of Silverton Quadrangle*. USGS Bulletin 182. Washington, D.C.: 1901.

Rathmell, Ruth. "Of Record and Reminiscence." *Ouray County Plaindealer & Herald*. N.d., 1976.

Rhoda, Franklin. *Report on the Topography of the San Juan Country*. Washington, D.C.: 1874.

Rice, Frank A. "A History of Ouray and Ouray County." Unpublished manuscript, 1961.

Rickard, T. A. *Across the San Juan Mountains*. San Francisco: Mining and Scientific Press, 1907.

Rickard, Thomas, et al. *The Economics of Mining*. 2d ed. New York: Hill Publishing Co., 1907.

Ridgway, Arthur. "The Mission of Colorado Toll Roads." *Colorado Magazine* 9, no. 5 (September 1932).

Ripley, Henry. *Hand Clasp of the East and West*. Denver: Williamson-Haffner, 1914.

Rockwell, Wilson. *Sunset Slope*. Denver: Big Mountain Press, 1956.

———. *Uncompahgre Country*. Denver: Sage Books, 1965.

———. "Gentlemen of Fortune," in *The 1966 Brand Book*. Denver, Colo.: Denver Posse, The Denver Westerners, 1967.

———. "Portrait in the Gallery, Otto Mears – Pathfinder of the San Juans," in *The 1967 Brand Book*, vol. 23. Denver, Colo.: The Denver Westerners, 1968.

Ronzio, Richard A. "Colorado Smelting and Reduction Works," in *The 1966 Brand Book*. Denver: The Denver Westerners, 1967.

Sabin, Edwin L. *Around the Circle*. Reprint, Colorado Springs: Century One Press, 1913.

Schneider, James G. "Otto Mears – Pathfinder of the San Juan," in *The Westerners Brand Book*. Denver: The Denver Westerners, 1975.

Schulze, Suzzane. *A Century of the Colorado Census*. Greeley: University of Northern Colorado, 1976.

Sloane, Howard, and Lucille Sloane. *A Pictorial History of American Mining*. New York: Crown Publishers, 1970.

Sloane, R. E. *The Silverton Railroad Companies*. Northglenn, Colo.: Mega Publications, 1975.

Sloan, Robert E., and Carl A. Skowronski. *The Rainbow Route*. Denver: Sundance Ltd., 1975.

Smith, Arthur E., and Tom Rosemeyer. "Great Pockets, The National Belle Mine." *The Mineralogical Record* (July, August 1986): 229–236.

Smith, Duane A. *Rocky Mountain Mining Camps.* Lincoln: University of Nebraska Press, 1967.

————. "Silver Coquette–The San Juans 1860–1875," in *The Brand Book 1969,* vol. 25. Denver: The Denver Westerners, 1970.

————. "The San Juaner: A Computerized Portrait." *Colorado Magazine* 52, no. 2 (Spring 1975).

————. *Colorado Mining, A Photographic History.* Albuquerque: University of New Mexico Press, 1977.

————. *Song of the Hammer and Drill.* Golden: Colorado School of Mines Press, 1982.

Smith, P. David. *Ouray: Chief of the Utes.* Ouray, Colo.: Wayfinder Press, 1986.

Sprague, Marshall. *The Great Gates, The Story of the Rocky Mountain Passes.* Boston: Little, Brown, 1974.

Stone, Wilbur Fisk. *History of Colorado,* 4 vols. Chicago: Clarke Publishing Co., 1918.

Ubbelohde, Carl, Maxine Benson, and Duane A. Smith. *A Colorado History.* Boulder, Colo.: Pruett Publishing Co., 1976.

Uchill, Ida Libert. *Pioneers, Peddlers and Tsadikim.* Denver: Sage Books, 1957.

United States Geological Survey. *Mineral and Water Resources of Colorado.* Washington, D.C., 1964.

United States Government. *First Annual Report on Statistics of Railroads in the United States for the Year Ending 1888.* Washington, D.C., N.d.

Vandenbusche, Duane, and Duane Smith. *A Land Alone: Colorado's Western Slope.* Boulder, Colo.: Pruett Publishing Co., 1981.

Vanderwilt, John W. *Mineral Resources of Colorado.* Denver: State of Colorado Mineral Resources Board, 1947.

Varnes, David J. *Geology and Ore Deposits of the South Silverton District, San Juan Mountains, Colorado.* USGS Professional Paper 378-A. Washington, D.C., 1963.

Westermeier, Clifford. *Colorado's First Portrait.* Albuquerque: University of New Mexico Press, 1970.

Wheeler, George. *U.S. Survey of Territories West of the 100th Meridian.* Washington, D.C., 1876.

Williams, Henry T. *Tourist Guide and Map of the San Juan Mines of Colorado.* Denver: Cuban Reprint, 1965.

Williamson, Ruby G. *Otto Mears, Pathfinder of the San Juan.* Gunnison, Colo.: B & B Printers, 1981.

Wolle, Muriel Sibell. *Stampede to Timberline.* Chicago: Swallow Press, 1974.

————. *Timberline Tailings.* Chicago: Swallow Press, 1977.

Wood, Dorothy, and Frances Wood. *I Hauled These Mountains In Here.* Caldwell, Idaho: The Caxton Printers, 1977.

Wormington, H. M. *Ancient Man in North America.* Denver: Denver Museum of Natural History, 1959.

Wormington, H. M., and Robert H. Lister. "Archaeological Investigations on the Uncompahgre Plateau," in *Proceedings of Denver Museum of Natural History* (March 1956).

Wyman, Louis. *Snowflakes and Quartz.* Silverton, Colo.: San Juan County Book Company, 1977.

Wyman, Mark. *Hard Rock Epic.* Berkeley: University of California Press, 1979.

Young, Otis E., Jr. *Western Mining.* Norman: University of Oklahoma Press, 1970.

Young, Robert G., and Joann W. Young. *Colorado West—Land of Geology and Wildflowers.* N.p.: Wheelright Press, 1977.

Zamonski, Stanley W., and Teddy Keller. *The Fifty-Niners.* Denver: Sage Books, 1961.

Index

217